Life Cycle Investing

Investing for
the times of your life

Life Cycle Investing

Investing for the times of your life

Donald R. Nichols

DOW JONES-IRWIN   Homewood, Illinois   60430

© DOW JONES-IRWIN, 1985

This publication is designed to provide accurate and
authoritative information in regard to the subject matter
covered. It is sold with the understanding that the
publisher is not engaged in rendering legal, accounting, or
other professional service. If legal advice or other expert
assistance is required, the services of a competent
professional person should be sought.

*From a Declaration of Principles jointly adopted by a Committee
of the American Bar Association and a Committee of Publishers.*

ISBN 0-87094-614-5

Library of Congress Catalog Card No. 85–70801

Printed in the United States of America

1 2 3 4 5 6 7 8 9 0 BC 2 1 0 9 8 7 6 5

For my parents, Ray and Katie Nichols

With special thanks to:

Prof. Jerry Rosenbloom of The University of Pennsylvania

Prof. Robert J. Gordon of Northwestern University and his publisher Little, Brown and Company, Inc.

T. Rowe Price Associates, Inc.

Preface

Even if you're only an occasional reader of brokerage reports and advertisements for securities, you've noticed they usually end with statements such as ". . . particularly recommended for purchase by income-oriented investors" or ". . . suitable for investors seeking long-term capital appreciation." Those conclusions may be accurate, but they aren't informative if you don't know who such investors are and whether you should be one of them. Providing that information is what *Life Cycle Investing* attempts to do.

Most people think the right investment is the one that makes the most money. To a large extent that sentiment is indisputable, for it's difficult to argue with success. However, with investing as in life, success isn't always evidence of good judgment, nor is failure proof of faulty judgment.

For example: A 70 year old pensioner invests his life savings in a futures contract and triples his money in a month. Most of us would applaud his success; few of us, his judgment. A 30 year old accountant does likewise and loses everything. Most of us would lament her misfortune, but we wouldn't necessarily doubt her judgment for becoming involved with speculative investments. The reason for opposing opinions about the same investment lies with the circumstances of the respective investors. Such a high-risk venture isn't particularly suited to the former investor, despite its success, whereas it is more appropriate for the younger investor, even though it didn't work out well.

The basic purpose of this book is to help people judge the kinds of investments that are suitable for their particular stage of life and personal circumstances. The book's basic theme is *appropriateness* of general categories of investments to our age and life circumstances. Its basic idea is that people should look more favorably upon certain types of investments throughout a growing and evolving life. It urges you to ask "Is this the kind of investment I need at this stage of my life?" before you ask "Is this the most potentially profitable investment of its kind?"

Life Cycle Investing reflects my bias that the purpose of investing is to enrich your life, not to create more money for its own sake. In other words, we should think about money and investments in the context of life, not the other way around.

The book assumes the reader has a modest knowledge of investment basics. For those who wish to delve more deeply into characteristics and techniques of particular investments and investment strategies, frequent references for further reading or information are included. Readers whose active lives and educations have not tutored them in fundamental understanding of investments might wish to review my first book, *Starting Small, Investing Smart*.

Apart from a passing familiarity with fundamentals, this book requires no more of you than a willingness to place investments within the proper place in your life. And that is an important place indeed.

Donald R. Nichols

Contents

Introduction   **1**

Part I   **The Elements of Life Cycle
                    Investing   7**
Chapter 1   Five Elements of the Life Cycle
                    Portfolio   **9**
Chapter 2   Stages of an Investor's Life   **16**

Part II   **The Investments of Life Cycle
                    Investing   27**
Chapter 3   Depository Institutions and the Life Cycle
                    Investor   **29**
Chapter 4   Corporate Stocks and the Life Cycle
                    Investor   **37**
Chapter 5   Stock Options and the Life Cycle
                    Investor   **52**
Chapter 6   Bonds and the Life Cycle Investor   **75**
Chapter 7   Mutual Funds and the Life Cycle
                    Investor   **89**
Chapter 8   Money Market Funds and the Life Cycle
                    Investor   **106**

Chapter 9   Limited Partnerships and the Life Cycle Investor   **114**

Chapter 10   Commodities and the Life Cycle Investor   **121**

Chapter 11   Precious Metals and the Life Cycle Investor   **131**

Chapter 12   Annuities and the Life Cycle Investor   **142**

Chapter 13   Employee Investment Plans and the Life Cycle Investor   **150**

Chapter 14   Individual Retirement Accounts and the Life Cycle Investor   **161**

Tri-Chapter Summary: Life Cycle Investors and Retirement-Anticipation Investments   **176**

Part III   **The Tools, Techniques, and Methods of Life Cycle Investing**   **187**

Chapter 15   Managing the Five Portfolio Elements   **189**

Chapter 16   Managing Inflation   **229**

Chapter 17   Dollar-Cost Averaging and Income Reinvestment   **236**

Chapter 18   The Mathematical Tools of Life Cycle Investing   **245**

Chapter 19   Taxes and the Life Cycle Investor   **259**

Chapter 20   Managing Investment Advisors   **269**

Part IV   **The Portfolios of Life Cycle Investing**   **281**

Chapter 21   The Minor's Portfolio— Birth to Age 21   **283**

Chapter 22   The Portfolio of Young Adulthood— Ages 22 to 30   **287**

Chapter 23   The Estate Building Portfolio— Ages 30 to 45   **293**

Chapter 24   The Mature Portfolio—Ages 45 to 55   **298**

Chapter 25   The Senior Portfolio—Ages 55 to 65   **303**

Chapter 26   The Retirement Portfolio— Age 65 and Beyond   **307**

Conclusion   **316**

Index   **319**

Introduction

Regardless of your age, income, or previous success as an investor, there will come a time when your money will have to work harder for you than it does now. That time may be decades away or it may arrive tomorrow morning, but it will come, and you need to be prepared for it.

Many investors try to make their money more productive by "playing the markets"—that is, by moving their investments out of one vehicle into another according to whatever seems to offer the greatest returns. For many investors that has been a rewarding strategy, but it presents two problems for most of us. First, success and profit last only as long as we hit both the right market and the right investment medium within that market. Second, that strategy enslaves us to financial markets, forever searching for the investment waters upon which we can throw our hard-earned bread for endless multiplication.

There is an alternative, and it comes not from what we know about investing, but by examining what we know about life.

1

"Seven are the ages of man," Shakespeare wrote, and his insightful categories have been amplified by countless sociologists and psychologists in the ensuing 300 years. Each life—each of us—undergoes relatively predictable passages at relatively predictable ages. Whatever we wish to believe about our personal uniqueness, realistically we know that others have had and are having life experiences similar to our own, and as we look at those who've walked further ahead on life's path, we see our own footprints paralleling theirs closely.

There is a uniformity about the human condition, a set of realities we all share with only a few personal twists, and as we age we realize something important: the demands that life makes upon our maturity and stamina are accompanied by demands upon our finances. A wise personal investment program needs more than hot dice. It needs to serve investors at each stage of their lives and to anticipate the demands so inevitable in the cycle of life. Out of this notion comes the concept of life cycle investing.

Although poets, philosophers, and psychologists have been captivated by this concept for hundreds of years, economists discovered the financial importance of the life cycle in this century, notably in the work of John Maynard Keynes, the brilliant English economist and originator of the "Keynesian Consumption Function," and of Nobel laureate Milton Friedman, who espoused the "Permanent Income Hypothesis."

But it was the esteemed Franco Modigliani who was able to capture so important an idea within a straightforward theory of simple elegance called the "Modigliani Life Cycle Hypothesis of Income, Consumption, and Saving." Modigliani observed that people progress from spending more than they earn (they are "net dis-savers") to earning more than they spend (they become "net savers") and back to their former condition. The young and the retired tend to spend more than they earn, the former because they live on the income of others and the latter because they draw down their lifetime savings. In their middle years, people are generally able to set aside greater portions of their income. The idea is illustrated by the following graph:

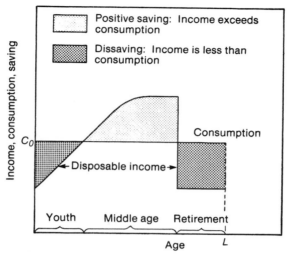

Income, consumption, saving

C_0

- Positive saving: Income exceeds consumption
- Dissaving: Income is less than consumption

Consumption

◄ Disposable income ►

Youth   Middle age   Retirement

Age L

From Robert J. Gordon, *Macroeconomics*, p. 379. Copyright ©
1978 by Little, Brown and Company (Inc.). Reprinted by per-
mission.

The vertical axis represents income and out-go, lumped together because income can only be spent or saved. Therefore, income must equal consumption plus saving, and that can be illustrated on a single axis.

The horizontal axis represents time—stages of life, in this case.

The line parallel to the horizontal axis represents total lifetime consumption averaged out as if it occurred equally each year of life. If, upon your death, someone added up your total lifetime income, subtracted saving, and divided the resulting figure by the number of years you'd lived, the result would be represented by the straight line.

The average consumption line is present to bring the income-consumption-saving schedule—the curved line—into sharper relief. As you can see, during infancy and youth people consume considerably more than they earn, and there is no saving. The schedule continues to reveal that during young adulthood they break into the net saving area of the graph, becoming financially able to set aside a portion of income as they enter the workforce. As they progress through greater personal and professional maturity, increments in income permit greater saving, represented by the ascending curve on the schedule. At retirement they begin to live on the savings accumulated during middle years, and again they become net dis-savers, consuming more income than they earn.

Obviously, Modigliani's hypothesis doesn't pertain specifically to every investor, for we all know people whose peak earning years occur after normal retirement, just as we all know people whose income and consumption deviate in other ways from norms at particular stages of their lives. As a generality, however, Modigliani's Life Cycle Hypothesis holds for millions of people, and it is a firm base for the concept of life cycle investing.

First, the life cycle hypothesis suggests that certain times of our lives are better served by different kinds of investments. The retiree's need for current income, for example, calls for a portfolio quite different from that of the younger investor, whose portfolio is likely to be smaller and centered around accumulation of capital.

Second, life cycle investing shows the need to anticipate emerging financial demands and to situate portfolios in expectation of future needs for money. Young parents, for instance, generally know that within the next 18 years they will likely need to pay for their children's college educations, just as midcareer investors can anticipate certain types of life/financial needs, such as funds to tide over periods of unemployment, to support an aging parent, and to provide for their own retirement.

Third, life cycle investing teaches that we must be prepared to change our investment program as we enter advancing stages of life. That doesn't mean that retirees, for instance, should abandon completely the more volatile components of their portfolio because they can't withstand losses, or that, say, people in peak earning years should shift hefty chunks of capital from certificates of deposit into commodity contracts because theory may call for them to do so. But life cycle investing does imply that our portfolios should change and mature as we do.

In general, that change involves realigning personal investments among the five elements that should be common in all portfolios. Those elements are stability of principal, current income, capital growth, aggressive income and/or growth, and lump sum accumulations. Although investors of all ages need to accommodate each of these five elements, each element is particularly important to investors at different stages of their life cycles. Therefore, as we begin to develop our strategy for life cycle investing, it's important that we understand the purpose of each separate element in a portfolio.

Accordingly, our first chapter discusses each element and illustrates its varying importance to investors of differing ages. Succeeding chapters cover selected investment vehicles as they pertain to investors at differing times in their lives. Finally, all the preceding information comes together in the concluding chapters, which construct sample portfolios for investors at identified stages in their life cycles.

In order to make life cycle investing work for you, you have to understand the fundamentals of constructing a portfolio and which types of investments meet those fundamentals. So let's begin with the beginning and an explanation of the fundamentals.

PART I

The Elements of Life Cycle Investing

CHAPTER 1

Five Elements of the Life Cycle Portfolio

Think of your financial house as you would any other structure you depend upon for comfort and security. Like your home, you want your financial structure to have a solid foundation. Your portfolio should provide what you want, should accommodate your needs, should reflect your taste and preferences, and should not be in danger of falling in around your ears. In putting your financial house in order you need to consider five key elements: stability of principal, current income, capital growth, aggressive income and growth, and lump sum investments. Let's examine each.

STABILITY OF PRINCIPAL

Stability of principal is accomplished through investments that offer optimum protection against market loss and fluctuations in value. Investing for stability of principal is called "preservation of capital." What that means is you want to set aside a portion of your financial assets in vehicles where you can get at it in emergencies, where you are assured you won't lose the money you set aside, and where it earns some returns. However, the important consideration is preserving the dollar you set aside. Earning high returns is a secondary consideration when investing for stability of principal, although many investments offer stability of principal and high current income.

Every investor must be concerned with preserving investments from loss. That's especially important for the savings component of the portfolio, and at this point we need to make a small distinction.

The economist speaks of "saving" as any part of income that's not spent. The economist subtracts what you spend from what you earn and calls the result "saving." It doesn't matter to the economist whether the unconsumed portion of income is set aside in stocks or bonds or inside the mattress; that money is said to be saved because it wasn't spent. Economists get even pickier about such things, for they also distinguish between "saving," which is a flow from income, and "savings," which is the accumulation of whatever unconsumed income flows into. In the economist's dictionary, "investment" is the purchase of plant, equipment, and productive capacity, not the purchase of financial instruments like stocks and bonds.

We, however, use the investor's dictionary, and in that book "saving" means choosing financial vehicles that emphasize stability of principal, whereas "investing" refers to financial vehicles like stocks or real estate partnerships that offer ownership. Therefore, the investor's dictionary makes saving a separate decision from investing, and the part of the portfolio devoted to savings is different from the part devoted to investments.

Generally speaking, these definitional discrepancies are of little practical importance, but there is one sense in which the distinction is highly important, because investing is what we do after we've saved. Having an adequate portion of your portfolio in stable, liquid, savings-type investments is important for all investors. Financial advisors generally counsel investors to set aside 10 percent of net income every payday into vehicles that preserve capital, and they also advise investors to have 25 to 50 percent of yearly net income in investments that preserve capital.

Without this reserve set aside for unforeseen contingencies, investors should postpone expanding their portfolio.

However, stability of principal and preservation of capital are especially important as we approach and enter retirement. When younger, we have time and alternate sources of income with which to recoup losses from more volatile investments. With increasing age, we need to be more greatly concerned with hanging onto what we've accumulated, and that means greater attention to investments offering stability of principal. Whereas investors in their 20s may need only small holdings of stable investments, those in their 60s will likely take substantial positions in investments offering capital stability.

Fortunately, an astonishing number of investment alternatives offer stability of principal. As we'll see, banks, money market funds, and near-term bonds offer good protection against capital loss, and investors can also follow investment techniques such as interest rate hedging and purchase of put options to defend against fluctuations in value of bonds and stocks.

INCOME

Income investments are those providing regular checks in the mail, notably dividends from common and preferred stocks and coupon payments from interest-bearing securities like bonds and certificates of deposit. Nearly all investors will want to have an income component in their portfolio, although the proportion of holdings that generates current receipts becomes more important as we age.

Most high tax-bracket investors prefer to concentrate their portfolio of income investments in municipal bonds and municipal bond funds, which pay interest exempt from federal, and in some cases state and local, income taxation. However, $100 of dividend income from stocks may be excluded from federal taxation for single taxpayers ($200 for married couples filing jointly), and investors at any stage of life can profit from this tax advantage. In addition, many

investors regardless of age prefer to invest for current income, reasoning that dividend and interest payments can be
reinvested for long-term compounding and that capital
gains from growth investments are too unpredictable.

Investments providing current income include corporate,
government, and municipal bonds, which pay interest semi-
annually; common and preferred corporate stocks, which
pay dividends quarterly; bond and stock mutual funds,
which disburse payments at varying times ranging from
monthly to yearly; unit investment trusts, which make payments on monthly, quarterly, semi-annual, or annual schedules; money market funds, with monthly payments; and
accounts with depository institutions that pay interest at
different times for different types of accounts.

CAPITAL GROWTH INVESTMENTS

Growth investments are those which provide long-term
capital appreciation—that is, increases in value—as opposed to income investments, which emphasize current receipts. The purpose of growth investments is to increase the
value of your total portfolio, and by "value" we mean "market price." Most investors pursue this goal through purchase of stocks, bonds, and mutual fund shares, for those
are the most commonly thought-of growth investments.

Common stocks and mutual funds dedicated to capital
growth provide capital gains through increases in share
prices, as we'll see in chapters explaining those investment
vehicles. The same is true for purchase of any financial asset, like precious metals or houses, which you sell at prices
higher than you paid. In fact, the possibility of long-term
capital growth attracts many investors to precious metals
and real estate.

In addition, company-sponsored employee investment programs often provide the chance for you to purchase stock in
the corporation you work for. These programs can be highly
useful for the investor seeking long-term capital growth, for
employee investment programs frequently permit you to
buy your company's stock at prices below market value,

potentially offering a built-in capital gain. In many cases, companies will match all or a portion of contributions to their stock purchase plans. Also, certain types of company-sponsored investment plans offer tax-deferred capital accumulations. We'll look at these considerations in a special chapter.

Many investors pursue capital growth through purchase of corporate, government, and municipal bonds. Although classified as income investments, these securities, as we'll learn in their chapters, often sell at depressed prices. Investors who buy them at discounted prices receive capital gains when these bonds increase in value. Capital appreciation is also available through mutual funds and investment trusts that purchase bonds.

AGGRESSIVE INCOME AND GROWTH INVESTMENTS

In the investor's dictionary, "aggressive" investments are those that offer greater possibility of reward as potential compensation for acceptance of greater risk of loss. Consequently, aggressive *growth* investments, such as some types of stocks and mutual funds as well as speculation in commodity futures, options on commodity futures and stocks, and commodity pools, offer the chance for very rapid gains—and equally dramatic financial losses.

There tends to be no middle ground for these investment vehicles, and they are suited for investors of any age who can risk capital in the hope of exceptional gains. Such investors generally are the young, who have many working years in which to recover losses, and the midcareer professional, whose growing income and financial wherewithal can sustain potential losses.

Aggressive *income* investments are generally those which provide interest and dividend payments above those on securities from similar issuers. Those issuers tend to be distressed corporations and municipalities whose securities—stocks and bonds—have been beaten down in price (and, accordingly, up in yield) because of their uncertainties.

For example, in early 1985 the common stock, preferred stock, and bonds of Public Service of Indiana, a nuclear utility, were yielding exceptional current income because of financial bloodletting associated with canceled construction projects. Among stocks during the same period, Continental Illinois National Bank offered a dividend yield almost twice that of higher grade bank stocks because of that company's many problems with nonperforming loans—until federal regulators forced Continental to kill its dividend.

In each case, these higher interest and dividend payments occurred because the threat of insolvency forced down the price of the issuer's securities. There are many securities by distressed issuers, and they are attractive to aggressive income investors. These investors, too, tend to occupy stages of life in which they can afford to tolerate uncertainties associated with higher-risk securities, although many investors in other life situations prefer aggressive income vehicles as a counterbalance to more stable and predictable elements of the portfolio.

In addition, continuing innovations in financial markets turn up new sources of income. In the chapters on stock options, for instance, we'll see how aggressive income investors can receive additional income from naked and covered puts and calls. Further, we'll also see whom to contact about receiving current income from holdings of precious metals, which normally pay no current income at all.

LUMP SUM INVESTMENTS

This category of investment differs from capital growth investments in that it generally operates within a fixed time period. The purpose of long-term capital growth investments is continual growth and appreciation. In contrast, lump sum investments are those which investors enter for the purpose of accumulating a sizable sum within a fixed period.

As we'll see, two types of lump sum investments are the zero-coupon bond and its companion, the zero-coupon certificate of deposit. Unlike conventional, income-producing bonds and CDs, these vehicles pay no current interest but are sold at deep discounts and pay interest as the difference between purchase price and maturity value. They can be highly useful in investment programs designed to provide for a child's college tuition or for anticipating retirement.

Annuities are a type of capital accumulation investment with lump sum characteristics. Most commonly, investors purchase annuities so that their capital can grow tax-deferred for years, even decades, and then be converted to investments providing current income. A similar type of investment is the Individual Retirement Account, which permits long-term tax-advantaged and tax-deferred accumulation of investment funds for retirement.

Lump sum investments are useful to investors at any stage in the life cycle. The principal criterion for investing in them is the willingness to permit capital to grow untouched until it reaches a critical investment mass.

SUMMARY

Those are the five components of a portfolio with which we'll be concerned. As we'll see, an important part of life cycle investing is selecting investments suited to certain stages of life, and inherent in the notion of selecting investments is the realization that portfolios must be altered to meet maturing needs. As always, the recurring issue in life cycle investing is not so much selecting one type of investment to the exclusion of another, but rather, apportioning the components of our portfolio to satisfy an investment strategy suited to changing life situations.

Most investors need to employ each of the five portfolio elements outlined here. But the need to weight our portfolios to emphasize different investment objectives at different stages of the life cycle remains paramount. That is central to the strategy of life cycle investing. Therefore, let's take a look at the varying stages of an investor's life and how investors should begin thinking about portfolio needs appropriate to each stage of the life cycle.

CHAPTER 2

Stages of an Investor's Life

In this chapter we discuss people and their need for money. Specifically, we look at investors ranging from the very young to the retired, and we examine which of the five portfolio elements of Chapter 1 is important within their general life situations.

CHILDHOOD: BIRTH TO AGE 21

Newborn children are the most extreme dis-savers. They not only consume more income than they produce, but they also consume a considerable portion of their parents' income. It may, therefore, seem strange to speak of a child's portfolio needs, because children don't provide for themselves for many, many years—in fact, not until they stop being children. However, children do have financial needs, other than customary parental support, which insightful parents can accommodate.

Above all, children need to be taught wise financial habits and the importance of prudent saving and investment. Providing example and instruction is among the most

16

important of parental responsibilities, and many parents impress financial values upon children by encouraging them to open savings accounts, purchase savings bonds, and set aside a portion of their allowances and childhood earnings in other low-cost instruments appropriate to their income. Important as this pedagogical portfolio is, a child's income doesn't go far in meeting his or her financial needs, and children require more than the type of portfolio that sets a pattern for lifetime financial habits. It remains for parents to meet investment needs of children by constructing that portfolio for them.

The first type of "investment" that most parents purchase for children is insurance on their own life. Given that children must be supported from parents' resources, parents will wish to assure offspring a source of income should they not be alive to provide it. Life insurance is outside our treatment of investments, but parents should be aware that rearing a child to age 18 requires about one third of their total income for those 18 years and should base insurance coverage accordingly.

More appropriate to our treatment of investments, though, is the realization that a child's largest single expenditure is likely to be college tuition. Parents have around 18 years after the birth of their children to accumulate sums for education, and that means two aspects of the parent-sponsored child's portfolio are important: capital growth and lump sum accumulations—that is, long-term growth and investments that mature within a specific time.

The key words are *child's portfolio*. Most parents seek to accumulate tuition for children by investing their resources in accounts owned by the parents, assuming they'll convert investments to cash when tuition bills arrive. That's a mistake because investment gains in an adult's portfolio are taxed at the adult's tax rate. That can reduce substantially the amount which actually goes toward capital growth and lump sum accumulations for children. Financially, it's best for parents to sponsor capital growth and lump sum accumulations by investing in accounts for which the child is owner of record. That way investment gains are taxable to the child, who is likely to escape taxation for many years until his or her portfolio generates $1,000 in interest, dividends, or capital gains.

Shifting the tax burden onto the children for whom the portfolio is constructed is possible through trusts and other legally constituted accounts, but all parents can achieve much the same goal through a Uniform Gifts to Minors Account (UGMA). This permits each parent to give each child $10,000 per year ($20,000 per couple) without incurring federal gift tax, and it doesn't require complicated legal arrangements.

The UGMA can be opened through banks, brokerages, and mutual funds after the child receives a social security number. The procedure is simple. When opening an account for your children, you merely check the appropriate block on the account application. That's sufficient to establish the child as owner of the account and yourself as contributor of funds, either cash or securities, for investment.

The account application will require you to appoint a custodian to manage the portfolio until the child attains majority. The custodian should be a trusted relative or the executor of your estate. Of course, you can name yourself as custodian, but if you die the UGMA would be part of your estate and subject to estate taxes. Therefore, it's best to name a custodian who isn't a contributor to the account.

Parents contribute to the UGMA, in effect making a gift to the child, and their contributions are invested in stocks, bonds, mutual funds, and other vehicles that the child then owns. Because the child owns the account, gains are taxable to the child, and that reduces the tax burden. However, it is particularly important to understand that once you open a UGMA your child owns the money or securities you contribute. As owner, the child may dispose of the money at whim. If your child prefers to take his or her money and spend it on a fleet of motorcycles instead of college tuition, he or she is legally free to do so. That takes us back to the importance of instilling financial responsibility in children.

It's also important to understand that all dividends, interest, and capital gains from the UGMA must be used for the child's benefit and may not be used to cover expenses for which a parent is normally responsible in supporting a child. If you use income from the UGMA for your benefit or for customary parental expenses, it will be taxable to you.

The Uniform Gifts to Minors Account is such a convenient and simple tool for meeting a child's portfolio needs that it will form the basis of all our subsequent discussion of a child's portfolio. Henceforth, when we discuss investment alternatives appropriate to people in this stage of their life, we will understand that the investments are held in a UGMA. For the time being, however, we need to understand that the elements of capital growth and lump sum accumulations are likely to be the most important in a child's portfolio.

YOUNG ADULTHOOD: AGES 22 TO 30

Investors at this stage of the life cycle are just beginning to earn an income that exceeds their consumption, and they have the greatest array of alternatives open to them. All else being equal, they are generally free to explore markets liberally, for they have many years in which to regain financial losses and they have few persons dependent upon them for livelihood.

The portfolio of young adulthood should, however, proceed from a firm base of savings, and it's important that investors at this stage of life recognize the wisdom of regulating financial habits. Therefore, this is an ideal time of life in which to begin setting aside a fixed percentage of net income with responsible regularity.

Once the savings imperative is met, though, young adults are free, within the constraints of their salary, to pursue other elements of their portfolio. In general, financial advisors counsel young investors to pursue capital growth and aggressive capital gains with their investments. The reason for this preference is two-fold. First, younger investors can afford to have funds tied up in long-term growth investments, for they generally need not supplement salaries with current income from investments. Second, they can invest for aggressive gains—investments that fluctuate dramatically in value—because they can withstand greater uncertainty in their portfolios.

Between ages 22 and 30, however, investors also need to consider other portfolio needs. For example, many in this age group are accumulating cash for the down payment on a house, meaning they lean toward investments that offer high interest and capital stability. In addition, during this period many people make the most important financial decision of their lives: the selection of a spouse. The financial implications of marriage are too numerous to recount, but today's dual-income lifestyles often give young investors greater discretionary income to invest, make tax considerations important at an early stage of life, and throw young investors into his-hers-and-ours portfolio situations. Further, many investors at this age begin to receive employment sweeteners like stock options and company-sponsored investment plans, further expanding investment alternatives.

Also during this period, many investors make a second critical financial decision by having children. The arrival of a child or three strains family income and adds new dimensions to portfolio structuring. For one thing, young parents will want to consider providing for a child's financial needs through the Uniform Gifts to Minors Account. For another, the expenses of raising children often mean that young investors have less discretionary income to scatter among diverse investment vehicles, forcing them to concentrate their investments.

As a consequence, the young nesters' portfolio often becomes weighted toward investments offering long-term capital growth and toward financial vehicles that permit them to set aside smaller sums at a time. These accommodations are made as young investors recognize the importance of lifetime financial planning and the gradual building of a financial estate. Nonetheless, this stage of life permits life cycle investors an enviable range of financial alternatives and world enough and time to investigate them.

ESTATE BUILDING: AGES 30 TO 45

During these years, the life cycle investor builds upon the portfolio started earlier, but the greater portion of his or her net worth is likely to be concentrated away from paper assets into property as the wage earner provides shelter and support for a family. Still, the growing income of this age group permits some portfolio expansion.

As long as children are in the nest, many investors at this stage of the life cycle concentrate on growth investments and the building of a financial estate. In many cases, however, investors of this age are comfortable enough to continue taking less moderate risks with aggressive income and growth investments, for they still have several decades of full-time employment ahead of them and can re-earn capital losses, if necessary.

Professional aspirations govern much of these investors' financial goals as well. Many find that "investment" in continuing education pays great personal and professional rewards, and many others become more earnestly involved in collecting stock of their employing corporation, either through open-market purchases or company-sponsored pension or stock plans. In addition, this is an ideal time in which to begin setting aside income for retirement, and many investors at this stage of the life cycle insist upon contributions to Individual Retirement Accounts, 401(k) plans, Keogh accounts, and company or union retirement plans before undertaking any other investments.

The tax considerations of investing generally become more pressing as investors of this age group enter higher income brackets. Somewhere during this 15-year spread, investors begin to look more seriously at tax-advantaged, tax-deferred, and tax-exempt investments, for those frequently provide greater returns than fully taxed investments. Also, long-term estate planning becomes a more immediate need as investors seek to preserve and perpetuate their growing net worth. Therefore, financial relationships with banks, brokers, and other advisors become almost as important as financial investments, for the pressures of a growing family, a growing career, and a growing income require superb financial counsel.

PORTFOLIO MATURITY: AGES 45 TO 55

This is the time of life when all the generalities seem to fall apart. During these years life seems to sort out its winners and losers. Some of us rise to greater personal achievements, professional advancement, and financial accomplishment. Others stagnate, careers in backwater, salaries relegated to inflation adjustments only. We shall assume the former and happier course to be generally true.

During these years, life cycle investors generally become greater net savers than at any previous time, whether from increases in income or because they aren't having more children. Although college tuition remains a formidable expense (unless wise parents opened that UGMA years ago), the major outlays of parenthood are behind them at a time when they're entering their peak earning years. Net worth will probably have increased substantially, giving investors access to larger credit.

During these years of personal and portfolio maturity, the life cycle investor needs to be actively concerned with all five elements of investing. He or she really cannot afford to let one lapse in favor of another, and the portfolio appropriate to this 10-year period is likely to be more balanced than at any other time of life. The reason for this pentagonal balancing act is amply clear in what we know to be true of life during these years.

For example, after age 45 the aging of one's parents may occasion drains not only on current income but also upon financial reserves. Constant-dollar investments are needed to assure that those funds are available. One's own retirement is a more tangible reality, meaning that IRAs and other retirement accumulations are essential investments. However, the investor still has 10 to 15 working years ahead, and these are normally years of increasing income. Both facts suggest that some aggressive investing is still in order, as are long-term capital growth vehicles. This life cycle investor also begins to look more earnestly at income investments, for tax-favored municipal bond interest is attractive to an investor confronting higher tax brackets. In addition, this is the period when many professionals are grooming for senior management rank, and they generally are expected to hold sizable chunks of company stock.

In short, whereas the 20s were a time of exciting experimentation, the maturing portfolio is a matter of keeping all the bases covered. During these years the portfolio is called upon to do more than at any previous time, and the astute life cycle investor must be prepared for all the eventualities this time of life brings.

THE SENIOR PORTFOLIO: AGES 55 TO 65

These years generally find the life cycle investor at the peak of his or her working income. With most of working life behind them, however, investors need to apportion portfolios away from aggressive income and growth investments, for they are no longer able to re-earn losses. Also, they moderate the long-term growth component of their portfolios, although they do not abandon it entirely, for most people will live into their 80s.

It is to be hoped that all investors at this stage of life have long since been regular contributors to retirement-anticipation investments. Tax-advantaged investments, especially those offering depreciation and other write-offs against income, are likely to have joined the tax-deferred and tax-exempt vehicles of the senior portfolio. And overall, the investor of this age will be looking more favorably upon capital stability and safety.

In addition, this life cycle investor becomes more interested in lump sum accumulation investments. With retirement a near reality, the investor will want to make the most of approaching time. This investor knows that upon retirement current income to supplement social security and pension payments is highly important. Therefore, the investor will be drawn to capital accumulation investments that provide a predictable lump sum which can be converted to current income investments.

In short, the investor at this stage of life is beginning to think seriously about re-aligning the portfolio grown over a lifetime. The *appropriateness* of investment vehicles becomes an ever-important question as the investor considers the disposition of invested dollars. Clearly, formerly appropriate investments no longer suit current needs. This life cycle investor will be redirecting his or her portfolio according to the realities of a new stage of life.

THE RETIREMENT PORTFOLIO

Once again, life cycle investors find themselves net dis-savers as they normally end their paycheck lives and begin to live on income from their portfolios. Generally, retirees receive current income from social security and pensions and perhaps from part-time work undertaken for activity or necessity. For the most part, however, this is the time in which investors must convert the portfolio accumulated over a lifetime into an income producer.

The life cycle investor in retirement needs to emphasize two elements of the portfolio in particular: maximum current income and maximum safety. The reason why these two elements dominate portfolio structure is obvious. In later years, paychecks diminish, requiring financial investments to provide current receipts, and investors no longer can withstand the volatility of the youthful portfolio.

There are two addenda that we should add to these twin imperatives of the retirement portfolio. First, besides maximum current income, the retirement portfolio needs to provide *regular* income—that is, dividend or interest checks in the mail at least quarterly and preferably monthly. Second, we must not confuse "safety" with "stability of principal," particularly as we get into later chapters and discuss the importance of U.S. government bonds in the retirement portfolio.

The two terms often may be used interchangeably, for investments offering stability of principal are frequently the safest—that is, they provide optimum protection against loss of principal. U.S. government bonds and notes, the foundation of a retirement portfolio, offer greatest safety, for if you hold them until maturity you'll receive their par value. However, prices of government securities fluctuate, meaning they aren't always the most stable investments. Thus, they are an exception to the notion that safety and stability are synonomous.

Further, the retirement portfolio must provide some capital growth. Investors live years beyond retirement, and few wish to contemplate 20 years or more living off a portfolio that ignores some measure of capital growth. Still, selective capital growth with maximum attention to safety is the critical issue.

Occasionally, the life cycle investor will have been so successful in his or her investments that taxes are an issue even at a time when most of us enter reduced tax brackets. These happy retirees will, of course, seek to arrange tax-favored current income and growth.

SUMMARY

In brief, we've seen that at different stages of the life cycle different parts of the portfolio need to be emphasized. As always, the issue is the relative weighting of investments offering stability, growth, income, aggressive receipts, and lump sum accumulations. Each is important to all investors, but each attains greater relative importance at progressing stages of the life cycle portfolio.

Thus, life cycle investors are concerned first with the strategy of their portfolios—that is, with apportioning emphasis among the five elements—and then they are concerned with portfolio tactics—that is, adding and deleting specific securities. Tactics are important, for they make strategy pay off. However, strategy has to be there for tactics to make sense.

What we must do now is learn how individual investment alternatives can serve the strategy of life cycle investing. Therefore, we'll examine several types of investments as they apply to each stage of the investor's life cycle. As we'll see, one type of investment can address many needs of life cycle investors. After we've covered the array of investment alternatives with reference to each stage of the investor's life cycle, we'll discuss some sample portfolios appropriate to each stage of life cycle investing.

So for now, let's look in more detail at securities appropriate to life cycle investors.

PART II

The Investments of Life Cycle Investing

In this part of *Life Cycle Investing,* we examine the different kinds of investments available through common financial markets and look at how each can be used at different stages of life. As we'll see, the same general type of investment can offer different types of rewards suited to investors at different points in their life cycles.

Although financial markets have been tremendously innovative in bringing new products to investors and in revitalizing old products in new forms, all investments are one of two kinds: those offering ownership and those offering a debtor-creditor relationship. From the former, investors profit according to the fortunes of the enterprise and from other investors' desire to hold an ownership interest. From the latter, they profit as the beneficiary of contractual arrangements providing a specified return.

Corporate stocks are the most commonly thought-of ownership investments, although precious metals, mutual funds, and partnerships are also ownership investments. The most frequent example of a debtor-creditor investment is a corporate, government, or municipal bond, by which investors lend money to an issuer and receive contractual returns, but certificates of deposit and other depository accounts also fall into this category.

But the important point is not so much the category of investments as it is the ability of differing investments to meet needs suited to investors of different ages and financial circumstances. Accordingly, this section of the book discusses several common investment vehicles and then examines how each can be of use to life cycle investors. A special feature of Part II is a detailed examination of retirement-anticipation investments, including a separate summary, because retirement planning has become a critical feature for nearly all American investors and because many types of investments can be used in setting aside funds for the time when we need to live off our portfolios.

CHAPTER 3

Depository Institutions and the Life Cycle Investor

Depository institutions are organizations such as banks, savings and loans, and credit unions that accept deposits from individuals and companies and put them to work through loans. In exchange for your making funds available to these institutions so they can lend them, they pay you interest. Depository institutions also make available other services to their depositors, including loans, lines of credit, and financial counsel. Principally, however, we're interested in the deposit accounts that these institutions offer, for as investments these accounts are of considerable use to life cycle investors.

Two advantages these accounts offer are a high degree of capital stability and investment security. Depository institutions are heavily regulated, and one purpose of such regulation is to ensure that the money you place in an account is there when you want it. If you place a dollar on account with a federally insured bank, S&L, or credit union, legions of governmental agencies monitor the institution to make sure it doesn't lose your dollar.

These are attractive advantages for conservative investors, and another is that depository institutions rarely charge fees to open and maintain accounts.

Almost everyone is familiar with the conventional checking account, formally known as a "demand deposit" because depositors can receive funds in the account on demand. Also becoming better known are *NOW Accounts,* which pay interest on checking account funds that otherwise lie fallow. NOW Accounts aren't really investments; they are "transactions balances," or receptacles for cash awaiting other uses. Another type of account frequently available from a depository institution is the *money market account.* We devote a whole chapter to money market accounts, so we'll postpone present discussion of those, too.

Equally familiar are *savings accounts* with banks and S&Ls and *share accounts* with credit unions. These accounts offer life cycle investors the opportunity to invest small sums of money, frequently as little as $5, on which they receive modest interest, usually 5½ percent to 7 percent, depending upon the institution. They are highly safe and liquid, meaning you can withdraw your deposit at any time. To be absolutely rigorous, depository institutions can require advance notice of your intention to remove funds from your account, but in practice they hardly ever do so.

Many advisors say there's no reason for today's investor to have a conventional savings account, for interest paid is much less than what is available through other investments. In general, this advice is valid. However, it may pay for any investor, regardless of his or her portfolio size, to have a small savings account as a means of gaining access to other services provided by the institution.

Of greater appeal to life cycle investors are *time certificates* and *certificates of deposit.* Financial institutions used to observe clearer distinctions between the two, but now almost every fixed-term deposit with a bank, S&L, or credit union is called a certificate of deposit or CD.

These are contractual obligations between you and the institution through which you agree to leave cash on deposit for a specified time and the institution agrees to pay you interest at rates that increase with the length of deposit. Unlike conventional savings accounts, certificates are not readily accessible. If you must withdraw your funds prior to maturity, the sponsoring institution will charge you interest penalties for early withdrawal.

With some of the changes in financial markets over the past few years, many institutions are issuing "designer CDs" that permit you to negotiate deposit amounts, interest rates, and maturity with your banker or savings and loan officer. For the most part, however, depository institutions offer CDs in $500 multiples with interest rates that increase one half of one percent for each six months your money is left on account. As of mid-1985, minimum deposits for certificates ranged from $500 to $10,000, interest rates ranged from 5¾ percent to 13 percent, and maturities ranged from 6 months to 12 years.

Investors with $10,000 or more may also take advantage of "floating rate CDs," which pay interest pegged to Treasury bills or another financial index. These instruments help offset one criticism of fixed-income securities: that they do not keep investors abreast of inflation. Because T-bill rates tend to rise for a variety of reasons, inflation expectations among them, CDs pegged to their rates are said to be better hedges against inflation.

In addition, investors with sizable sums may be attracted to "jumbo CDs," which are available in minimum deposits of $100,000 with interest rates established by market conditions. Whereas most CDs credit interest at a stated compounding period and pay the accumulated amount upon maturity, larger-denomination CDs may be arranged to pay direct interest via a check in the mail semi-annually, quarterly, or even monthly in some cases. Thus, CDs can be useful as current income investments as well as savings vehicles.

One type of CD that is useful in obtaining lump sum accumulations is the *zero-coupon certificate of deposit*. "Zero CDs" are offered by banks and brokerage institutions, which purchase conventional certificates of deposit and break them down into lesser denomination packages for resale.

Available in amounts as small as $250, zero CDs do not pay conventional interest. Instead, they pay accrued interest as the difference between purchase price and maturity value, nearly always $1,000. Say, for example, that you purchased a zero CD for $250 to mature in 12 years at a value of $1,000. The $750 difference between purchase price and maturity value is interest, and it is paid only when the CD matures. There is no interim interest as was the case with other certificates.

There are two general drawbacks to CDs. The first is their illiquidity prior to maturity. This means that investors must keep maturities short if they're treating CDs as high-interest savings vehicles, for otherwise they may not be able to get their money in case of emergency without an interest penalty. Second, the maturities of CDs must be monitored. If you overlook a maturing CD, your financial institution often can renew it automatically at the same maturity of the initial deposit. If you had planned to do something else with a maturing CD, you will suffer interest penalties and delays in extracting your renewed deposit.

Let's look at how investments through depository institutions can serve life cycle investors.

DEPOSITORY INSTITUTIONS AND THE MINOR'S PORTFOLIO

Because the minimum initial investment is so small, conventional savings accounts have long been convenient receptacles for teaching children the habits of prudent saving. For parents wishing to establish longer-term savings programs for their children, savings accounts are easily opened and require no elaborate custody and trust arrangements.

As the value of the savings account increases, it will prove profitable to switch funds into certificates paying higher interest. The range of maturities available on CDs permits the child and his or her custodian to leave funds on account for whatever period is suitable to overall financial objectives.

Further, the child's need to plan for lump sum accumulations makes zero-coupon CDs an attractive addition to whatever other investment program has been established on his or her behalf.

DEPOSITORY INSTITUTIONS AND THE YOUNG ADULT'S PORTFOLIO

Investors at this stage of their life cycle most likely will forsake the conventional savings account, as other savings-type vehicles, notably money market funds, offer similar features and pay higher interest. In addition, the illiquidity of CDs prior to maturity may make them less desirable for this age group than other investments paying similar yields.

However, young investors with very modest capital may find that conventional savings accounts serve to help them establish an investment program of some kind, so they ought not to be dismissed out of hand. In addition, the savings component of their portfolio can be accommodated by CDs, with the proviso that investors will need to keep maturities short to assure ready accessibility.

Further, we've noted that at this stage of their lives, young investors need to establish financial relationships with institutions. These accounts give them access to the other financial services offered by depository institutions and, accordingly, can be significant to total financial planning.

DEPOSITORY INSTITUTIONS AND THE ESTATE BUILDING PORTFOLIO

Between the ages of 30 and 45, investors find that accounts with depository institutions are important in securing collateral for other financial activities. Other things being equal, these investors have outgrown the conventional savings account. However, as they build their family estate, certificates of deposit can provide ready collateral, secure savings, regular interest, and a firm financial foundation.

Whether they choose long or short maturities depends upon other financial considerations such as adequacy of current salary, employment stability, and the liquidity of other investments.

Also, we noted that at this age investors likely will want to start planning for retirement. Individual Retirement Accounts and Keogh Plan Accounts, on which we have a whole chapter later, can be opened through depository institutions. Again, zero CDs purchased through brokerages are excellent vehicles for obtaining lump sum accumulations when purchased for tax-deferred retirement accounts.

DEPOSITORY INSTITUTIONS AND THE MATURE PORTFOLIO

One disadvantage to the interest received from depository accounts is that it's fully taxable. Having entered their peak income years, investors in the 45 to 55 year old age group often find that tax-advantaged investments offer greater ultimate yields, and for this reason allocate a greater portion of their investments away from depository accounts. In addition, these life cycle investors are concerned with capital growth, for which savings accounts and CDs are less suited.

However, conventional CDs can serve as high-interest savings accounts, providing that maturities are, once again, kept short. Further, investors at this stage should by all means be setting funds aside in Individual Retirement Accounts. Both standard and zero-coupon CDs are suitable for IRAs and Keoghs.

DEPOSITORY INSTITUTIONS AND THE SENIOR PORTFOLIO

Investors beyond age 55 will be attracted to the capital stability and security of depository accounts, although their fully taxed status will also be a drawback as these investors reach peak earning years. At this stage, life cycle investors often prefer to reduce substantially their holdings of more speculative income and growth securities, and CDs—even those with longer-maturities—become more attractive as alternatives for that portion of their portfolio.

It is especially important that these life cycle investors sequester funds into IRAs, and, as always, all types of CDs are available.

DEPOSITORY INSTITUTIONS AND THE RETIREMENT PORTFOLIO

Again, capital stability and security are compelling reasons for retirees to consider keeping substantial portions of liquid assets in depository institutions. By and large, these investors are in reduced tax brackets, so the fully taxable status of interest from depositaries is a minimal price to pay for their advantages. Account holders can arrange for interest payments to be paid directly rather than left to compound, serving the important current income needs of retirees.

As we'll see in later chapters, U.S. government securities also offer great safety, and near-term maturities are vulnerable to lesser price fluctuations. These securities compete with CDs in the retirement portfolio, and their interest isn't taxable by state and local governments.

SUMMARY

All in all, depository institutions offer a number of alternatives for life cycle investors. Financial deregulation and the widespread comfort that investors seem to be finding in investing in markets that aren't represented by a large, gray building have drawn many people away from depository institutions. Fortunately, banks, S&Ls, and credit unions have responded to these competitive challenges, and they provide many other financial services that life cycle investors should be aware of. For the time being, though, deposits in these institutions can be extremely attractive, quite apart from other relationships with depositaries.

CHAPTER 4

Corporate Stocks and the Life Cycle Investor

Corporate stocks can be a critical component of the life cycle investor's portfolio at any age. Depending upon the type purchased, stocks, also called shares and equities, can meet three of the five basic portfolio needs, the exceptions being capital stability and lump sum accumulations. Because stock prices fluctuate, and often dramatically, stocks aren't suited to the savings component of the portfolio. In addition, they don't provide absolutely known returns within a specific time, so they don't qualify under our definition as lump sum investments. However, they can provide growth, income, and aggressive gains, assuming you are an astute picker among the thousands of stocks traded on the listed exchanges.

INCOME STOCKS

Stocks that provide high yields are called *income stocks* because they generate a higher level of dividend payments than competing issues. As a rule of thumb, stocks paying at least an 8 percent yield (yield is dividend divided by share price) are considered income stocks. That somewhat arbitrary level may be increasing, however, for in today's high interest rate environment a stock that pays less than a 10 percent dividend really isn't competitive with other income investments. Traditionally, several categories of common stocks classify as income investments, notably the issues of power companies, telephone companies, and banks. Preferred stocks issued by hundreds of corporations throughout many industries are also classified as income stocks because their dividends provide above-average returns to shareholders.

Although many income stocks have long histories of substantial dividend payments, there are two considerations worth noting about this category of equity investment.

First, industries and corporations go through life cycles just like individuals, and many companies that were once classified as aggressive growth investments mature into "dividend plays." A good example is Xerox Corporation, a high-growth darling of the 60s that more recently has been touted for its attractive dividend. Therefore, a company need not have been renowned for decades as an income security in order to become one.

Second, many companies, particularly electric utilities, that have been considered havens for income investors are in danger of losing their status as they, too, enter a new stage of economic life. It's no secret that dividends of utilities that have paid generous returns for decades are now in jeopardy, and perhaps the same will prove true of bank stocks in this era of financial deregulation. Conversely, stocks formerly classified as income investments—like American Telephone & Telegraph—suddenly find themselves reborn as growth investments, having been divested of traditional lines of business and thrust into new competitive territory. Consequently, stocks don't necessarily remain income securities even if they've been classified so for years, nor should they be dismissed as income investments just because they've never been thought of as such.

Investment advisors generally counsel retirees and unsophisticated investors to concentrate the stock component of their portfolio in income investments because these investors need dividends to supplement current income from other sources. Accordingly, these income securities are often pejoratively nick-named "widow and orphan stocks."

However, nearly all investors should have some stocks that pay steady dividends, for each taxpayer may exempt $100 per year in dividend income from federal taxation ($200 for marrieds filing jointly). Although dividends beyond the $100 or $200 threshold are fully taxed at the investor's marginal rates, some stocks, usually those of utilities with major construction projects, pay dividends that are legally defined as tax-free returns of capital. These securities appeal to investors in substantial tax brackets.

Further, during the volatile stock market and high interest rate climate of the past few years many younger and better-heeled investors have opted for high-dividend securities. They've grown disgusted with gyrations in prices of quality stocks, and they've discovered that steady dividends can be reinvested at attractive interest to produce exceptional returns. For example, investors who receive $100 per month in dividends can accumulate almost $150,000 over 30 years if they reinvest in a money market fund paying 8 percent compounded monthly. For all of these reasons, income stocks are useful to life cycle investors who are by no means in the company of widows and orphans.

GROWTH STOCKS

The second general category of equities is *growth stocks,* so named because they can provide long-term capital growth. Although many growth equities pay dividends, stocks in this category are noted for their gradual increase in share prices rather than their income potential.

The chief disadvantage of growth stocks is that which applies to all stocks: you've got to pick the right security. That can be a trying task for professionals, much less personal investors without the resources in capital and research available to professionals. Achieving long-term gains also requires patience, sometimes many years of it, before a stock finally takes off.

A second problem is that today's securities markets are not oriented toward long-term stocks. Most investors buy securities upon recommendation of their brokers. Brokerage firms, particularly full-service brokers, earn money from commissions as investors add and delete securities in their portfolios. Consequently, brokers gear their recommendations toward short-term gains, which generate larger commissions through frequent buying and selling. That tends to mean investors don't always receive adequate attention to long-term growth from brokers.

Our tax code reinforces account churning and cavalier attention to long-term growth. At mid-1985, the taxman considers securities held longer than six months as "long-term" and entitled to favorable capital gains treatment, and he has lengthened and shortened the definition of long-term many times in recent years. Six months is somewhat out of keeping with the notion of long-term as it applies to other human dimensions. At the least, the tax code is on the side of investors who sell appreciated securities a couple of times a year.

Further, a cursory glance at the recent history of broad stock market indexes makes one wonder whether stocks provide long-term growth. Over lengthy periods—20 years and longer—investments in broad categories of stocks have tended to provide capital growth, and there's no question that many individual stocks have shown handsome capital growth. As of mid-1984, however, many stock indexes stood at levels no greater than five years earlier, and they suffered many bumps and bursts along the way. Erratic markets have driven many investors out of stocks entirely, having convinced them that pursuing long-term growth through stocks is unproductive.

In counterpoint, high interest rates have provided two attractive alternatives to long-term growth through stock purchases. First, interest on certificates of deposit and newly issued bonds has exceeded the average growth of many broad stock indexes. Second, stratospheric interest rates have depressed prices of long-term bonds in secondary markets. Availability of bonds at deep discounts from par adds built-in capital growth to the high yields of long-term bonds. We'll discuss deep discount bonds, and we'll see why many investors prefer them over stocks for capital growth.

Compensating, one hopes, for these disadvantages are several attractive features of growth stocks. We've mentioned one already. If you've owned an appreciated stock for at least six months, you receive favored capital gains tax rates when you sell. Additionally, gains aren't taxed until shares are sold. Investors who've picked a long string of winning stocks have increased their net worth substantially without taxes. Of course, that's also true for any capital asset, including bonds, precious metals, and collectibles. So long as you don't sell an appreciated asset, you aren't taxed on the gains. Favored capital gains treatment makes growth stocks appealing to investors in upper tax brackets, and to the extent that growth stocks produce greater appreciation than other investments, they are still the first choice for many life cycle investors seeking long-term capital growth.

One type of long-term growth investment is the "turn-around," in which investors purchase shares of distressed companies, corporations that have changed managements, or generally give some indication that they are undervalued. Another growth investment strategy is purchasing shares of companies in cyclical industries—those tied to the general economic cycle—when the economy is in doldrums. These securities can often be purchased at low price multiples, and when better economic times arrive, these shares often produce rewarding price increases.

AGGRESSIVE GROWTH AND INCOME STOCKS

Aggressive growth and income stocks are our third category of equities. Often called "speculative" to distinguish them from longer-term growth stocks, these securities appeal to investors seeking fast capital growth or truly exceptional levels of dividends, often from distressed corporations that have maintained dividends despite taking a beating in their financial condition. As you'd expect, aggressive securities require investors to accept greater risk of losing money on investments, either because share prices fluctuate violently or because management isn't able to maintain dividends.

One problem for investors pursuing speculative gains is defining what an aggressive growth stock is. In the past, these were issues of young or marginally capitalized companies or corporations in speculative industries like computer leasing, gambling, and precious metals mining. Although it wasn't always the case, they tended to be very low-priced stocks, like today's penny stocks, and the risks were relatively obvious to estimate. Today, all of the customary definitions of aggressive growth candidates aren't so watertight.

For one thing, security markets' definition of "long-term" as six months makes it difficult to separate long-term investments from aggressive growth investments. For another, the volatile stock prices of many established, well-capitalized blue-chip corporations make them look more like speculative stocks than growth stocks.

For a third consideration, economic rerationalization of American industries has thrust many formerly solid and entrenched companies onto shakier ground, making their stocks more speculative. For a fourth, many investment advisors, to say nothing of many investors, now regard most conventional stocks as paths to ruin. In their view, the formerly aggressive growth investments, like gold mining stocks, are now the only place where conservative investors should be putting their money. These advisors also argue that customarily conservative investments like corporate and government bonds are now highly speculative investments because fluctuating interest rates mean aggressive moves in their selling prices.

The consequence of all this is that aggressive growth seems to be more a function of market timing, economic cycles, industrial change, and world view than a function of a stock's individual characteristics. The same is true of aggressive income stocks. It used to be, for example, that a portfolio of utility stocks was considered a safe, conventional choice for regular income investors. Today, many public power companies are considered aggressive income investments because their financial circumstances make dividend payments less secure. Today's aggressive income investor tends to concentrate on lower-rated corporate bonds rather than stocks, on long-term government bonds, and on income-generating vehicles like writing stock options. We'll discuss each of these in later chapters.

In today's financial environment, aggressive growth investors tend to concentrate stock holdings in securities of emerging companies, newly issued stocks, and in special situations like corporate mergers, arbitrage, and liquidations. These issues often provide very rapid price appreciation, albeit more for reasons of emotionalism than of investment fundamentals, and they are more closely associated with conventional notions of aggressive capital growth. Publicly traded stock options (calls and puts) also provide aggressive gains from stocks, and we have a separate chapter devoted to those.

Aggressive growth investors are often drawn to certain types of investment techniques that provide aggressive gains as well as to certain stocks themselves. Two such techniques are buying stocks on *margin* and *short sales* of stocks.

Let's say that you expect AT&T to increase one point within the month. You could buy 100 shares, currently at the price of $15.25 per share, for an investment of $1,525 plus commissions. If the stock increases one point, you've made $100. However, if you margined your purchase, you could make even more on your investment.

Margin purchases are accomplished by borrowing money from your stock broker in order to buy stock. This loan is collateralized by cash, securities in your brokerage account, and the stock you're buying. At present, margin requirements (established by the Federal Reserve Board) are 50 percent of investment, having fluctuated between 10 percent or less and 100 percent in this century. So under 1985 margin rules, you could put up $1,525, borrow $1,525 from your broker, and purchase 200 shares of AT&T. If the stock moves one point, you've made $200 on your investment of $1,525. You then sell the 200 shares, repay the loan from your broker, and take your gain.

There are two warnings about margin purchases, however. The first is that you must pay interest on your loan from the broker. If your stock doesn't promptly produce the anticipated gain, interest payments can eat up your capital, for brokerage loan rates average 1 to 2 percent above the prime rate.

Second, if your stock falls in price beyond certain limits, your broker will require you to sell your shares or put up additional equity in your account. This is the famed "margin call" that ruined many investors during the speculative fever of the 1920s and 1930s.

And, of course, you must pay brokerage commissions on purchase and sale of securities, further offsetting any gains that margin purchases may produce. The advent of call options has made margined stock purchases less attractive, as we'll see in a later chapter.

Short sales are an ingenious device of American securities markets that make it possible for you not only to profit from price declines but also to do so without owning the stock that's falling in price. Essentially, short sales involve selling stock you don't own so that you can repurchase it after the price has (you hope) fallen.

Although that sounds complicated, it's not. Let's say you expect the price of AT&T to fall. You phone your broker and issue an order for a short sale. The broker sells the AT&T, having borrowed the securities from another investor, and credits your account with the cash from the sale. When (if!) AT&T declines in price, you repurchase the stock at the lower price, and the difference between the higher sale price and the lower purchase price is your gain. You're still following the old dictum to "buy low and sell high," except in this case you sold before you bought.

Fortunately, investors must be very well capitalized before brokerages will permit short sales, because the potential for loss is infinite. If the stock rises in price, you could end up having to repurchase the shares at a much higher price than you sold them for. Also, while you're waiting for the shares to fall you owe the owner of the borrowed shares all dividends paid by the stock.

One offshoot of the short sale is called *shorting against the box*. In this case, you're shorting stock that you hold in your portfolio. This technique is useful for guarding against price declines in your portfolio and there are also some tax advantages. However, the advent of put options has made short sales and shorts against the box less attractive.

As a reminder, though, margin purchases and short sales are techniques for receiving aggressive gains from a particular stock. The underlying security is not necessarily an aggressive investment; the manner of buying and selling it is.

Two investments of growing popularity for aggressive gains are *stock index futures* and *options on stock index futures*. These financial instruments make it possible for investors to profit from increases and decreases in broad indexes of stocks, like the trademarked S&P 500 Index and S&P 100 Index, not merely from the movement of a single issue. Because investors expect to anticipate the direction of the whole market (as represented by the index) more accurately than movement of a single stock, index futures and options on index futures have become exceptionally popular investments.

Advisors caution that investing in these instruments is not a substitute for selection of individual stocks. They are suited for aggressive gains, but index futures and index options also have conservative uses. For a thorough treatment of these vehicles, consult *The Dow Jones-Irwin Guide to Stock Index Futures and Options* by William Nix and Susan Nix (Homewood, Ill.: Dow Jones-Irwin, 1984). Another text that is useful to aggressive investors is *Special Situation Investing* by Brian J. Stark (Homewood, Ill.: Dow Jones-Irwin, 1983).

Finally, we need to say a word about preferred stocks. Unlike common stocks, preferreds are hybrid securities. Many have special features, such as conversion privileges and variable dividends, that make them useful in many stock strategies. Income investors may be attracted to them because of their high dividends, whereas growth investors may choose them because preferred shares can be converted to common shares, allowing the preferred stock investor to participate in the price movements of the corporation's common stock. Accordingly, preferred stocks are the choice of more sophisticated investors and of corporate investors who receive a tax break on dividends.

With the foregoing as background, let's look at how stocks can fit into the portfolios of life cycle investors.

STOCKS AND THE MINOR'S PORTFOLIO

Many parents consider corporate stocks to be an important element in the portfolio they establish for their children. Typically, long-term growth stocks are the favored equity investment, for these securities offer the chance for accumulations over a lengthy period, and commissions are minimized when securities are held for many years instead of traded frequently. Thus, the buy-and-hold strategy is frequently followed when choosing equities for the child's portfolio.

However, some advisors say the minor's portfolio is better served through aggressive portfolio management. In the case of children, tax advantages of long-term gains are generally inconsequential, and when returns can be maximized during shorter periods and compounded frequently, the aggressive strategy may pay greater overall returns despite their fully taxable status. The problem, of course, is picking a steady string of winning stocks. When the account custodian lacks the time or talent for active purchase and sale of profitable securities, the minor's portfolio may be better off staying with one winning stock.

More frequently of late, many custodians of minors' accounts are opting for income investments, including stocks that produce rewarding dividends. Followers of this strategy reason that the dividends' fully taxable income doesn't occasion tax liability until the child receives $1,000 yearly in unearned income from dividends, interest, and capital gains or $3,000 yearly from all sources. Therefore, all dividend payments are likely to go untaxed for many years. Reinvested, these dividends can accumulate to impressive magnitudes in 20 years or so, the life of most minors' accounts.

Dividends often are a more assured source of return than capital gains, and account custodians, who usually are part-time portfolio managers, can achieve substantial increases through dividend stocks without constant monitoring of the portfolio. Also, many prognosticators see only increased volatility for share prices during the coming years. Accordingly, reinvesting high dividends may remain a favored course for managers of children's portfolios.

STOCKS AND THE PORTFOLIO OF YOUNG ADULTHOOD

Throughout their 20s, investors can afford to pursue aggressive growth investments, largely because they have a productive lifetime in which to regain portfolio losses. Making mistakes and learning from them are important in any investment program, and it's generally best to make mistakes early. Aggressive growth investments offer their share of mistakes as well as rewards, and as such they can be both instructional and profitable.

Aggressive gains are only one alternative open to younger investors. With many decades of productive life ahead of them, these life cycle investors can accumulate substantial gains through long-term growth stocks and income stocks. Over a productive life of three and four decades, even modest rates of return can compound to enormous sums. The growth strategy requires discipline, especially the discipline to reinvest dividends as they're received, but the rewards of disciplined investment and reinvestment can be highly profitable—perhaps even more profitable than pursuing aggressive gains.

STOCKS AND THE ESTATE BUILDING PORTFOLIO

Gradual accumulation of financial assets is important during the years between 30 and 45, and this 15-year span is suited to long-term growth from well-chosen stocks. In addition, taxes become more of a consideration as income begins to increase, and favored capital gains treatment is necessary to reduce the tax bite.

With two-income households more prevalent in this stage of the life cycle, investment capital is somewhat more readily available, and in such cases aggressive gain through stocks is a reasonable goal to pursue.

Also, investors at this stage of their life need to plan for their nonworking years with investments in Individual Retirement Accounts, Keogh Plans, and other vehicles. As we'll see in the chapter devoted to those vehicles, all three types of stocks can provide funds for a distant retirement, and they should be considered by investors in the estate building years.

STOCKS AND THE MATURE PORTFOLIO

The same circumstances apply to investors between ages 45 and 55. By all means, these life cycle investors should set aside funds regularly for retirement, and that implies some investment in equities. In addition, they are likely to be participating in an employer's investment program, and that may occasion purchases of their company's stock.

It's important, however, that investors in this group have a well-balanced portfolio, for their financial demands are at their heaviest. Fortunately, during these years expenses diminish as children begin to leave home and income from a maturing career increases. That fortuitously frees capital for a range of investments.

By and large, income stocks are unimportant during this time, although many dedicated income investors prefer to follow their earlier pattern of investing for maximum dividends and rigidly reinvesting them. If temperament permits, though, these life cycle investors should strive for long-term growth and aggressive gains from their equities. With 10 to 20 working years remaining ahead of them, long-term growth is a wise strategy. With greater discretionary income, some risk-taking through aggressive gains is warranted.

These life cycle investors have begun to accumulate greater net worth, and brokerage accounts may be large enough to permit margin purchases and short sales. Accordingly, aggressive investment strategies, as well as aggressive investments themselves, are available to investors in this phase of life, although many will not use them. That's probably just as well, even though these years represent the waning of life cycle investors' ability to accept high risk in exchange for high reward. Beyond age 55, capital preservation becomes more important, and aggressive gains are less tolerable because of the risk of capital loss.

STOCKS AND THE SENIOR PORTFOLIO

For reasons outlined above, capital growth dominates the stock selections of investors beyond age 55. The 10 working years ahead of these life cycle investors is a reasonable time in which to pursue the goal of capital growth, and the advanced tax brackets of a peaking career make tax-favored gains necessary. Investors who are quite well-off may still chase aggressive gains, and their greater investment experience may help them do so more profitably.

Still, stocks with generous dividends permit growth through income reinvestment, and many investors of this age group are drawn to high-income stocks, especially for their retirement portfolios, which defer taxation on dividends. Anticipating retirement is absolutely critical for investors in this stage of their life cycle, and that means giving careful consideration to equities that fit the strategy they're following in constructing their tax-deferred retirement portfolios.

Elsewhere in the portfolio of this period, hybrid stocks—those that feature a balanced mix of dividend income and capital growth—are ideal selections, and many investment advisors are armed with stocks appropriate to a balanced objective. The dividend payments of these stocks tend to buoy them in erratic markets, and during good markets their growth prospects aid in securing capital gains.

Still, capital preservation achieves greater importance, and many investors take advantage of stock index futures, options on index futures, and listed options on individual stocks to hedge their investment in common stocks. If you're in this age group and considering these investment vehicles, *Stock Index Futures,* edited by Frank J. Fabozzi and Gregory Kipnis (Homewood, Ill.: Dow Jones-Irwin, 1984), is an informative collection of essays on the subject.

STOCKS AND THE RETIREMENT PORTFOLIO

During retirement, income from investments becomes particularly important. Consequently, retired life cycle investors tend to emphasize stocks paying steady and reliable dividends as a supplement to current income from other sources.

Capital stability and safety are more important than at any previous time, and many retirees delete stocks from their portfolios entirely in favor of high-paying certificates of deposit, government bonds, and other creditor instruments that are obligated to pay returns. These investors are disinclined to tolerate the fluctuations in capital inevitably associated with stock ownership.

Capital growth is still important for retired investors, however, and many of these life cycle investors devote a portion of their stock holdings to growth stocks. At age 65, most people can anticipate 10 to 20 more years of life, making capital growth still important. As we'll see, corporate and government bonds selling at discounts from par often substitute for growth through stocks, yet growth stocks shouldn't be totally ignored in the retirement portfolio.

SUMMARY

Income, growth, and aggressive gains are three possible consequences of investment in common and preferred corporate stocks. At each stage of the life cycle, stocks can provide returns suitable to an investor's needs and temperament.

It's important to remember, though, that our discussion of corporate stocks has covered only direct investment in equities. That is, we've assumed investors have phoned their broker and purchased stocks directly. There is an alternative—indirect investment in corporate stocks—that is also open to life cycle investors through purchase of shares in mutual funds. We'll discuss this alternative at length in a separate chapter, for mutual funds can prove to be a highly advantageous way to participate in the gains of stock ownership.

CHAPTER 5

Stock Options and the Life Cycle Investor

Buying and selling options are an excellent means of extending the usefulness of common stocks for life cycle investors. As we'll see in this chapter, publicly listed stock options can increase portfolio income, reduce risk of losses on common stocks, increase or decrease the speculative content of a portfolio, and even permit investors to profit from declines in stock prices.

As the name implies, an option is a financial instrument that gives investors control—the right to buy or sell—stocks at a specified price during a specified period. Most of us are probably familiar with options as employment sweeteners for the higher echelons of corporate management. If you're among the high-priced help of an American corporation, you likely have company-sponsored stock options that permit you to buy a certain quantity of your corporation's stock sometime during your employment, often for a period of 10 years.

What we're talking about, however, are publicly listed stock options traded through formal securities exchanges like the Chicago Board Options Exchange. Like stocks and bonds, these options have broad public markets, and they are purchased through brokers. Unlike company-sponsored options, public options apply to hundreds of stocks, and their effective life is months, not years.

Listed options are of two types: calls and puts.

A *call option,* or simply a "call," gives its purchaser the right to buy 100 shares of its underlying security at a specific price during a specific period. Investors buy a call believing that the security it pertains to will increase in price.

A *put option,* or "put," is the converse. It gives the purchaser the right to sell 100 shares of the representative stock at a specific price for a specific period. Investors buy a put believing its underlying stock will fall in price.

Calls and puts have two distinct features. The first is the strike price. That is the price at which you may exercise your option. The second is the expiration date. That limits the period of time in which you may control the 100 shares of stock.

Here's a sample quotation for the calls and puts of American Telephone & Telegraph from *The Wall Street Journal.*

Option and NYSE Close	Strike Price	July	October Calls-Last	January	July	October Puts-Last	January
AT&T	10	r	5⅜	r	r	⅛	s
15¼	15	9⁄16	1	1½	9⁄16	¾	15⁄16
15¼	20	1⁄16	⅛	5⁄16	r	4⅝	4¾

The first column names the stock to which the option applies—AT&T—and the closing price for AT&T stock the previous day on the New York Stock Exchange. (By the way, a stock may trade on one exchange and its options on another, as is the case here, where AT&T trades on the New York Stock Exchange and its options on the Chicago Board Options Exchange.) In this case, AT&T closed at a price of $15.25 per share.

The second column identifies the strike price, the price of the underlying stock at which the option may be exercised. We see here that the calls and puts of AT&T may be exercised at prices of $10, $15, and $20 per share. Those prices are referred to as the $10, $15, or $20 series of options.

Next, our attention is directed to the identification of calls and puts (the class of options) and the final prices at which they closed in the previous day's trading. We also see that each of the prices pertains to a specific month, each 90 days distant from the closest—July, October, and January in this case. At 4 P.M. New York time on the third Friday of each of those months, your options expire, and you no longer control the underlying shares. (The options actually expire on noon of the following Saturday, for reasons that defy everyone, because the exchanges are closed on Saturday). At any time from the instant of purchase to the hour of expiration, you may exercise your option.

The strike price and the expiration date are particularly important because they are the two key determinants of the option's premium. The premium is the price of the call or put.

Let's look for a moment at the calls with a strike price of 15, that is, those giving you the option to buy AT&T at $15 per share. Notice that the calls expiring in July are annotated 9/16; October, 1; January, 1½. To decode into trading prices, convert fractions to decimals, multiply by 100, and add a dollar sign. The fraction 9/16 converts to .5625. Multiplying by 100 because calls give you control of 100 shares reveals a premium of $56.25. Thus, you pay $56.25 plus commission for the right to purchase 100 shares of AT&T for $15 per share, or $1,500 for the minimum of 100 shares.

The symbol *r* means that a particular option wasn't traded that day. You may occasionally also see an *s,* indicating that a particular option is no longer available.

As you would expect, the longer you have the right to exercise an option the more you pay for it. Therefore, calls maturing in July cost $56.25, whereas those maturing in October cost $100, and the January calls cost $150. The same is also true of the July, October, and January puts. The longer you wish to control an option, the higher its premium.

However, expiration date is only one influence on the option's premium. Another important consideration is the relationship of the option's strike price to the stock's selling price.

In this example, AT&T stock is selling for $15.25 per share, and we have three strike prices for calls and puts: $10, $15, and $20 per share. Looking still at the calls expiring in October, we see that the right to purchase AT&T at $10 per share costs us 5⅜ per share, or $537.50 ($5.375 times 100). The right to purchase at $15 per share costs $100, and the premium for the option to buy AT&T at $20 per share is $12.50.

Although that may look complicated at first, the logic is clear. With AT&T selling at $15.25, an option to buy at $10 gives you the opportunity to purchase the stock below current market price. So the premium is high. The option to buy AT&T at $15, slightly below the $15.25 market price, is cheaper because the advantage of owning the option is less. The premium for buying AT&T at $20 per share is worth very little, because who would pay $20 for stock selling at $15.25?

With AT&T at $15.25 per share, a call with a strike price of $10 is said to be "in the money." The strike price of $15 is "on the money," and a strike price of $20 is "out of the money."

The same idea holds for puts, except in reverse. Remember, a put gives you the right to sell a stock at a specified price that may be higher or lower than the current price. Therefore, with AT&T selling at $15.25, the right to sell a stock at $20 would logically be more valuable than the right to sell it at $15, and it would be much more valuable than the right to sell it at $10.

If we examine the premiums for the October puts, we see our logic confirmed. The right to sell AT&T at $20 per share by the third week in October costs $462.50. The right to sell at $15 costs $75, and the right to sell at $10 per share costs $12.50. Thus, in the case of puts, the $20 strike price is in the money, the $15 strike price is on the money, and the $10 strike price is out of the money.

Now let's look at how purchase of options works.

Let's say you're interested in the common stock of American Telephone & Telegraph when it is selling at $15.25 per share. You could purchase the stock outright, paying $1,525 for 100 shares, and if the price rises to $16.25, you'll make $100 on your investment.

However, that may not be the best course. Maybe you don't have $1,525 at the moment, or perhaps you'd rather invest the $1,525 elsewhere while you're waiting out the price move. Perhaps you already own some AT&T stock and you're thinking about increasing your holdings, but you want to buy at a favorable price. Maybe you don't want to risk $1,525 in the stock market, but you also don't want to miss out if AT&T starts to move. Buying a call on AT&T can serve you in all these situations.

You phone your broker and buy one, or however many, AT&T calls. Each call you purchase entitles you to buy 100 shares of AT&T for the strike price at your discretion any time between now and the expiration date. Your decision to buy in the money, on the money, or out of the money depends upon your optimism about AT&T, your willingness to accept risk, and the amount you have available for investment.

If you're conservative, you may choose in-the-money calls, which already assure you a gain but which have a higher premium. If you're optimistic about the prospects for AT&T, perhaps you'll buy out of the money, which costs less, but that means the stock has to increase substantially.

Let's say that you select the October on-the-money call at $15. You pay $100 plus brokerage commissions. Fortunately, AT&T rises to $16.25. At this point you have two choices.

First, you may exercise your option. You phone the broker, inform him or her that you wish to exercise, and mail off a check for $1,500 plus commission for the purchase of the stock, and the AT&T is yours. It doesn't matter that the stock's price has risen, for you have the option to buy at $15 per share.

Second, you may sell the call rather than exercise it. Remember that the option to buy a stock at less than market value is in the money and, therefore, valuable. With AT&T selling at $16.25, your right to purchase at $15 is now in the money by $1.25 per share or $125. Remember also that options are publicly traded. Consequently, you can trade options like any liquid financial instrument, and if the option is worth more than you paid for it, you can sell it for a capital gain. Many investors buy options with no intention of exercising them. Rather, they wish to take advantage of increases in their premiums, just as they would with any other investment that increases in value.

Before moving to puts, let's observe one more advantage of buying calls over buying their underlying stock. Take the unhappy case of AT&T falling in price from, say, $15.25 to $13.25. If you'd invested $1,525 in 100 shares, you'd be out $200. However, if you'd purchased an October call costing $100, you can't lose more than the premium. In this case, your loss is half what it would be otherwise. Bear in mind, though, that you'd receive dividends if you'd bought the stock rather than the option, and remember also that the stock could turn around and increase in price. If AT&T increases after your call has expired, you're still out the premium.

Now for the purchase of put options.

As we noted, buying puts entitles the purchaser to sell 100 shares of stock at a specified price within a specified period. Calls gave us the right to buy at an established price. If the stock rose in price, no matter, for we had locked in our purchase price. Puts do the opposite. They give us the right to sell at a known price, even if the market price is lower than our contracted price. The right to sell a stock at a specified price is important to several kinds of investors.

First, there's the speculator who sees an opportunity to profit from other people's losses. A speculative investor could profit from declines in stock price by selling short, but doing so has all the risks we noted in our discussion of short sales

Next, there are investors who own a stock and lose money when its price declines. They could sell to curtail losses, but perhaps the stock is an excellent long-term investment and the investor doesn't want to be in and out of the market with every price fluctuation just to prevent losses. The owner of stock that's falling in price could defend himself or herself with a short against the box, but that maneuver might also have negative consequences, as we discussed.

In addition, consider the case of someone about to receive stock from a company pension plan in several months. Say, for example, that you work for AT&T and you will receive 1,000 shares from a retirement distribution in October. You're planning to convert those shares to another type of investment, but you have no way to know what 1,000 shares of AT&T will be worth in October. You could take your chances on your stock falling by the time you receive it, or you could purchase 10 puts that allow you to lock in a price for your 1,000 shares. That way, you know that whatever happens to your stock you will be able to sell all 1,000 shares at a known price.

Someone who's used stock as collateral for a loan is in a similar situation. If the price of that stock collapses, you could be required to put up more collateral. With puts, the collateralized stock retains its price.

All of these investors can find benefit from being able to sell a stock at a fixed price if its value falls, and that's exactly the benefit they receive from buying put options.

Let's concentrate on uses of puts by people who own the underlying stock. Let's say you've just bought 100 shares of AT&T at $1,525 and you want to defend your investment against loss. In this case, all you need to do is purchase a put.

Referring back to the reprinted quotations, we see that investors may purchase puts giving them the option to sell AT&T at $10, $15, and $20. Whether you purchase in the money, on the money, or out of the money depends upon your willingness to tolerate price declines of your stock and the amount you have available to invest. For the sake of consistency in our examples, let's say you decide to purchase on the money and choose the $15 puts expiring in October, for which you pay $75 plus commissions. (In reality, investors purchasing puts for this defensive purpose would probably select the longest put, which is January here.)

As with calls, you merely phone your broker and buy the desired number of puts. From that point forward, you have the right to sell 100 shares of AT&T at $15 per share. In other words, you have locked in a selling price that prevents your being forced to sell AT&T for less than you paid for it. If the price of AT&T falls to, say, $12 per share, you again have two choices.

First, you may exercise the put by calling your broker, informing him or her that you wish to enforce your option, and mailing your AT&T to the brokerage. You receive $15 per share for the sale, minus commissions.

Second, as was the case with calls, you may simply sell the put. Again, your on-the-money put is now in the money because the value of the underlying stock has fallen. In this example, we purchased AT&T at $15, and now it's selling at $12. However, we also purchased a $15 series put, which is in the money by $3 per share. So what we lost on the stock we gained on the put. Thus, by keeping the stock and selling the put we're still even, not counting commissions, even though the price of AT&T declined.

Of course, it's possible that AT&T will rise in price after you've purchased the put. In that case, the premium of your put will diminish, becoming worth less as the price of its underlying stock rises. However, you can't lose more than the $75 premium you paid for the put, in contrast to losses possible with short sales.

Minimal downside risk is an important advantage to investors entering into puts for aggressive gains—that is, investors who don't own the stock on which they've purchased a put. If you buy a put expecting the price of the underlying security to fall, you can't lose more than the premium for the put. On the other hand, aggressive investors can profit in two ways from buying puts.

They, too, can exercise their option to sell. They call their broker, buy AT&T at its then-current price of $12 per share in a standard market transaction, exercise their option, and sell it immediately for $15 per share, all of which also means paying commissions.

They can also sell the put at a gain. As was the case with calls, many people buy puts never intending to exercise them. Instead, they take advantage of the rules of price movements for options:

1. Premiums for calls increase as the price of the underlying stock increases.

2. Premiums for puts increase as the price of the underlying stock falls.

3. Premiums for calls decrease as the price of the underlying stock falls.

4. Premiums for puts will decrease as the price of the underlying stock rises.

If your position in either calls or puts begins to turn against you, you may close out your position by selling the options before expiration, for which you pay a commission. If you neither exercise the option nor sell it, your option expires, and the premium you paid is lost. By the way, that loss is deductable on your federal income tax return if you itemize.

Where does your lost premium go? It goes to whoever *wrote* the option, and that brings us to the other side of calls and puts. We've been talking about the uses and advantages of purchasing options. In the case of calls, we noted that buying allowed us to lock in a fixed price for a stock, permitted us to invest capital elsewhere while awaiting price moves, and offered capital gains from selling the instrument itself instead of exercising the option. In the case of puts, we observed that purchase enabled us to lock in a selling price for stock, permitted speculative gains, defended us against price decreases of stock, and compensated us for declines in stock by selling the instrument itself.

There are several risks to writing options—that is, in being on the other side of a transaction in options.

The investor who writes a call agrees to undertake the risk of having 100 shares of stock called away from him or her. Let's say you own 100 shares of AT&T and that you write a call at $15. That means whoever bought the call may purchase your 100 shares at $15, even if the market price of AT&T is higher.

Investors who write puts undertake the risk of someone forcing them to purchase 100 shares of stock at the strike price, even if the stock is selling below the strike price.

In exchange for undertaking these risks, the writer of a call or put receives the premium, minus commissions, that the purchaser paid.

A note on terminology: writers of options are sometimes called sellers. In other financial texts, you'll sometimes read about sellers receiving the premium that buyers paid. We will avoid that term, instead referring to someone who receives money from options as *writers of options,* which is the more accurate and legitimate term. We'll refer to options sellers strictly as investors who have purchased an option and who sell the option itself in public markets as they would sell stocks or bonds.

Let's look at how writing calls works.

In our example, our first investor bought an AT&T October 15 call for $100, giving him the right to purchase 100 shares of AT&T at $15 per share. On the other side of that transaction is an investor who accepted that $100 in exchange for the risk that the price of his AT&T would increase and that the buyer would exercise the call.

Just as the buyer phoned a broker and bought the call, so did the writer of the call phone a broker and say, "I'd like to write an October 15 call on 100 shares of AT&T." Or, to put those instructions in every day parlance, "In exchange for a premium, I will accept the obligation to sell someone 100 shares of AT&T at $15 per share between now and the third week of October."

That obligation holds whether the writer actually owns 100 shares of AT&T, in which case he or she has written a "covered call," or whether the writer doesn't own the stock, called writing a "naked call."

The broker executes the transaction and mails the writer of the call a check for the premium, minus commissions. The writer may do whatever he or she wishes with the check. It is cash in hand.

Why would someone write a call? For the premium. Writing calls is a means of generating additional current income from holdings of common stock (or, in the case of naked calls, income from stocks the investor doesn't own).

Let's say you bought 100 shares of AT&T and wrote an October 15 call at the same time. This is a covered call.

Right away, you receive $100 minus commissions on your investment. That's roughly the equivalent of a one point per share increase. In addition, you receive all dividends that the stock pays while the option is unexercised.

A special note: we have a chapter devoted to life cycle investors and Individual Retirement Accounts. There we learn that self-directed IRAs and Keogh Plans allow investors to write covered calls and that tax on the option premium is deferred until retirement. Therefore, writing covered calls can be an excellent way to increase the value of an IRA.

Also, the writer may receive capital gains if he or she writes an out-of-the-money call. Let's say that instead of writing the October 15 call the investor writes the October 20 call. In this case, he or she won't have to sell the AT&T for a price below $20 per share. If the investor bought the AT&T at $15 per share and it is called away at $20 per share, he or she receives $5 per share in capital gains as well as the premium, which, of course, is smaller in this case.

Further, writing calls can generate income on stocks that are falling in price. Let's say you wrote a call for the 15 series and the price of AT&T falls to $12, as in our earlier example. Odds are good that the call won't be exercised, because its purchaser won't pay $15 for stock he could buy in the market for $12. Therefore, you'll probably keep your stock and the dividends it pays and the option premium. All of that can help offset losses in your portfolio.

However, you can't always have everything. Let's say you bought 100 shares of AT&T, wrote an October 15 call, and the price of your shares increased to $25. If the call is exercised—and it most likely would be under these conditions—you will have to sell your stock at $15 per share even though you could sell it on the open market for $25.

Of course, having written a call, you can buy it back so long as you haven't received an execution notice. You merely phone the broker to whom you wrote the call and say, "I've written an October 15 call, and I want to buy it back." The broker will execute an offsetting transaction, charge you a commission plus the cost of the new premium in October 15 calls, and you're back where you started.

We've been talking about covered calls, those written by investors who own the underlying securities. If you have a substantial account with a brokerage, your broker may permit you to write naked calls. Fortunately, investors must be very well capitalized before a brokerage will permit this maneuver, because the potential for loss is high.

Let's say you write a naked October 15 call on AT&T, for which you receive the $100 premium. In this case, you do not own the underlying shares of AT&T. If the price of AT&T falls, you've scooted out with $100 on stock you never owned, for the call likely won't be exercised. However, if the price of AT&T rises to, say, $25, and the purchaser exercises the option, you're in trouble.

The market price is now $25. You've promised to sell at $15. The buyer of the option wants his shares. Unless you want the brokerage to freeze your account, the Securities Exchange Commission to embargo your assets, and the FBI to come knocking on your door, you must buy 100 shares of AT&T at $25 per share (for which you also pay a commission) and sell them at $15 (for which you also pay a commission) to the holder of the option.

The $100 minus commission that you received as a premium doesn't go far in covering losses like that. Of course, writers of naked calls are usually active market observers and frequent traders, so they likely will have bought back their option before things get out of hand.

The same scenario in the opposite direction occurs with writers of puts. Writing puts is also restricted to investors with heavy positions in cash and securities with a brokerage, and many discount brokerages (which we'll discuss later) won't even bother with writers of puts. The reason is that writing a put is inherently a naked position, for the writer agrees to purchase 100 shares of stock at the strike price, regardless of the market price, in exchange for the premium on the put.

We saw how buyers of puts could use them as conservative vehicles to offset losses in a portfolio. Writing a put is strictly a speculative, aggressive income investment maneuver.

Writers of puts have the same conversation with brokers that writers of calls had. They phone and, in effect, say, "Send me the premium minus commissions, and I'll be liable for purchase of 100 shares of AT&T at $15 per share between now and the third week of October."

Writers of puts want one thing: they want the price of the underlying shares to increase. Let's say the writer of the put agrees to buy 100 shares of AT&T at $15. He or she receives the premium, presumably having mastered the art of opening envelopes with crossed fingers. The price of AT&T rises to $25. In this case, the put likely won't be exercised, for someone could sell the shares in the open market for more than $15.

However, let's say the price of AT&T falls to $10. At this point, the writer of the put will have to pay $15 per share for stock selling at $10 if the buyer of the put exercises it, and if the writer of the put hasn't bought back the position.

Calls and puts are among the more recent of financial innovations, having been around in quantity only since the mid-1970s, so we're just now beginning to see some formal studies of who profits from buying and selling puts and calls. All of the academic material aside, though, one has to wonder why anyone would write a put.

In this case, for instance, the premium for the October 15 puts is $75. The commission will be $30 to $40 for writing a put, even at a discount brokerage. That leaves us with a potential reward of $35 to $45 for the risk of losing hundreds of dollars. One has to be quite a risk-seeker—or else desperate for money—to play those odds.

One explanation is that writers of puts know something about buyers of puts. They know, for instance, that speculative buyers likely will sell their put for a gain rather than exercise it and that conservative buyers of puts usually purchase them as compensation for declines in long-term holdings of stock. Therefore, for the most part, investors usually buy puts for their uses as investment instruments, not for the sake of exercising them. Writers of puts know this, and they're willing to accept the odds of being forced to make good on their promise to buy stock at a price higher than market value.

There are two more points we need to raise before discussing how life cycle investors can use options to advantage: commissions and combinations.

You will notice that the phrases "plus commissions" and "minus commissions" appear quite frequently in our study of options. That's because every move you make with options requires you to pay them. Buy a call or put, and you pay a commission. Sell a call or put, and you pay a commission. Execute an offsetting transaction with calls and puts, and you pay a commission. Exercise your call or put, and you pay commissions to purchase or sell the underlying stock. In sum, you can figure it will cost you $40 to $100 everytime you do anything with an option, and that's only for purchase and sale. Commissions can be a deterrent to dealing in options at all.

Second, we've been talking about one-sided options transactions only—either buying or writing options. By now you've probably figured that you can do both simultaneously. Here are some examples of combinations:

1. Let's say you own 100 shares of AT&T. You can simultaneously write a call, giving you premium income, and buy a put, giving you downside protection.

2. You can write a call and write a put, whether in the same option series or a different one. If you, as an owner of AT&T, think it is poised for a marked upward move, you can write an out-of-the-money call, giving you premium income plus capital appreciation, and write an in-the-money put, which won't be exercised if you're right about the direction of the price move.

3. Let's say you don't own AT&T but you think AT&T is about to move one way or the other. You can buy both a put and a call, and you're poised to profit whichever way the stock moves, either by executing the winning option or by selling it.

Multiple-sided options transactions are known as "strips," "straps," and "straddles," and by this time a few more varieties have probably been discovered. We'll not cover the more complicated transactions, but there are several excellent texts that do. For a thorough, if somewhat academic, treatment of options, consult *Handbook of Financial Markets* edited by Frank J. Fabozzi and Frank G. Zarb (Homewood, Ill.: Dow Jones-Irwin, 1981). Two other worthy books by the same publisher are *Option Pricing* (1983), a professional trader's treatment by Robert Jarrow and Andrew Rudd, and *The Dow Jones Guide to Put and Call Options* (1975) by Henry K. Clasing, Jr., probably the best explanation of the subject available to the lay investor.

OPTIONS AND THE MINOR'S PORTFOLIO

In general, calls and puts are not particularly well-suited to the minor's portfolio of common stocks, although exceptions to that generality do, of course, exist. First, let's look at buying calls and puts.

The custodian who manages a minor's portfolio is interested largely in investing for long-term gains, for high current income that can be reinvested, or for lump sum accumulations to be expended for a single purpose such as college tuition. Buying call options doesn't generally suit any of those three objectives, because a call is a wasting asset. It exists for less than a year, and the premium plus commissions could likely be invested in vehicles of longer duration. In addition, there is always the likelihood that the purchased call could expire worthless if the underlying stock doesn't produce the hoped-for upward price movement. In that case, the funds invested on the minor's behalf are lost.

For similar reasons, buying put options is generally a misdirection of capital. The money the custodian pays for a put could be more suitably used, if nowhere else than in a savings account paying compounded interest. Further, the put could expire without producing any investment gain.

There is one possible exception to the inadvisability of

buying puts. If the minor's parents have contributed sizable shares of a single stock, or if, over time, the minor's account custodian has accumulated several hundred shares of a single stock, then perhaps it's wise to defend against downward price fluctuations by purchasing puts. However, the warning about the option expiring worthless still applies, and someone will have used contributed funds for no purpose if that happens.

Other problems exist for the minor's portfolio in writing calls and puts. For one thing, the custodian who invests in stocks on behalf of a minor is generally interested in long-term capital gains. If the custodian writes a call on the minor's stock holdings, it's possible that he or she will miss out on dramatic price moves if the call option is exercised.

However, writing options does generate current income on a portfolio of stocks, and it also provides some compensation for declines in stock intended to be held for long periods. And as we've seen, writing out-of-the-money calls can still permit some capital appreciation.

Writing puts for a minor's portfolio is considered imprudent management, and if a professional investment custodian does so for a minor's portfolio he or she could be held legally liable for losses. If a professional is prohibited from doing it, you shouldn't do it either.

OPTIONS AND THE YOUNG ADULT'S PORTFOLIO

Investors in their 20s can afford to take some risks with their capital, and the purchase of calls and puts can prove lucrative, providing the investor is a wise picker among options. Otherwise, options trading—that is, buying calls and puts with the intention of selling the instruments themselves at a gain—can be an expensive investment lesson.

One problem with investors at this stage of the life cycle is a fledgling income. Investors who can't come up with the funds for outright purchases of stock can nonetheless lock in share prices through buying calls, assuming they can come up with the required purchase price if they wish to exercise a successfully purchased call before it expires.

Similarly, young investors who have accumulated a position in stocks can buy puts to protect against losses. For the most part, however, this is a capital preservation maneuver, and younger investors needn't be overwhelmingly concerned with capital preservation.

Writing calls, as always, can generate additional income for the younger investor's stock holdings, particularly if he or she has the discipline to reinvest premium income. But again, not many investors in this age group need to be concerned excessively with current income from their investments.

Finally, writing puts is a rather aggressive move that can cost the younger investor a considerable portion of capital if the position proves unwise.

OPTIONS AND THE ESTATE BUILDING PORTFOLIO

As we noted, during the span between ages 30 and 45 the investor's net worth is frequently weighted in house and property. In addition, we also observed that long-term investments, particularly capital growth vehicles and retirement plans, begin to assume importance. Also, we observed that continuing demands upon current income—mortgage payments, support of children—eat into investable capital. Further, tax-preferred investments also become more attractive, and option premiums provide fully taxed returns.

For all of these reasons, many investors at this stage of their lives do not select options among their first investment choices. However, for life cycle investors in their estate building stage, there is an alternative that can provide some of the rewards of calls and puts. That alternative is a mutual fund concentrating in options.

We have an extended discussion of mutual funds shortly, and when we get to that chapter we'll learn that these funds pool small amounts of capital from many investors and put them to work in an extraordinary assortment of investments. One such investment is options, mainly calls. As we've seen, there are many option strategies—growth, income, aggressive gains—and there are also mutual funds dealing in options to pursue those objectives.

Several funds offering portfolios of options and securities on which call options are written are available through The Colonial Group of Funds. A "load fund" available through fee-charging brokers, Colonial's option funds require a very low $250 minimum initial investment and subsequent investments of only $25. For investors whose income is strained by current demands, these low minimums offer the chance for indirect purchase and sale of options and underlying stocks managed by professionals.

For further information and a prospectus write:

The Colonial Group of Funds
75 Federal Street
Boston, MA   02110
Phone: (617)425–3750

Of course, investors at this stage of their life cycle who are in more fortunate financial circumstances can buy, write, and sell options for the full range of advantages that they provide.

OPTIONS AND THE MATURING PORTFOLIO

As we noted in Chapter 2, the years between 45 and 55 are when investors generally find their available income increasing as their children leave home and their careers move them into higher-paying positions. We also noted that investors at this stage of their life cycle need to be concerned with all five portfolio elements, and options can help them achieve the balance they need among capital stability, income, growth, and aggressive gains (options aren't too useful in achieving lump sum accumulations).

First, let's look at buying calls and puts for the mature portfolio.

We learned that buying calls can be a highly useful technique for giving investors a position in a stock without actually having to buy that stock. Calls entitle investors to purchase shares at a specified price. If you've bought a call on a stock that increases in value, you may exercise the call, thus helping you fill your need for capital growth.

In addition, while you're waiting for the stock to appreciate, cash earmarked to buy it earns interest in a money market fund or bank account. Thus, buying calls can help you meet your need for savings and liquidity.

If you've picked a successful call, you can sell it for a capital gain rather than exercising the option. This makes purchase of calls an aggressive growth investment, for percentage gains from buying and selling calls may be greater than if you'd bought the stock outright.

To illustrate, assume you bought 100 shares of stock at $10 per share, for an investment of $1,000. If the stock increases one point, you've earned $100 and received a 10 percent return. However, if you'd bought 10 calls at $100 each and the calls increased one point, your $1,000 would become $2,000, for a 100 percent return. That's a pretty aggressive return. On the other hand, the option may eventually expire worthless, and that's not likely to happen with the stock. Such is the risk one takes for aggressive gains.

In comparison, buying puts can help you achieve capital stability on your stocks. As we've seen, if you hold stock at $15 per share and buy puts at $15 per share, you've immunized yourself against losses because you can always sell the underlying stock for that price by exercising the option. If you wish to hold the stock for long-term growth, gains from the put increasing in price as your stock price falls will help offset the capital loss. (Use of puts to offset declines in share price makes them particularly valuable for investors in the next stage of their life cycles.) Of course, in order to pursue this protection against downside risk you must continually renew your puts as they expire.

Further, puts provide aggressive gains of the type available from buying calls. If you invested that $1,000 in 10 puts at $100 each and the puts increased by one point as the underlying stock fell, there's that aggressive gain again.

Now for the advantages of writing calls and puts for the maturing portfolio.

Writing calls provides the mature portfolio all of the current income advantages we mentioned in the general discussion of calls. Thus, this life cycle investor can improve the current income portion of his portfolio by writing covered calls. In addition, writing out-of-the-money calls can provide income and permit capital gains.

Writing naked calls provides aggressive income, serving that portfolio need by giving you option income on stocks you don't own. You may not write naked calls for an IRA.

Writing puts can also provide aggressive receipts, albeit for great risk, as we've talked about.

The mature portfolio can be served well by the full range of aggressive and conservative uses for calls an puts. Using them fruitfully requires great attention and active management of your portfolio, to say nothing about a steady cash flow to keep renewing your position in options and a willingness to pay frequent commissions. Still, for investors at this stage of their life cycle the rewards can be worth it.

OPTIONS AND THE SENIOR PORTFOLIO

By and large, our discussion of options and the mature portfolio applies to investors in the 55 to 65 age group as well. However, these investors likely will avoid the more aggressive techniques of calls and puts, for they must be concerned with conserving capital. We also noted that senior investors become more attentive to lump sum accumulation investments as retirement nears, and options don't serve that portfolio need well.

Still, there's a special point to be made about many investors in this age group, and it can be a telling inducement to include options as part of the portfolio. Recall that many 55 to 65 year old investors hold a substantial position in their company's stock, having purchased shares in the open market or through tax-preferred investment plans. These holdings often represent a major portion of the senior investor's total assets, and as such they should be protected against loss.

If your company's stock is listed on one of the various options exchanges, one way to protect against major price declines is to buy puts. Investors may not be able to exercise their puts because their shares are held in corporate custody, or they may not want to sell their personally held shares, regarding them as long-term investments, but in buying puts they can offset declines in their holdings.

As we saw, the price of publicly traded puts increases as the price of their underlying shares declines. Thus, puts can be sold at a gain when their underlying stock can't. That means investors can secure protection for holdings of company stock by selling the puts they've bought, for increases in the price of the puts offsets declines in the price of the company stock.

Many investors, however, would rather buy more of their company's shares when the price declines, preferring to increase their holdings instead of preserving the price of what they already own.

Of course, this senior investor can write calls on all holdings of stocks for which options are listed, including personal holdings of company stocks, thereby adding to current income. He or she must remember, however, that the stock can be called away if the option is exercised.

In addition, IRA investors—and IRAs are important in the senior portfolio—can write calls on stock in their IRA accounts, thereby increasing the income from this tax-deferred vehicle.

OPTIONS AND THE RETIREMENT PORTFOLIO

In retirement, the critical portfolio elements are safety and current income, with some continuing capital growth also being necessary. As we noted in the chapters on stocks and bonds, many retired investors do not invest heavily in common stocks. These investors need greater stability than stocks provide, and they often choose to achieve capital growth through a stock mutual fund or through purchase of bonds selling at a discount from par. With stocks being reduced as a component of the retirement portfolio, options frequently are of lesser appeal to retired investors.

However, many life cycle investors do hold stocks during retirement, and options can be useful to them. By and large, this category of investor won't be interested in buying calls as capital growth vehicles, for there is always the danger that the underlying stock won't produce hoped-for gains and the call will expire worthless. During retirement even the most well-heeled investor is averse to the risk of a wasting asset.

Buying puts can, as we've observed several times, assure the investor of price protection for his stock holdings, and retired investors may wish to take advantage of puts for this purpose if they have the inclination to be active in the markets and if they have the income to expend in constantly renewing their puts as they expire or are sold.

Writing covered calls will generate additional current income for the retirement portfolio, assuming investors are willing to risk their stock being called away from them. Presumably, the risks of writing naked calls will deter even the most well-off retiree.

There is an additional inducement for writing calls that the newly retired investor may wish to consider. Let's say that you've just received a sizable number of your company's shares as part of your retirement plan distribution. For various reasons, you may prefer to sell these shares rather than hold them (perhaps your company's stock is too volatile for a retirement portfolio, or it doesn't pay sufficient dividends, or it no longer offers the level of gains it offered in the past). Under these circumstances, you can receive an additional boost by writing calls on these shares. The premium you receive will be an enhancement to your cash position, and if the stock is called away from you, you had planned to sell it anyway. In addition, by writing calls you secure a known selling price, and that enables you to make other portfolio decisions with greater assurance.

SUMMARY

Buying, writing, and selling call and put options offer the life cycle investor an exceptional array of possibilities for holdings of common stock. Whether for capital stability, income, growth, or aggressive gains, calls and puts can serve many uses—and many people. They can generate income, great fun, and even peace of mind if used judiciously and accurately. Even if, for reasons of temperament or ability, calls and puts don't appeal to you, they are certainly an investment vehicle that all life cycle investors should consider before rejecting.

CHAPTER 6

Bonds and the Life Cycle Investor

Corporate, government, and municipal bonds probably offer life cycle investors more advantages than any other investment vehicle. During the past few years, financial institutions have developed an exceptional array of innovations with fixed-income securities, and private investors have flocked to bonds as alternatives to other investments, including stocks. Even the federal government has jazzed up dull old conventional savings bonds.

Bonds are exciting investments these days. Part of that excitement has to do with financial innovations like zero-coupon bonds, and a greater part is caused by fantastic price fluctuations that have characterized bond markets in the past few years of heated interest rates and hot-and-cold inflation rates. Bonds are no longer the staid investments they used to be. Sometimes that's good, and sometimes that's not so good, but life cycle investors can't afford to overlook bonds as important elements in their portfolios, because bonds serve all five portfolio needs.

First, corporate, government, and municipal bonds can be used to achieve capital stability for the savings component of the portfolio. Instruments like U.S. Treasury bills, which

75

can be purchased without commissions from federal reserve banks and branches, are especially useful as savings vehicles because they mature in less than one year and, like all U.S. government obligations, are considered free from risk of default. They are the ultimate in safety and liquidity, although their prices ($10,000 minimum) make them somewhat inaccessible.

However, as all bonds approach maturity, their prices approach par. Life cycle investors who purchase near-term bonds (those maturing within two or three years) will not suffer a great deal of capital fluctuation. In addition, coupon rates from conventional bonds are generally equal to interest from long-term CDs and greater than interest and dividends from other sources. Thus, near-term bonds provide stability of principal and generally higher returns than other savings-type investments. Bonds purchased through a broker will cost you commissions (except when originally issued), but the federal government issues two-year notes every month that may be purchased free of fees from federal reserve banks and branches for a minimum investment of $5,000.

Second, bonds provide current income. With the exception of zero-coupon issues, discussed in a moment, bonds pay interest at stated intervals, usually semi-annually. Interest payments are an obligation of the issuer, unlike stock dividends which must be declared in order to be paid, so bonds are favored by income-oriented investors. In addition, bonds can offer tax advantages. Interest from municipal bonds is exempt from federal income tax, and sometimes municipal bonds (munies) can provide greater returns to high-bracket investors than other investments can. Also, some states don't tax interest on their own bonds. Interest from U.S. government bills, notes, and bonds is free of all state and local income tax, making these securities advantageous to investors residing in locations with onerous tax rates.

Third, bonds can offer capital growth. As we noted earlier, high interest rates depress prices of longer-term corporate, government, and municipal bonds. Bond prices move inversely to interest rates, and the further a bond is from maturity the greater will be its price declines as interest rates increase. As of spring 1985, for example, some bonds with 15- and 20-year maturities sold for $500 to $700 per each $1,000 of par. Life cycle investors who purchase these bonds at discounts from par and hold them to maturity receive substantial capital appreciation in addition to regular interest income.

In addition, some corporate bonds can be exchanged for stock of the issuing corporation. These convertible bonds offer bond investors capital growth through price appreciation of the bond's underlying shares. Convertibles frequently provide more capital stability than other bonds because their coupon rate makes them valuable as fixed-income securities and their conversion privilege makes them valuable as stock surrogates. Convertibles require a bit more analysis than conventional bonds, but they can be well worth the extra effort for many life cycle investors. For an excellent treatment of this type of bond consult *The Investor's Guide to Convertible Bonds* by Thomas C. Noddings (Homewood, Ill.: Dow Jones-Irwin, 1982).

Fourth, bonds can provide aggressive income and aggressive gains. In Chapter 1 we mentioned "junk bonds," identifying them as securities from distressed issuers. These bonds pay above-average returns, either because their coupon payments are high or because their prices have been beaten down in secondary markets. Corporate and municipal bonds are monitored by independent agencies—Moody's and Standard & Poor's are the best-known—that rate bonds according to their security. The four highest categories of bonds are called "investment grade," and lower-rated bonds are identified according to degree of default risk. Lower-rated securities appeal to aggressive income investors, who accept greater default risk for higher current income (and capital gains if buying these bonds at discounts in secondary markets). Consult your broker or business library for information about bond ratings.

Life cycle investors who follow interest rates astutely can also receive aggressive capital gains from their bond purchases. Regrettably for all but aggressive bond traders, swings in interest rates have been extreme in recent years. Many investors have profited from the inverse relationship between bond prices and general interest rates by purchasing long-term bonds when interest rates are high and selling them when rates decline. Sharp declines in interest rates are accompanied by equally sharp price increases in long-term securities and by equally sharp gains for the aggressive investor who guesses right about the direction of rates.

In one of the great paradoxes of recent financial markets, many investment advisors now consider bond purchases suitable only for aggressive investors because bond prices have moved so dramatically on several occasions and show a continued inclination to do so. Aggressive bond traders often leverage their investment by buying on margin, as we covered in Chapter 4.

Both aggressive and conservative fixed-income investors have been drawn to financial futures, which are short-term contracts that permit investors to profit from increases and declines in general interest rates and which permit investors to reduce their exposure to interest-rate risk. Most life cycle investors hedge against interest-rate increases by keeping bond maturities short. However, many also buy long-term bonds selling at deep discounts so as to profit from capital appreciation. Investors whose portfolio of long-term bonds is extensive might want to consult *Financial Futures and Investment Strategy* (Homewood, Ill.: Dow Jones-Irwin, 1984) by Arthur L. Rebell and Gail Gordon with Kenneth B. Platnick, which is devoted to interest-rate hedging. Another work on the subject in general is *Interest Rate Futures* by Allan M. Loosigian (Homewood, Ill.: Dow Jones-Irwin, 1980).

Fifth, bonds can be useful in achieving lump sum accumulations. By their nature as fixed-income investments, all bonds generate predictable returns: you get a stated par value and a stated amount of interest for a stated period. That circumstance makes bonds highly predictable investments when held to maturity. Even so, your total return from conventional bonds is still decided by the interest rate you receive from reinvesting your semi-annual income. However, a recent financial innovation, the zero-coupon bond, is ideal for life cycle investors interested in achieving the utmost predictability and a known return.

Unlike conventional bonds that pay semi-annual interest and are issued at or near par, zeros pay no coupon interest and are issued at very deep discounts from par. The difference between purchase price and maturity value is accrued interest (with conventional bonds, the difference between purchase price and maturity value is a capital gain). Therefore, if you hold a zero to maturity, you receive no current interest, but you do receive a known par value. Your total return does not depend upon the rate at which you can reinvest semi-annual coupons. In a sense, your accruing interest is continually reinvested at the rate you obtained when initially purchasing the zero.

Zeros are particularly useful for Uniform Gifts to Minors Accounts and for tax-deferred investments like IRAs and Keogh Plans. Say, for example, that your children will be starting college in 10 years. You review the investment pages and discover that a zero maturing in 10 years currently sells for $420. You know that every $420 you invest today on behalf of your children will be worth $1,000 in 10 years. If you estimate tuition at $10,000, you can invest $4,200 now and have $10,000 later. The same calculations apply to your retirement planning. Life cycle investors many years from retirement will be gratified by exceptional prices available on long-term zeros. You can buy $1,000 in retirement accumulations over 30 years for less than $100 today.

By and large, zeros are suited for lesser-taxed investors and for tax-deferred retirement plans because of the bizarre manner in which interest is taxed. Even though holders receive no interest until the zero matures, the IRS forces investors to declare the average annual interest accretion as if it were actually paid yearly. Therefore, zeros generate phantom interest income that is taxable. The partial exception to this rule is zero-coupon municipal bonds. Zero munies are free of federal tax, but the phantom interest income may still be taxable by your state, even though it isn't paid until maturity.

Zeros are advisable for UGMAs because children's minimal tax brackets allow them to escape the tax burden on zeros. For the same reason, municipal zeros aren't suited for minors because they don't need the tax break.

Many life cycle investors like zeros because they lack the wisdom or discipline to reinvest regular interest payments from conventional bonds. These investors consider it an advantage to have a bond generate interest that they can't spend right away, and for these people zeros represent one of the few investments that short-circuit their spendthrift habits.

Life cycle investors have many sources of further reading about bonds and other fixed-income securities. Two useful texts are *The Dow Jones-Irwin Guide to Buying and Selling Treasury Securities* (1984) by Howard M. Berlin and *The Handbook of Fixed Income Securities* (1983) edited by Frank J. Fabozzi and Irving M. Pollack. Both are published by Dow Jones-Irwin.

Now it's time to take a more detailed look at how bonds can benefit investors at each stage of their life cycle.

BONDS AND THE MINOR'S PORTFOLIO

Given that one general purpose of the minor's portfolio is to accumulate funds for education and self-sufficiency, zero-coupon bonds are ideally suited for the UGMA. Zeros are readily available in convenient maturities that coincide with college years and attainment of majority. They are also suited to the buy-and-hold strategy that we noted was of advantage in our discussion of stocks and the minor's portfolio. Although many corporations issue zeros, maximum security against default is available through zero-coupon "packages" backed by U.S. government securities. National brokerage firms purchase millions of dollars in conventional government bonds of varying maturities and reassemble the securities into smaller denomination instruments. They are safe, liquid, and available for very small initial amounts that accrue to hefty sums.

In addition, conventional bonds are also suited to the portfolios of these very young investors. Although interest is fully taxable, that is usually of minimal consequence. Account custodians may opt to purchase high-paying securities at or near par, or they may select among the hundreds of issues selling at discounts, obtaining capital gains as well as reinvestable interest payments. As a very general rule, aggressive gains aren't really needed in the minor's portfolio, for custodians have many years in which to allow interest to compound, and the extra percentage or two available from lower-rated securities often doesn't compensate for the higher level of risk, just as the cost and attention required for frequent trading may rule out pursuit of aggressive gains.

As we mentioned a moment ago, municipal bonds are less suited for the minor's portfolio because their tax advantages generally don't offset taxable income. Of course, children born with the proverbial silver spoon may find that municipals can generate greater returns than taxable investments.

Advisors are divided about the suitability of government bonds for minors' accounts. In the case of the buy-and-hold strategy, government and agency securities offer maximum protection against default, and custodians who plan simply to buy bonds and hold them may prefer this safety factor. However, government paper generally pays one percentage point or so less than competing corporate bonds.

BONDS AND THE PORTFOLIO OF YOUNG ADULTHOOD

For the most part, investors in their 20s are not active bond buyers. Generally, they don't need current income from semi-annual interest payments, nor do they have the income with which to purchase the quantities of bonds needed to generate adequate supplemental income if they do need it. In addition, municipals usually provide smaller gains than fully taxed bonds for investors in lower tax brackets, reducing their advantage to younger investors. Near-term bonds are useful as savings vehicles, although commissions required for their purchase may reduce total returns, and other vehicles, such as bank accounts and money market funds, permit younger investors to set aside savings in more convenient amounts.

As we've seen, younger investors with discipline can serve themselves well by reinvesting semi-annual coupon payments promptly as they're received. This is not an exciting investment plan, but it can be profitable, especially given the number of years these life cycle investors have before them in which to permit interest to compound.

Also, bonds do provide some opportunity for aggressive capital gains, thus making them acceptable vehicles for the aggressive growth that many advisors say is appropriate for these young investors. However, aggressive growth from a bond portfolio entails greater market savvy than most younger investors have developed, and the spectacular gains from aggressive bond trading require margin purchases. Most younger investors can't meet the financial requirements necessary before a brokerage will permit them to open a margin account, and if our economy stabilizes it might not provide the interest rate volatility needed for profitable speculative gains.

Long-term growth can certainly be achieved through bonds. Younger investors can take advantage of the slow and steady course of growth that comes from purchasing bonds at a discount and holding them to maturity, although bonds must compete with stocks to supply this component of the portfolio. For that reason, a hybrid like convertible bonds may be a well-advised choice for obtaining capital growth.

Zero-coupon bonds are very useful additions to the retirement portfolio that many younger investors are wise in starting, and there's no question that zeros will make millionaire retirees out of young investors who buy long-term at today's exceptional prices and interest rates.

There's a further consideration for which bonds are useful

to these young life cycle investors, and that has to do with dual-income households. It may be that young married couples should consider balancing their aggressive holdings with slightly more conservative vehicles. In this case, a conservative selection of bonds may serve as a counterpoint to an aggressive stock portfolio.

BONDS AND THE ESTATE BUILDING PORTFOLIO

Between ages 30 and 45, investors tend to concentrate on gradual accumulation of financial assets. Bonds selling at a discount permit gradual accumulations of capital, and consequently they are more reasonable choices at this age than they were in the previous stage of life cycle investing. Convertible bonds may also meet this need.

Taxes often begin to become a consideration as careers and income mature, and during these years investors begin to examine federally tax-free municipals. Of course, zero-coupon municipals are a good choice for tax-free accumulations of income, and they are more sought-after by investors at this stage.

After age 30, life cycle investors must give greater consideration to retirement planning, and bonds can be useful additions to an IRA and to other retirement-anticipation plans.

BONDS AND THE MATURE PORTFOLIO

Although bonds are of ancillary use to younger investors, they become more seriously important after age 45. The need for capital growth and the uncertainties associated with price fluctuations of stocks make bonds more attactive alternatives after that time.

Deep-discount bonds offer such long-term growth. Convertibles may also grow more attractive. Municipal bonds, as we've noted frequently, offer federally tax-free interest, and tax considerations do become more pressing as income and tax brackets increase.

Mature life cycle investors can still afford to risk capital in aggressive growth and income investments, therefore lower-rated bonds may become more interesting. Investors at this stage generally have the financial wherewithal to open margin accounts with brokerage firms, so margined purchases are a possibility for investors who have the temperament to strive for short-term gains on borrowed money.

As we've noted before and will note again, retirement planning is exceedingly important during these years. Bonds definitely should be considered as components of retirement planning.

BONDS AND THE SENIOR PORTFOLIO

Between ages 55 and 65 capital stability and capital growth become highly important. With retirement looming, lump sum accumulations also become a greater concern, and occasionally current income is a greater requirement for increasing numbers of Americans choosing early retirement. As we've seen, bonds accomplish all of these objectives.

With higher income and a life of financial accumulations behind them, many of these life cycle investors choose to hold their savings in near-term bonds that generally offer higher interest and greater liquidity than competing instruments. With many thousands of dollars in the savings component of their portfolios, these investors have accumulated sums necessary to achieve higher returns to scale from their capital. They aren't in the position of younger investors who could buy only a bond or two, making other instruments more attractive for saving.

Deep-discount bonds offer a relatively assured source of long-term capital growth, and older life cycle investors look upon them with more favor.

As always, municipal bonds may provide preferred returns for these investors, who are likely in more restrictive tax brackets, and zero municipals provide the appropriate tax-exempt capital growth. In addition, ultimate security of capital becomes more important, and investors at this stage of life often restrict their bond purchases to U.S. government issues and to municipals backed by an insuring agency.

With retirement approaching, if it hasn't actually arrived, senior life cycle investors give greater weight to lump sum accumulations. They have greater concern with achieving a known quantity of capital from which they can make retirement income plans, and they tend to prefer government-backed zero-coupon bond packages for this purpose.

BONDS AND THE RETIREMENT PORTFOLIO

For retired life cycle investors, bonds are essential elements of the portfolio. Their use as current-income vehicles becomes exceedingly important, and they may also be used to provide capital stability and security of principal as well as modest capital growth.

Among the most liquid and stable "bond" investments are U.S. Treasury bills. These short-term instruments offer three maturities—13, 26, and 52 weeks—and they pay interest immediately after purchase if you renew them during the Treasury's frequent auctions. Otherwise, they pay interest like zero-coupon bonds upon maturity. They are great savings vehicles for investors who can come up with the $10,000 purchase price.

We've already seen that semi-annual coupon payments can be an ideal source of current income. What we've not discussed, and will at greater length in an example retirement portfolio, is the exceptional usefulness of U.S. government and agency securities for this purpose. Most corporate and municipal bonds pay interest in June and December, with January and July being the next most popular payment periods. Obviously, you'd have to have very sizable sums invested in order to make twice-yearly interest payments provide enough income for a whole year. However, a quick review of the financial pages reveals that Uncle Sam has bonds and notes maturing almost every month from now until well into the next century (although May–November and August–February payment periods seem to be most prevalent for distant maturities).

Consequently, six series of U.S. government bonds and notes can provide retired investors with income every month. An issue maturing in January or July of any year, for instance, will provide interest in January and July; a February or August maturity will provide income in those months; a March or September maturity provides a check then, and so on through the calendar. Further, HH savings bonds pay coupon interest (a straight 7½ percent) at six month intervals from the date of purchase. Therefore, it's possible to arrange highly convenient payments from HH bonds, which offer added advantages of immunity to market fluctuations and freedom from commissions.

U.S. government securities are free of default risk, making them comfortable investments for a lifetime of accrued income, and their interest is exempt from local taxation. However, market prices of government bonds will fluctuate with interest rates, and some of the lengthy maturities have generated substantial losses because prices are more volatile the more distant the maturity. Consequently, it's important that retirees keep bond maturities brief, often within five years. That's a convenient period over which to monitor a portfolio of bonds, yields for five-year paper are still competitive with other investments, and capital stability is much greater.

One exception to the five-year rule is deep-discount bonds, which retirees frequently prefer over stocks as sources of capital growth. By extending maturities beyond five years, investors can find attractive prices below par, securing capital gains as well as current income. Gains from discount bonds are more assured than, though perhaps not as great as, those from stocks. Of course, convertibles are also possibilities for achieving capital growth in combination with current income.

Well-financed retirees may still find that municipals pay greater post-tax income, although they should restrict purchases to short-maturity, insured issues for greater security against default. Observing this preference will cost them a bit in yield, but the trade-off is a wise one. For obvious reasons, retired investors shy from junk bonds and other aggressive income investments.

Despite retirees' need for current income, they shouldn't overlook zero-coupon issues as a source of lump sum accumulations. Now that retirement can last a quarter of a century, retirees still need to plan for their future. Particularly as more Americans retire before age 65, it's become useful to separate retirement into stages of its own, just as we've identified separate stages of the rest of the life cycle.

In early retirement, for example, many investors are not yet eligible for social security income. During this period, while they are young enough to be active and able to reward themselves with that world cruise or other long-postponed dream, they may actually need greater current income than in later stages of retirement. When social security and pension income kick in, retirees have an additional source of midretirement income, and they may opt to transfer a portion of their portfolio from income investments into growth investments. Zero-coupon bond packages backed by U.S. government securities can be useful in achieving capital growth. If they outlive annuity payments or conversion of IRAs and Keoghs into cash during late retirement, they can convert growth investments back to income investments. Presumably their investment capital will have grown, providing a larger source of income when converted.

SUMMARY

"Bonds can do it all," to paraphrase the sports pages. At each stage of the life cycle, a bond investment can serve each of the portfolio goals important at that stage. Far from being the staid and conventional codgers that their reputation claims they are, bonds can serve an exceptional range of uses.

In fact, bonds are even more ingenious and useful than the previous discussion would indicate, for we've not covered such instruments as variable-rate bonds, indexed bonds, bonds with put features, bonds convertible into precious metals, foreign bonds that pay interest in foreign currencies with the potential to appreciate against the dollar, and bonds with other attractive features. By all means, you should consult the referenced readings for greater information about these securities. In the meantime, there are many other investments available to life cycle investors, and we need to examine those.

CHAPTER 7

Mutual Funds and the Life Cycle Investor

Mutual funds, formally known as open-end investment companies, can be the most versatile, useful, and profitable vehicles available for life cycle investors. These pools of shared capital managed by major investment houses make it possible for all investors of any age to participate in portfolios of stocks, bonds, and other financial instruments as indirect owners of securities.

We talked about direct ownership in our preceeding chapters, where we discussed advantages available to investors who purchased stocks and bonds for their own accounts. Indirect ownership of securities through mutual funds differs from direct ownership in that the investor does not have personal control of a particular security. Instead, investors contribute capital to professional investment managers who purchase securities on behalf of all participants in the mutual fund. Mutual fund investors own shares in the particular fund, thereby participating in the gains and losses of the fund's portfolio. Mutual funds are available from giant mutual fund "families" like Fidelity, Dreyfus, and T. Rowe Price; from major national brokerage firms that sponsor their own funds; and from discount brokerages that purchase and sell other institutions' mutual funds as a client service.

Apart from professional management, the chief advantage to mutual fund investment is the ability to diversify a portfolio of securities with a single investment. For initial investments ranging from $250 to $25,000, life cycle investors can own part of a portfolio containing hundreds of stocks or bonds, whereas they might be able to own only a few individual securities if investing those sums directly. In addition, mutual funds permit investors to purchase additional shares in minimum amounts ranging from no minimum to $500. That means investors can add to their holdings in small amounts determined by their budgets.

For a refresher on how mutual funds work and their many advantages, investors can consult almost any basic investment primer, including three books published by Dow Jones-Irwin. *Starting Small, Investing Smart* (1984) contains a long chapter on mutual funds, and two other books, *Mutual Funds Yearbook, 1984* by William G. Droms and *The Dow Jones-Irwin Guide to Mutual Funds,* Revised Edition (1983) by Donald D. Rugg and Norman B. Hale, are particularly useful in discussing investment strategies with mutual funds.

For life cycle investors, two particular features of mutual funds are especially important.

First, mutual funds enable life cycle investors to accommodate all five of the basic portfolio elements. This is possible because different funds invest in different kinds of stocks, bonds, and financial instruments according to the goals of the fund's charter. Money market mutual funds, which we'll discuss in their own chapter, permit investors to hold the savings component of their portfolio in high-yielding, short-term investments with an unvarying net asset value. Some funds invest in stocks and bonds that offer high current income. Other funds concentrate on long-term capital growth. Another type of fund pursues aggressive income, and yet another pursues aggressive capital growth. There is a mutual fund suitable for developing each of the five components of the portfolio.

(Special note: At present, only one type of fund offers investors the chance to achieve lump sum accumulations through indirect investment, and that's the municipal securities investment trust. Most municipal trusts, as the name implies, invest only in tax-free municipal securities, meaning their main advantage benefits investors above the 30 percent federal income tax bracket. Strictly speaking, trusts are not mutual funds, although they hold some similarities, one being the ability to own a diversified portfolio with a single investment. More recently of late, trusts have been featuring substantial holdings of zero-coupon municipal bonds, which provide investors some lump sum accumulations when the trust matures. At present, no conventional mutual fund offers a diversified portfolio of zeros, but that could change as zeros become more popular.)

Within these broad categories, mutual funds offer even greater specificity in meeting the components of a portfolio. Consider mutual funds that invest in bonds. Some bond funds invest only in U.S. government obligations for maximum safety, making them appealing to older and more conservative investors. Municipal bond mutual funds invest for federally tax-free income—an attractive choice for high-bracket taxpayers, made more so by the range of portfolio maturities available to the mutual fund investor. Some bond funds are comprised largely of convertible issues, adding a dimension of stock growth to the bond portfolio. Life cycle investors who find bonds appropriate to their needs can locate a mutual fund to suit them.

Mutual funds that invest in common stocks are even more diverse in their appeal. In addition to standard distinctions among funds that invest for income, growth, and aggressive gains, there are funds that invest only in utility stocks, only in gold stocks, only in technology or leisure or medical or blue-chip stocks, or only in aerospace and defense stocks. Some stock funds invest in market trends, such as those that purchase stocks comprising broad market indexes. Some concentrate on special situations like stock in companies that are takeover candidates. Other mutual funds invest in market-related instruments like publicly traded stock options. Owners of shares in these types of mutual funds are able to participate in highly selective market segments, adding additional dimensions to their life cycle portfolios.

The second important feature of mutual funds shares is that they permit life cycle investors to alter the composition of their portfolios as they enter new stages of life. This is possible through switch privileges available from mutual fund families. Large fund families permit investors to exchange shares in one fund for shares in another sponsored by the family, usually, but not always, without a fee. The younger life cycle investor who owns shares in an aggressive growth fund can switch to shares in a more conservative fund appropriate for advancing years. Investors can switch from stocks to bonds, or vice versa, as one investment becomes more appropriate for a different stage of life. When taxes become burdensome, life cycle investors can instruct their fund to redirect holdings into municipal bond funds. Similarly, they can move capital out of the savings component of a money market fund into another fund serving a different portfolio element.

As a consequence of these two advantages, life cycle investors can progress through their entire investment lives as owners of mutual fund shares, selecting the portfolio appropriate to their needs and altering their selection as time progresses. All life cycle investors need to do is phone their mutual fund with the appropriate instructions, and they are repositioned for a different stage of life. That makes mutual funds very attractive for life cycle investors.

In addition, mutual funds are very adept at handling two particular accounts of importance for life cycle investors, the UGMA and the IRA. Fund advisors have long experience in these matters, and many types of stock and bond mutual funds are suited for investment goals of minors and investors preparing for retirement. Switch privileges still apply, providing additional versatility, and a phone call to your fund of choice will give you all the necessary paperwork.

As we noted earlier, mutual funds permit investors to purchase additional shares in the fund for very modest amounts. If you wanted to reinvest $250, you couldn't phone your broker and buy part of one bond, for instance, but for that amount you could buy part of a diversified portfolio of bonds, and you also achieve economies and advantages when buying stocks through mutual fund reinvestment. For younger investors with substantial demands upon disposable income, reinvestment of modest amounts is a compelling advantage of mutual fund ownership. However, reinvestment advantages of mutual funds are acutely important for long-term accumulations of capital.

Finally, mutual funds permit life cycle investors one type of investment flexibility that no other vehicle provides: the ability to convert all types of investments into income-generating investments. Mutual funds typically give shareholders the option to take gains from the fund in additional shares or as current income. Long-term investors prefer the former option, plowing interest, dividends, and capital gains from the fund back into their holdings for further growth. However, income investors frequently prefer to take gains from the fund as they're declared, whether monthly, quarterly, or yearly. That works in three ways.

First, life cycle investors who need current income can invest in funds dedicated to that purpose, usually selecting those that concentrate on high-dividend stocks; corporate, government, and municipal bonds; money market funds; and equity-income funds. They elect to receive dividends and interest generated by the funds in the form of regular checks. Straight out, they elect the advantage of greatest use.

Second, investors can utilize their switch privileges, transferring shares of, say, a growth fund for holdings of income funds and electing to receive regular payments of dividends and interest. Doing so means that investors abandon the advantages of growth investments for the advantages of current income investments.

Third, investors can opt to receive some gains as regular payments, securing advantages of both growth and income investments. Mutual fund investors can usually choose an intermediate option, such as receiving dividends and interest in cash and reinvesting capital gains in additional mutual fund shares. That's another way of having your growth cake while eating your income cake.

For example, an older life cycle investor holds shares in a growth fund that is performing quite well. If he or she keeps reinvesting all returns, the fund may generate handsome capital growth but no income. However, by electing to receive dividends in cash while reinvesting capital gains in additional fund shares, the investor receives both current income and capital growth.

That advantage simply isn't available through direct ownership of stocks and bonds. If investors own a stock or bond that's increasing in price, they can receive quarterly dividends or semi-annual interest, but price gains aren't cash until the security is sold. That means investors have to sell securities producing gains in order to receive additional current income. By electing to receive part of mutual fund distributions in cash, investors receive interest, dividends, and/or capital gains cash-in-hand while the value of mutual fund holdings is increasing. They needn't sell securities producing gains.

Finally, other forms of indirect ownership of financial investments are available to life cycle investors. We'll discuss many of them in later chapters, when we cover commodities funds, real estate investment trusts, and partnerships of various kinds. For stock and bond investors, two other types of indirect securities ownership may be appropriate.

One is the trust, which is established through legal arrangements with financial institutions or advisors. In general, establishing a trust involves disposition of financial assets by one person to be invested by an intermediary for the benefit of another person, who often has restricted access to investments made by the intermediary.

Trusts have many uses. Wealthier parents often establish them for children in place of the simpler Uniform Gifts to Minors Accounts. Also, one spouse can arrange them to care for a husband, wife, or other family member whose financial familiarity or responsibility is scant. Life cycle investors who have substantial estates and portfolios would be well-advised to seek legal counsel to determine the usefulness of trusts, for the many types available may repay investigation. Trusts often are complicated, expensive, and a source of domestic hostility, so they're not suited for every investor or family.

A second type of indirect ownership of stocks and bonds is available through the closed-end investment company. Closed-end funds are similar to mutual funds in that shareholders are owners of a company that holds assets in the shares of other companies. However, those shares are purchased and sold through brokers, not through a sponsoring fund, and prices are determined by market transactions, not the net asset value of stocks in the fund. By and large, closed-end funds are less versatile than their open-end counterparts and offer fewer investment attractions. Life cycle investors can construct successful portfolios without them, but they are worthy of consideration.

Let's now take a longer look at how different life cycle investors can make use of mutual funds.

MUTUAL FUNDS AND THE MINOR'S PORTFOLIO

Virtually any type of mutual fund can be highly useful as part of the minor's portfolio, with the possible exception of municipal bond funds because children are likely to be in negligible tax brackets. If the UGMA custodian pursues aggressive gains or long-term growth through the account, he or she can find a mutual fund directed to that strategy. The same is true for custodians who seek aggressive income, intending to reinvest high levels of dividends or interest for optimum compounding. If the custodian is interested in particular industries for their investment potential, there's likely to be a fund emphasizing shares of that industry.

Mutual funds are of greatest use in the minor's portfolio when all distributions are reinvested for additional growth rather than taken in the form of current income. As we noted, mutual funds are accustomed to dealing with

UGMAs, and they are an excellent way to minimize the administrative burden of investing on behalf of children.

MUTUAL FUNDS AND THE YOUNG ADULT'S PORTFOLIO

In general, aggressive growth funds and long-term growth funds are excellent choices for these life cycle investors. Relatively low minimums for initial investment enable younger investors to include many portfolio components on modest incomes. They may subscribe to several funds without draining their income and without tilting their portfolios heavily in favor of one component. Low reinvestment minimums make it possible for investors in their 20s to establish a disciplined approach to investment.

Especially important, these younger investors need to learn about investing and financial markets. Mutual funds can serve this instructional purpose, and regular records from the fund free them from unfamiliar paperwork. Switch privileges among mutual funds permit them to experiment with the alteration of portfolios that is crucial to the concept of life cycle investing, preparing them for the changes they must make in portfolio composition as they age.

With taxes a minor consideration for this group, younger investors can afford to take short-term gains from one fund and switch them to another for maximum returns. For this same reason, municipal bond funds are of less appeal to this age group. We've already noted that income investments aren't generally needed by investors in their 20s. Nonetheless, younger investors who wish to establish a bond component in their portfolios can do so easily through any of the varieties of bond funds available.

Young married couples may discover that each newlywed brings both a highly disparate portfolio and different investment preferences into marriage. Mutual funds offer an excellent means either of consolidating financial assets or of serving the investment preferences of one partner without disrupting the choices of the other.

Many younger investors begin to anticipate retirement as they approach 30, and they will find mutual funds a convenient way to establish Individual Retirement Accounts.

MUTUAL FUNDS AND THE ESTATE BUILDING PORTFOLIO

Between ages 30 and 45 the gradual accumulation of financial assets plays a great role in investment strategy, and mutual funds can be important in achieving that purpose.

Many life cycle investors prefer to extend the aggressive growth and long-term growth funds established during younger years into this next stage of their lives. These life cycle investors are still young enough to risk capital in aggressive vehicles, and the number of working years ahead of them makes long-term growth attractive. Although current income from investments isn't a critical need during these years, some 30 to 45 year-old investors are inclined to buy shares in an aggressive income fund as an alternative to an aggressive growth fund. They feel that long-term compounding of high interest and dividend payments is a more assured source of long-term returns than an aggressive growth fund.

However, as investors mature in their careers and investment judgment, many wish to diversify their holdings into areas of greater familiarity. The exceptional array of funds emphasizing one industry or segment of the economy can parallel the investor's growing area of career expertise and investment acquaintance. Accordingly, many investors at this stage of their lives are attracted to specialty mutual funds holding shares in specific industry groups.

Further, many investors during this stage begin planning for lump sum accumulations upon retirement. Those plans may draw the investors into municipal securities investment trusts featuring a zero-coupon bond element for maximum federally untaxed growth. Otherwise, they may subscribe to conventional municipal bond funds and allow returns to be reinvested in additional fund shares for long-term growth. As always, the investor's tax status will determine the advantage of municipal funds over corporate and government bond funds.

At this stage of life, the decision to participate in bond funds is a judgment call. A bond fund can be very useful in achieving long-term capital growth, especially given mutual funds' low reinvestment minimums and the impossibility of buying part of a bond otherwise. However, equities funds seeking long-term capital growth compete with bond funds in meeting this goal.

Investors beyond age 30 should look upon retirement planning more seriously, and, as always, mutual funds can be an appropriate instrument for IRAs and Keogh Plans. We'll discuss retirement plan investment strategies via mutual fund IRAs in their own chapter.

MUTUAL FUNDS AND THE MATURE PORTFOLIO

Between ages 45 and 55, life cycle investors often find themselves at the peak of their ability to diversify financial holdings. With a decade or two of work ahead of them, they're still young enough to risk aggressive gains while planning for long-term capital growth. Their income generally places them in higher tax brackets, making tax-favored returns more attractive, and they are more earnestly setting aside money for retirement. As we would expect, these investors can be served well through combinations of mutual funds in their portfolios.

Many of these life cycle investors find equity-income funds—those striving for a balance of high current income and long-term capital growth—to be particularly useful. These investors reason that over their remaining 10 to 20 working years balanced funds offer the best prospects for sound returns, for they combine dividends and growth in optimum combinations. Equity-income funds tend to offer steadier gains than funds concentrating on either income or growth. When market conditions favor income stocks, growth funds tend to underperform markets, and when conditions favor growth stocks, income funds often languish. Funds attempting a balance of returns from income and growth can usually offer some increase in net asset value during most markets.

Bond funds of all types can be useful components of the mature portfolio. Municipal bond funds can provide federally untaxed returns, except that whatever capital appreciation they may accrue will be fully taxable. Funds trading U.S. government securities offer maximum assurance against default—although not against capital loss from fluctuating net asset value—and corporate bond funds can provide high returns. The former is of attraction to high-bracket investors, the latter to lower-bracket investors and the middle to conservatively minded investors. As always, mutual funds' low minimums for subsequent investment and opportunity to reinvest returns in additional shares make them fine choices for growth via bonds as well as stocks.

Investors seeking aggressive gains can do so through funds that pursue a quick market killing, or they may prefer funds investing in lower-rated bonds for compounding of higher current income. In addition, the maturing life cycle investor can usually afford to direct holdings into funds exploring particular market segments. If one particular investment group is outperforming the general market, life cycle investors in the 45 to 55 age group can pursue capital growth through mutual funds concentrating in those segments.

During these years, many investors confront their mortality, and husbands, especially, consider reapportioning their estates into their wives' names. Often, one spouse is less familiar with investments than the other, and more often these days it's the husband who is less savvy. With their advantage of professional management, mutual funds can be a comforting receptacle for financial assets realigned between partners, regardless of which is the financial maven. However, wise investors will always consult tax and estate counsel before moving assets under these circumstances.

By all means, these life cycle investors should be placing the maximum affordable amount each year into retirement-anticipation investments. Mutual funds can be a profitable choice for doing so.

MUTUAL FUNDS AND THE SENIOR PORTFOLIO

Beyond age 55, most life cycle investors redirect portfolios away from volatile investments. Switch privileges among mutual funds in the same fund family are always convenient and often profitable, but they are exceptionally important as mature investors reconsider what they need in a portfolio.

Of course, some investors at this age still want and can afford an aggressive growth element, and aggressive growth funds are reasonable for investors beyond age 50. Portfolio diversification afforded through mutual funds means that aggressive growth isn't concentrated in a single equity, cutting the prospect of drastic losses if a single investment turns sour.

Nonetheless, most aggressively oriented investors of this age group prefer aggressive income gains. Even with holdings of more speculative bonds through a fund, payment of interest is still more assured than are aggressive capital gains. Therefore, these investors feel that they can still invest aggressively but with greater prudence by selecting aggressive income funds over aggressive growth funds.

For the most part, however, conservatism governs the senior portfolio. These life cycle investors generally opt for reduced market risk, meaning that they tilt their portfolios away from aggressive elements. Regrettably, they cannot easily avoid capital risk. However, they can moderate their exposure to capital fluctuations through some types of bond funds.

As we noted in our introductory section on mutual funds, bond funds are quite diverse in their market approaches. One type of bond fund of interest to older investors is one that restricts its portfolio of bonds to near-term maturities. These funds offer reduced fluctuation in net asset value because the closer bonds are to maturity, the less is their volatility. Of course, all bond fund managers are free to shorten maturities in their holdings, but managers of near-term funds are obligated to do so by the restrictions of their fund's intentions.

Funds with restricted maturities go by many names. Some, for instance, are called "short-intermediate funds," indicating their holdings are not long-term. Others reveal the same strategy through titles like "limited-term." For the most part, these funds purchase obligations maturing from within two to seven years, although a fund's definition of short-term or limited-term will be specified in the prospectus. In some cases, an intermediate term fund may hold maturities out to 10 years, and that still provides quite a bit of room for capital fluctuation.

One particular fund of precise maturity is the target fund. These funds purchase obligations maturing no later than a specified year. No matter when you subscribe to a target fund, the entire amount of your investment is devoted to obligations maturing in the fund's year of final maturity. Although still mutual funds, target funds differ from their counterpart bond funds in that their holdings all mature no later than the named year, whereas most funds will have a weighted average maturity.

Further, target funds are not in business indefinitely, as conventional mutual bond funds are. Say, for instance, that a mutual fund holds a weighted average maturity of five years. In this case, the arithmetic mean maturity of the fund's bonds is five years. Not every bond in the fund's portfolio will mature in five years. Five years from now, this fund will still have weighted average maturity of five years. If, however, you subscribe to a target fund maturing in five years, five years from now that fund will close its books and distribute returns to shareholders. In short, target funds mature when their holdings mature. That's not the case with conventional bond funds, which are in business more or less indefinitely.

Investing in a fund with a known maturity offers all the

advantages of mutual funds and most of the advantages of direct ownership of bonds. Still, whether an investor chooses a target fund or a conventional bond fund, older life cycle investors prefer to keep a rein on their bond maturities to avoid capital instability. There are many types of government, municipal, and corporate bond funds that feature restricted maturities, so investors have a wide selection to choose from.

Obviously, government bond funds are more favored choices for these life cycle investors. Freedom from default risk is a compelling feature of these bond funds. However, many investors prefer to hold government bonds directly rather than as indirect owners for reasons that will appear later.

Long-term capital growth is still an important consideration during the years after age 55. Equity-income funds and long-term growth funds remain suitable vehicles for meeting those needs for older investors.

These life cycle investors need to look at the mix of all their mutual fund holdings. In many cases, they'll discover that all their funds are directed toward a single objective, particularly if they're participating in a mutual fund as part of a company-sponsored employee investment program. It may be wise to have several funds with a common investment objective, for they can compete to the investor's advantage for his or her continued participation. However, it's as unwise to have all your fund holdings devoted to a single objective as it is to concentrate financial holdings in any other sense. Arrange mutual funds to complement each other's objectives, particularly at this time of life.

MUTUAL FUNDS AND THE RETIREMENT PORTFOLIO

As we've noted before, the critical issues of the retirement portfolio are capital stability, security, current income, and some degree of capital growth. As we've noted frequently, retired investors usually avoid aggressive gains, being generally unable to tolerate prospective losses. As they do throughout the life cycle, mutual funds can provide all the elements important to portfolios of retired investors.

One of the surest sources of stability, security, and current income is the money market mutual fund. We'll discuss the many advantages of this investment in the next chapter.

One chief advantage for retired investors of mutual funds is the alternative of taking gains as reinvested shares or as current receipts. In the case of the growth element of the retirement portfolio, reinvested returns can compound for continued growth, and retirees may choose to postpone current income in favor of the growth element. An intermediate alternative is to receive dividend or interest income as current receipts and to reinvest capital gains distributions in additional fund shares. This alternative may be especially useful for investors in equity-income funds. In general, however, retired investors prefer to take gains in the form of current income. Mutual funds declare distributions on varying schedules, so investors must be selective in timing mutual fund distributions to coincide with other current income.

Bond funds achieve growing importance in the retired investor's portfolio, for they generally declare distributions monthly. This distribution schedule is more frequent than those of stock funds, which often make payments quarterly or even annually. Consequently, bond funds are favored choices for current income.

For maximum assurance against default, U.S. government bond funds are wise choices, and investors who still find taxes a consideration after retirement may select municipal bond funds or municipal investment trusts that pay current income exempt from federal taxes. Retired investors who can afford moderate risks in their portfolios can choose aggressive income funds for slightly higher returns. In addition, income funds concentrating on high-yielding stocks can serve as a companion to bond funds. Some types of selected stock funds, particularly those buying utility shares, may generate above-average current income.

However, these life cycle investors must bear in mind that current income from all mutual funds will vary with market conditions. Therefore, retired investors who elect to be paid fund distributions as they're declared will not receive predictable amounts. If you buy a stock or bond that pays $100 in yearly dividends or interest, you will receive a predictable payment of $25 per quarter in dividends or $50 semi-annually in interest. Not so with funds. Dividend and interest income will vary as fund managers alter the securities in their fund. Capital gains received as current income will fluctuate considerably, which may dissuade some retired investors from leaving money in an aggressive growth fund and taking distributions in cash.

For very sizable accounts—usually $10,000 or more—some funds will permit shareholders to make withdrawals of a constant amount at fixed intervals—for example, $500 per month or quarter. The withdrawal option overcomes the unpredictability of receiving cash distributions, but at a cost. In this case, regular payments may be comprised of returned capital as well as dividends, interest, or capital gains. Consequently, these payments are different from receiving only distributions in cash, for regular withdrawals may constitute drawing down your total investment in the fund. Nonetheless, regular withdrawals are a possibility for investors who wish to assure themselves of predictable payments from their mutual funds.

SUMMARY

Mutual funds provide all life cycle investors access to securities markets, professional management, portfolio diversification, record-keeping services, and an exceptional selection of investment possibilities. These highly versatile investment vehicles permit everyone to invest indirectly for the same purposes served by direct ownership of stocks and bonds. The low minimums for initial and subsequent investments often make mutual funds preferred choices over direct investment, and the ability to switch portfolios among funds in the same investment family is a singular advantage offered by no other investment medium. Investors may choose to permit returns to compound, or they may elect to receive cash distributions. For every investor at every stage of life, there's a mutual fund to meet the needs of life and of life cycle investing.

CHAPTER 8

Money Market Funds and the Life Cycle Investor

If there's one investment of universal use to life cycle investors at every stage of life, it must be the money market fund. In the decade or so they've been available to American investors, they've become the most popular financial vehicle since the cookie jar.

One reason for this justified popularity is their high yield. Money fund managers purchase certificates of deposit, repurchase agreements, commercial paper, banker's acceptances, Treasury bills, and other short-term financial instruments that pay market-level rates of interest. Fund managers then pass these high returns on to the fund's participants. In recent years, fund yields have ranged from 5 to 20 percent and are usually compounded monthly.

Another cause of popularity is their accessibility. Money market funds are available from depository institutions, major brokerage houses, and mutual funds with minimum investments of $500 to $10,000. Some money funds require no minimum for initial investment, and required minimums for adding to the account are generally within the limits of every investor's pocketbook.

Accessibility is matched by other conveniences, such as

checking privileges that permit immediate liquidity. Fund investors may receive distributions in cash, or they may choose to leave their money in the account to compound. Investors who open a money fund through a depository institution receive governmental guarantees against loss, and those who open accounts through mutual funds enjoy switch privileges with other funds in the family, as we noted in the preceeding chapter. Investors who hold money funds through a brokerage may use their account balance as margin collateral, and they can also arrange to pay for securities purchases directly from the money fund.

Another reason for the popularity of money funds is their diversity. The most common type of money fund invests in short-term paper of corporations and financial institutions for the highest yield. Yet some money funds invest in municipal obligations that provide federally untaxed returns, and other money funds invest solely in U.S. government and agency obligations for maximum safety. Consequently, investors seeking the highest yield, the highest post-tax yield, and the highest level of safety against default can find a money fund that meets their needs.

Finally, money funds offer capital stability. Unlike other mutual funds, the net asset value of money market mutual funds never varies from $1, hence their designation as "constant-dollar investments." This same capital stability is also available from funds sponsored by depository institutions and brokerages. That means all offer the same advantages as savings accounts, time certificates, certificates of deposit, and other investments that never fluctuate in price, and money funds are free from length-of-deposit requirements associated with certificates. Consequently, money funds are ideal savings vehicles—safe, liquid, stable, and high-yielding. Their usefulness as savings-type accounts is enhanced by automatic deposit arrangements between your bank and your money fund. You may arrange to have a fixed amount withdrawn from a checking account and deposited to a money fund at regular intervals, enforcing discipline upon your savings program.

In addition to their usefulness as savings, money funds are also excellent temporary repositories for funds awaiting investment elsewhere. If you hold your money fund through a broker, you may request proceeds from sale of securities to be deposited in the fund pending reinvestment, and you can instruct the broker to deposit all interest and dividends in the money fund as they're paid. Otherwise, you can make such deposits in a fund with another sponsor, although you'll lose interest while the deposit is in the mails.

The ability to deposit modest amounts in a money fund makes them well-suited for holding dividends, interest, and other payments you may receive occasionally. Every investor, no matter how experienced or disciplined, is tempted to fritter away a small dividend or interest payment with the excuse that it isn't enough money to invest fruitfully. Of course, over one year and several years, those dissipated payments could have accumulated to an investable mass if they hadn't been spent idly. By forcing yourself to take advantage of the low minimums for subsequent investment in a money fund, you compound growth of your investments and prevent attenuation of your capital.

Money funds are also excellent receptacles during periods of uncertainty and declines in other financial markets. If, for whatever reason, you want to stay out of securities markets for a time, deposits in a money fund will generate returns safely and without capital risk. When the time is right to reinvest elsewhere, your money is readily available. In fact, several investment advisory services counsel investors about the wise timing of movement into and out of money funds and other investments. When the market for certain types of investments appears gloomy, switching your holdings to a money fund will permit you to ride out a downward trend. Conversely, when markets look promising in other securities, money can be moved easily out of its parking place in a money fund into investments offering higher returns. Movement back and forth between money funds and other investments is especially easy through the switch privileges offered by mutual fund families.

Money funds are useful not only for this intermarket maneuvering but also for long-term accumulation of a critical capital mass. Investors who prefer direct investment in stocks and bonds often find it necessary to work with at least $5,000 to $10,000 in order to diversify holdings, to achieve efficiencies of cost, and to gain entry to investments costing many thousands of dollars. Collecting capital for direct investment is made easier through the higher interest and capital stability afforded by money funds. Investors allow their capital to grow in a money fund, and when they've achieved a desired amount, they are able to invest with appropriate economies and diversification.

On the other side of the investment coin, money funds are useful for divesting financial assets. Retired investors, particularly, favor an investment that offers capital stability and frequent payments. For that reason, many life cycle investors beyond age 65 collect their stocks and bonds and place proceeds from securities sales into money funds. They then elect to receive cash payments of earned interest, or they arrange to receive regular payments of interest and, if necessary, principal from the fund.

And, of course, money funds are suitable investments for IRAs and Keogh Plans. They are easy to open, simple to operate, and highly secure against capital loss.

If the first rule of investing is not to lose money, money market funds certainly qualify as one of the first investments anyone should make, and they definitely are the first investment life cycle investors should examine.

MONEY FUNDS AND THE MINOR'S PORTFOLIO

Money funds can enter the life cycle portfolio with the very first investment parents make on their children's behalf. Money market funds available through mutual fund families are acquainted with the paperwork necessary for a UGMA. Parents who recognize the importance of investing for their children's future but who are not especially conversant with financial markets can meet their responsibilities easily by opening a money fund. They can be the modern counterpart of yesterday's parents who opened a savings account for their children at birth, except that savings in a money fund pay greater returns. Regular deposits will have compounded handsomely by the time children are ready for college, even if the UGMA isn't resituated in more sophisticated and potentially more volatile investments.

MONEY FUNDS AND THE YOUNG ADULT'S PORTFOLIO

These life cycle investors will discover that a money fund opened after receiving their first full-time paycheck can become the basis of a lifetime saving plan. They may wish to open a money fund account at a bank, or they can take advantage of the generally lower minimums required by mutual fund families, in which case they also eventually have the option of moving cash into and out of other affiliated funds. In any event, once younger investors strike out on their own, money funds are most likely the first place they should put savings and investment dollars. Their decision to do so could start a lifetime financial arrangement.

MONEY FUNDS AND THE ESTATE BUILDING PORTFOLIO

Money funds are particularly important to the 30 to 45 year old age group, for during these years a source of stable, liquid, high-yielding savings is a paramount consideration. Although the general weighting of the portfolio at this time is toward long-term capital growth with a bit of consideration to aggressive gains, we must remember that during these years people can have many unanticipated demands upon their finances. The liquidity and stability of money funds, as well as the ease of rebuilding the account if it's drawn down, make them excellent havens of cash for a rainy day.

In addition, money market mutual funds give these life cycle investors constant access to other funds in the family. While residing in a money market mutual fund, their cash can be away from stocks and bonds without being totally divorced from access to them. A phone call can move these investors back into the other portfolio elements that cater to this time of life.

MONEY FUNDS AND THE MATURE PORTFOLIO

Being in the mature category doesn't mean that investors have outgrown the usefulness of money funds. Between ages 45 and 55, investors must confront many portfolio needs, and money funds can help meet them.

With higher tax brackets usually a consideration during these years, investors may opt to keep the savings component of their portfolios in a tax-exempt money fund. Like money funds that mainly invest in fully taxable corporate paper, tax-exempts also maintain a constant-dollar price, but they provide returns untouched by the IRS (although state and local taxes usually apply).

With many years of investment experience behind them, life cycle investors at this stage often like to manage their finances more actively. Again, money funds permit stable, convenient receptacles for cash temporarily out of one investment medium and awaiting reinvestment. Money funds serve mature investors' portfolio reallocations.

By all means, investors in this age group should establish IRAs and, where appropriate, Keogh Plans. These tax-deferred retirement-anticipation plans can be served well by money funds, for they provide optimum security against capital loss, market-level rates of interest, and frequent compounding. Money funds serve these life cycle investors' retirement planning.

MONEY FUNDS AND THE SENIOR PORTFOLIO

Between ages 55 and 65, investors begin reorienting portfolios away from high-risk investments, and money funds certainly help them do so. In addition to exceptional capital stability, money funds investing exclusively in U.S. government obligations provide near-certainty against default.

There is, however, an important point to bear in mind before these life cycle investors should commit themselves heavily to money funds emphasizing U.S. government obligations. Many investors in this age group have the financial wherewithal to purchase directly the kinds of high-cost investments commonly purchased by money funds, and there may be good reasons for them to take advantage of their capital by direct rather than indirect investment. One reason is that the IRS defines the distributions of money funds as fully taxable dividends, tax-exempt funds invested in municipal obligations being excepted. Therefore, if an investor deposited, say, $25,000 in a money fund invested in government securities, returns from the fund are taxable by states and municipalities. If he or she had invested the $25,000 directly in U.S. government obligations, interest payments would be exempt from all but federal taxation.

Contradictory tax treatment won't influence investors who place large sums in tax-exempt money funds instead of buying municipal obligations directly. With only occasional exceptions, the returns provided by tax-exempt money funds are nearly identical to the returns of the underlying securities themselves, and both are free of federal tax.

Tax considerations aside, money funds of all types can serve the senior portfolio as well as, and in the same ways, they serve portfolios appropriate to other times of life.

MONEY FUNDS AND THE RETIREMENT PORTFOLIO

Even retirees need to set money aside for unforseen occasions—or, better yet, for spur-of-the-moment enthusiasms they denied themselves earlier in life—and, as we've seen, money funds are the vehicle of choice for doing so. As we've also seen, money funds can meet retirees' needs for current income if investors arrange to receive distributions in cash rather than have them reinvested to compound. In addition, investors can arrange for set monthly payments of fund income and principal if they hold a sizable account in a money fund.

As retired investors begin to draw down their IRAs, many prefer to sell stocks and bonds and place the proceeds in a money fund from which they then receive regular income distributions. Money funds make it possible for them to convert IRA investments, especially zero-coupon securities, into investments providing current income.

SUMMARY

In conclusion, money market funds provide safety, stability, liquidity, convenience, compounded returns, and current income for investors of every age. Funds can handle investments of almost any size, making them useful to investors with the smallest and largest sums to set aside. They are ideal savings accounts, temporary parking spots for capital between investments, safe havens during market uncertainty, and instruments to create income-producing assets. Some money funds provide federally tax-exempt returns along with all the other advantages associated with conventional funds. With all of this going for them, money funds are investments for a lifetime and for every time of life.

CHAPTER 9

Limited Partnerships and the Life Cycle Investor

In addition to indirect ownership of financial securities, life cycle investors can also be indirect owners of some types of business entities. The term *indirect* lacks legal precision in this context, but the general idea is similar to what we discussed in chapters on mutual funds and money market funds. Through the legal arrangement of the limited partnership, life cycle investors turn money over to professionals experienced in management of certain businesses.

The kind of partnership we're talking about isn't exactly what is normally meant by a partnership—that is, a couple of people pooling money and expertise and going into business together. Rather, what we mean is a bunch of unrelated investors, who probably never see each other, contributing only capital to a business arrangement operated by a third party. This third party is an established group of entrepreneurs, usually called "general partners," who specialize in a particular business. Occasionally, general partners will solicit limited partners directly, but most often investors gain access to the business through brokerages that sell limited partnerships much as they sell financial securities.

Everyone associated with this arrangement benefits—
potentially. As an intermediary, the brokerage collects sales
fees for matching general and limited partners. The general
partners, who often have sizable personal or company capital at risk, receive additional capital from private investors
without having to enter expensive borrowing markets. The
limited partners receive several advantages.

First, they can gain entry to a business that might otherwise be closed to them. For example, most limited partnerships cost $5,000 to $25,000, and sometimes they sell for as
little as $2,000 when they are eligible to be included in In-
dividual Retirement Accounts. Considering the types of
partnerships offered through this arrangement—and we'll
do exactly that in a moment—minimum capital requirements for the total venture are usually much, much higher,
frequently in the $250,000 to $1 million range.

Second, as limited partners, investors are not usually
liable for losses beyond the amount of initial investment.
That can be important in the case of more speculative businesses where rewards are not assured and where downside
risks can be considerable. These risks are usually borne by
the general partners, who, of course, receive returns com-
mensurate with their greater risk if the enterprise pays off.

Third, limited partners not only receive pro rata returns
from the business, but they are also eligible for certain
types of tax credits and tax exemptions from their share in
the business. In many cases, as we'll see, these credits and
exemptions are more lucrative than the income from the
partnerships.

Fourth, the paperwork and accounting are the responsibility of the general partners, freeing life cycle investors
from the necessity of dealing with administration.

In contrast to these advantages, limited partners must
also be aware of disadvantages to this type of investment.

First, the Securities Exchange Commission and other
regulatory bodies often establish minimum net worth requirements that investors must meet before they're eligible
to participate in some businesses. Many times partnership
ventures are so speculative that governmental bodies insist
that private investors meet requirements of liquid net

worth (cash and securities) and total net worth (all financial assets) as proof they can withstand losses. Therefore, even if you can meet the minimum partnership requirements, you might not meet minimum requirements for your total financial position. That means you might not be able to become a limited partner in some types of ventures.

Second, not all partnerships are liquid, meaning you may not be able to sell your partnership interest when you wish. Often, brokerages that act as middlemen for your entry into the partnership will maintain markets in the partnership, but such isn't always the case. If your investment turns against you, you might not be able to exit as easily as if you'd invested in stocks and bonds. Sometimes partnership agreements will contain a proviso that requires general partners to buy back interests from limited partners. Even where such arrangements exist, though, the repurchase price may be determined by an unattractive formula, or in other cases limited partners can't enforce buy-back requirements for several years.

Third, the government constantly examines partnerships to assure they meet Internal Revenue Service requirements pertaining to prospective return as contrasted with advantages of tax credits. In the past, many investors have purchased partnership interests only to find the IRS disallows deductions the investor had hoped to claim. Further, Congress has an unsavory history of altering rules for income and tax credits from partnerships after the fact. Consequently, limited partners can discover that legal changes no longer make their investment as desirable as it previously was. This circumstance alters not only returns from the partnership but also the value it commands in resale.

Fourth, partnerships require close examination by investors not intimately conversant with the business undertaken. As a limited partner, you are essentially going into business with a group of strangers. This relationship is different from the relationship you have as owner of stocks and bonds and mutual funds. In the former case, you have partners; in the latter case, you essentially have employees. As a shareholder in a company, you employ management. As a shareholder in a mutual fund, you employ fund managers. True, you're something of an absentee employer, but that is still quite different from being a distant partner.

With those advantages and disadvantages behind us, let's look at three types of partnerships into which life cycle investors can most easily enter by virtue of the partnerships' widespread accessibility via financial intermediaries.

The first type of limited partnership is the commodity pool. Because commodities investments serve a rather constrained purpose among the five portfolio elements, we have a separate chapter—the next one, in fact—devoted to them. More important for our purposes are two other widely available partnerships, the real estate partnership and the oil and gas partnership.

To take great liberties in explaining what these latter two types of partnerships accomplish, we will say, for the sake of consistency within our own categories, that their purpose is to produce current income. They can do that in two ways. First, they produce, immediately or eventually, cash-in-hand receipts. That is, they are constituted for the purpose of generating current income. Second, they produce tax credits and offsets that reduce federal tax liability, thereby increasing other personal income by reducing federal taxes. That is, their chief purpose is to maximize an investor's offsets against other income, leaving more of that income available after taxes. The partnership's intentions to concentrate on current income, tax advantages, or combinations of the two will be stated clearly in the offering circulars and companion documents.

In the case of real estate partnerships, investors can choose among partnerships that deal in commercial, industrial, and residential real estate and structures. In some cases, the partnership may be involved in constructing and leasing buildings to businesses or individuals. In other cases, the partnership may purchase and lease constructed buildings, leaving the actual construction to others.

Depending upon the intentions of the partnership, limited partners may find themselves fortunately graced with regular payments representing pro rata shares of rent paid to the partnership. In almost all cases, limited partners will be entitled to claim depreciation and other business-related costs as offsets against federal tax. Again, the relative weighting of current income versus tax write-offs depends upon the nature of the partnership.

For obvious reasons, real estate partnerships offering high depreciation and tax write-offs will be most attractive to high tax-bracket investors. Equally obvious, income-oriented partnerships will be more attractive to investors needing high levels of current income to supplement other sources or to investors preferring to reinvest current receipts for compounded growth.

Much has been written about the desirability of real estate investments, and many life cycle investors own rental property—duplexes, apartments, condominiums, and time-share arrangements. However, many investors are discovering that tax and income advantages applying to personal real estate ownership are equally accessible through real estate partnerships. In addition, as an indirect landlord you don't receive midnight phone calls about broken refrigerators.

Oil and gas partnerships are slightly more complicated, for they come in many types, are constantly subject to revised laws, and rarely generate predictable income or tax write-offs. There are three general types of O&Gs.

Drilling partnerships deal largely in finding hydrocarbons in unproven areas, an undertaking fraught with exceptional risks and favored by the prospect of exponential returns. In addition, at least under current law, drilling partnerships offer the highest tax write-offs, particularly as a percentage of investment. Many of these write-offs, such as intangible drilling costs, dry-hole costs, and abandoned-lease costs, are immediately deductible, meaning that investors receive greater deductible costs early in their participation. High up-front write-offs often attract the attention of the IRS, however.

Development partnerships, also called completion programs, exploit proven hydrocarbon reserves. Risks and rewards are lower than for drilling partnerships, and tax offsets are still available, although generally over a longer period for fewer immediate credits.

Income partnerships generally purchase proven, producing wells at discounts from the initial developer and attempt to operate them productively. Their purpose is to produce current income for as long as possible. Income partnerships feature fewer write-offs, but they offer the lowest risks. The investor's chief worry is how long the hydrocarbon field will remain productive. As a generality, investors historically have received 12 to 16 percent returns on O&G income partnerships.

Unfortunately, limited partnerships don't apply broadly to all categories of life cycle investors. Therefore, there's little point in running through the life cycle stages to see how this investment can benefit various times of an investor's life.

For starters, meeting investor suitability standards is quite difficult for younger investors. O&G income funds, for instance, typically require a net worth that is four times the amount of your investment and at least $90,000. Unless investors achieve fortunate financial status relatively early in life, these requirements will bar them from partnership participation.

Similarly, partnerships featuring extensive tax advantages are less attractive to younger investors, who typically do not face tax considerations appearing in more mature career years. In order to receive maximum advantage from most types of partnerships, investors must meet suitability standards and be in a high-enough income bracket to warrant tax-advantaged investments.

The speculative elements of some types of partnerships, particularly O&G drilling partnerships, make them unsuited for all but the aggressive income component of the portfolio. In addition, the $5,000, or so that is usually required to participate as a limited partner may tilt the portfolio in favor of one element, preventing balance and diversification.

The one area in which limited partnerships may be of broadest appeal to life cycle investors is in their applicability to retirement planning. As we noted, some limited partnerships in real estate and oil and gas are approved for Individual Retirement Accounts. Typically, IRA-approved partnerships are those concentrating on current income, which can be reinvested for tax-deferred returns. Tax-offsets do not apply to IRA investments, and highly leveraged investments that provide the greatest potential returns also don't qualify.

Chiefly, therefore, limited partnerships are of most advantage to the senior portfolio and to the retirement portfolio. Between ages 55 and 65, investors typically have accumulated the net worth to qualify them as suitable participants, and they are then more likely to be in tax brackets that receive the advantages of partnership write-offs. The combination of income and/or write-offs can serve these life cycle investors well. In addition, retired life cycle investors can profit from the current income of limited partnerships constructed to provide current receipts. Steady payments of pro rated rent or drilling royalties are a handsome companion to interest, dividends, and pension checks, and as a generality, these investors don't require tax offsets as they did when fully employed.

SUMMARY

For investors who have amassed the necessary net worth and who can afford to concentrate some of their assets in limited partnerships, these investments can provide tax-advantaged returns and current income, making them attractive companions to the other elements of the portfolio. They can provide aggressive gains, current income, and the tax offsets to make other income less vulnerable to the IRS. More than any other category of investments that we've covered thus far, however, investing in limited partnerships requires earnest discussion with both your investment advisor and your tax planner, and many life cycle investors can construct successful portfolios without limited partnerships. Nonetheless, they deserve a look.

CHAPTER 10

Commodities and the Life Cycle Investor

Another financial vehicle frequently offered as a limited partnership is the commodity pool. Just as life cycle investors can contribute capital to general partners for investment in real estate and hydrocarbons, so can they also become limited partners in businesses that trade commodity contracts.

Commodities trading has become enormously popular in recent years, with trading volume often exceeding stock and bond markets by sizable margins. Reasons for this popularity boom are many, but chief among them is the possibility of achieving fantastic gains for very small investments. Unlike stock and bond markets, in which investors pay the full price for securities or purchase them on 50 percent margin, commodities markets permit investors to put up miniscule deposits to hold positions. Favorable price moves create profits many times the size of the initial outlay.

Until relatively recently, commodities contracts were written only on what you might think of as produce of the earth—wheat, corn, sugar, potatoes—or on other agricultural products—chickens, swine, cattle. Closely affiliated are agricultural/commercial products, such as lumber, feeds and fats, and industrial commodities such as heating oil.

In the not-too-distant past, international trade made necessary trading of futures contracts in foreign currencies and precious metals. More recently, trading in financial abstractions like interest rate futures has grown to exceptional popularity.

Many investors are direct participants in commodities and futures markets. That is, like direct purchasers of stocks and bonds, they phone a broker and place orders for their personal accounts. Those orders are one of two types: contracts obligating them to deliver the commodity in question and contracts obligating them to purchase the commodity in question. These contracts can be bought, creating "long" positions, or they can be sold, creating "short" positions. Those who "go long" on contracts are expecting rising prices for the commodity; those who "go short" are anticipating declines in price of the commodity.

In many cases, these direct participants are individuals involved in producing the commodities, or they are corporations involved in commodity-sensitive enterprises. Let's say, for example, that you're a wheat farmer. If you plant your wheat today, many months elapse before you take your product to market. By entering into a commodity contract to deliver your wheat at a specific price on that distant date, you can fix the price per bushel that you will receive. Otherwise, you are subject to the vagaries of markets in your particular commodity. Through commodities contracts, you, the wheat farmer, know what you will receive for your labors.

On the other side of this transaction could be large corporations. Say, for instance, that you're the chief buyer of wheat for the General Mills Cereal Division. It would be to your advantage to know what you'll have to pay many months from now for the tons of wheat your company will need to produce breakfast foods. By entering commodities markets, you can fix the price at which your company will buy wheat, removing the risk of escalating markets and correspondingly declining profits.

In addition, there are many other uses for commodities and futures trading. Let's say that you're the treasurer for an international corporation expecting a payment in Swiss francs later this year. As an American corporation, you must convert those francs to American dollars. Your chief worry in this case is that the price of Swiss francs will decline against the American dollar by the time your company receives the payment. As treasurer, you can enter foreign exchange markets and today fix the price at which you can sell francs for dollars. Or let's say that you're a building contractor whose chief business worries are the price of lumber and interest rates. Commodities markets can be quite useful to you in reducing the costs and risks associated with your business.

For the most part, however, commodities and futures trades do not involve actual purchase and delivery of the commodity in question. Instead, they involve purchase, sale, and offsetting transactions through which the contract itself is an instrument of financial value. You need not have a business need for trading commodities, merely the desire to profit from the transactions and the acumen to do so. Most people certainly have the desire, but few have the acumen. That's where commodity pools can be useful.

Commodity pools are limited partnerships that make it possible for untutored investors to achieve profits in commodity markets through professional money management. As was the case with the limited partnerships we examined in the previous chapter, private investors—the limited partners—purchase units of participation in commodity pools managed by general partners. General partners make investments on behalf of the total partnerships and usually assume the risks in going short. In return, general partners receive profits from the trading activities and usually also receive a management fee that is a percentage of funds invested.

One important difference between commodities pools and other partnerships is that you usually don't know beforehand the kinds of investments the general partners will make. Unlike the O&G or real estate partnerships, commodities trading involves many completely different kinds of investments. Your general partner could be trading pork bellies or platinum one day and soybeans or sugar the next. He or she could be long in contracts or short. Although you will receive financial reports, you have no prior knowledge of where your money will be invested. More than any other financial undertaking, investing in commodity pools is irreducibly a matter of giving a stranger your money and hoping he or she can be trusted with it.

When entering a commodity pool it is especially important that you ask whether you can lose more money than your initial investment. The general advantage of the limited partnership in commodities is that you can't. However, in some cases you can be liable for more than your initial investment, which can be disastrous if you hook up with general partners whose dice turn cold.

The chief disadvantage to all commodities and futures trading is the exceedingly high likelihood of loss. Commodities markets are a "zero-sum game": for every winner, there is a loser. In order for you to make money, someone has to lose money, and in order for someone to make money, you might have to lose. Research confirms that the great majority of small investors lose in commodities trading, and in many cases having a professional in your corner is no assurance of winning.

Consequently, you must regard commodities pools strictly as an aggressive gains investment, although some pools occasionally produce long-term gains and can be arranged to provide some current, if unpredictable, income. They serve no other purpose within the five portfolio elements.

However, having declared that commodities pools are strictly aggressive gains investments, we need to back away from that blanket assertion. In some cases, *direct* commodities investments—not commodities pools—can serve conservative purposes. Let's say that you hold a very sizable position in gold as a long-term investment. Given that gold prices occasionally move with great volatility, it could be that you want to defend your position against adverse declines by entering into commodities contracts. In a related circumstance, let's say that you want to receive current income from your holdings of gold. You can sell commodities options against your holdings, much as you could sell listed options on your stocks, and receive income from your metals. Therefore, some types of commodities transactions can be used for stability and income.

It seems reasonable to assume, though, that very few

readers are in such circumstances as to warrant use of commodities and commodities options for conservative and income purposes. Those who are, no doubt, are much more sophisticated than the average life cycle investor. Therefore, we'll stick with our original assertion: virtually all life cycle investors must enter commodities pools with the understanding that they are striving for aggressive gains and also with the understanding that this course is fraught with much-above-average possibility for loss.

Generally, investors enter commodities pools as a consequence of contact with agents of the managing partners, and only rarely do they have access through financial intermediaries like brokers. Most investors will have to meet suitability standards regarding income and net worth, total and liquid, although these standards are not generally as high as for the other limited partnerships we discussed. Nonetheless, never invest a cent more than you can afford to lose entirely in a commodity pool.

In general, limited partnerships cost $5,000 to $25,000. In some cases, commodities pools are qualified for Individual Retirement Accounts at a maximum $2,000 investment, although many advisors question whether anything as volatile as a commodity investment is appropriate for an IRA. For these amounts of money, you can join forces with account managers who'll trade on your behalf.

Two of the more successful and reputable commodities firms offering partnerships are Collins Commodities and R. J. O'Brien & Associates.

Collins Commodities	R. J. O'Brien & Associates, Inc.
160 Broadway, Suite 802	550 West Jackson Blvd.
New York, NY 10038	Chicago, IL 60606
Phone: (800) 221–3183	Phone: (800)621–0757
(212) 608–7451	(312) 648–7304

These firms can provide you both contract specifications and additional readings about markets. There are, however, other sources that you can and should consult on your own, for there is a great deal more to know about these markets than we've covered in this scanty introduction. A very informative, if somewhat detailed, book on the subject is *The*

Dow Jones-Irwin Guide to Commodities Trading by Bruce G. Gould (Homewood, Ill.: Dow Jones-Irwin, 1981). Commodities exchanges also publish free pamphlets about various commodities and futures investments. You might wish to write The Chicago Mercantile Exchange at 44 W. Jackson Blvd., Chicago, IL 60606, or phone (312) 648–1000.

While you're waiting for those publications to arrive, let's look at how commodities pools can serve the aggressive gains component of the portfolio.

COMMODITIES POOLS AND THE MINOR'S PORTFOLIO

For the most part, the aggressive gains offered by commodities investments are not the type suited for the UGMA. Unlike the kinds of gains offered by aggressive stock or mutual fund investments, custodians who invest in commodities on behalf of minors run the risk of invested capital dwindling to nothing in a brief time. Usually with stocks there's something left if an investment doesn't pay off, but if a commodities position turns against you, you can lose everything. That's imprudent management, and given the lengthy period in which custodians can afford to let investments run in a UGMA, there is little reason to take such risks with an investment in commodities. In addition, capital gains losses are of no consolation to minors, whose tax bracket is negligible. Therefore, Uncle Sam won't underwrite part of the commodities loss. All of these circumstances combine to make commodities pools generally ill-suited to the minor's portfolio.

COMMODITIES POOLS AND THE PORTFOLIO OF YOUNG ADULTHOOD

Between ages 22 and 30, few investors can meet the suitability requirements for a commodities investment, and for those who can, the minimums required to participate will likely tilt their portfolios heavily in favor of aggressive gains. In practice, absence of diversification and concentration on a single portfolio element might not be so awful, but in principle it's an unwise course. Even though these young life cycle investors can afford to take aggressive risks, they must be mindful of the time ahead of them in which to invest for long-term accumulations.

As a practical matter for investors of this age group, money invested in commodities pools is likely to be spent to the detriment of other portfolio needs, particularly personal savings. There will be time enough in their lives for the kind of high-risk investments represented by commodities. They can afford—and *afford* is probably the best word—to wait.

COMMODITIES POOLS AND THE ESTATE BUILDING PORTFOLIO

During this time of life, investors generally feel they can take some aggressive risks with their portfolios. Assuming they've been conscientious about meeting the long-term growth requirements of their portfolios, allocating a sensible amount of their capital to commodities pools can be a reasonable way for these life cycle investors to pursue more vigorous gains. However, these investors must be exceedingly disciplined in electing this investment choice, for they have many demands upon their finances and investment capital.

If there are children in the family, investors will want to assure that they set aside prudent sums in UGMAs, and it's also important that these life cycle investors devote funds to IRAs. Especially, they must remember that the boom-and-bust amplitudes of commodities are not suited to the long-term building of financial estates that should be the key consideration at this time of life.

Nonetheless, if these life cycle investors have attended to their other portfolio elements, they're justified in directing capital into commodities for the aggressive gains component, as long as they don't invest any money the loss of which would alter their personal circumstances severely.

COMMODITIES POOLS AND THE MATURE PORTFOLIO

Life cycle investors in the 45 to 55 year old age group must be particularly sensitive to retirement planning and to the tax consequences of their investments. The instability of commodities gains and their payment of some fully taxable gains are incompatible with other investment goals. They must also be aware that aging parents, career aspirations, and maturing children can cause unexpected drains upon savings. Still, once these considerations have been accommodated, it's reasonable that these life cycle investors would consider establishing or expanding the aggressive gains component of their portfolios with a commodity partnership.

By this age, investors generally can meet financial suitability requirements necessary for entering commodities pools, and they still have a working life long enough to recover losses. Although temperament usually inclines one to conservatism at this age, investors shouldn't dismiss commodities entirely.

COMMODITIES POOLS AND THE SENIOR PORTFOLIO

Between ages 55 and 65, investors should participate in commodities pools only if they have fully accommodated the growth component of their portfolios and they have truly "extra" money on their hands. If these life cycle investors can look into their mirrors and checkbooks and genuinely decide that $5,000 and up isn't a lot of money to lose, then they should consider the gains possible from commodity pools. Otherwise, they're better off emotionally and financially to undertake less volatile investments.

The question of what constitutes "a lot of money" is an individual one, of course, but life cycle investors must evaluate that term with reference to prospective income, and not merely cash-on-hand. For most of us, $5,000 is a lot of money in an emotional sense at almost any age. But if you're 25, that isn't a lot of money with respect to anticipated lifetime earnings, even if it is a fair chunk of all the cash you could lay your hands on. Conversely, at age 60, $5,000 may not be a lot of money with respect to on-hand resources, but it could be a noteworthy sum as measured by the income stream remaining to be earned. That's why it frequently makes more sense for a younger investor to be involved in commodities even if older investors could more easily come up with the money. Investors who've reached the stage of the senior portfolio must evaluate a commodity pool investment with respect to anticipated earnings, not merely with regard to on-hand funds.

COMMODITIES POOLS AND THE RETIREMENT PORTFOLIO

Life cycle investors who are quite comfortably situated for retirement might still wish to have a small participation in commodities for the sake of the action. But that's only if they are very comfortably situated indeed. This simply isn't the time of life in which people can usually afford to lose money. In addition, it's not the time of life they should be investing for aggressive gains. Given that commodity investments meet no other portfolio element, most retired investors should stay away from them.

SUMMARY

Commodities pools are a type of limited partnership that makes it possible for life cycle investors to receive dramatic short-term gains by entrusting capital to others. Although we have discussed pools as generally acceptable investments for investors between ages 30 and 55, the real issue is the investor's ability and willingness to lose everything in an investment, and that's not always a matter of age. Commodities pools can serve a legitimate portfolio purpose—a very restricted purpose, served at great risk to be sure, but serve it they can. For all but the most sophisticated investors, commodities pools are preferable to direct personal participation in commodities markets, but many life cycle investors can construct very successful portfolios without commodities at all. That doesn't mean they should be ignored, but it does mean they should be examined as one of many vehicles that meet the aggressive gains component of the portfolio.

CHAPTER 11

Precious Metals and the Life Cycle Investor

Since the late 1970s, few investments have attracted as much attention as precious metals, particularly gold and silver. During the past 10 years, precious metals have developed an avid following among market newsletter services, private investors, and professional money managers. Mutual funds now offer portfolios of mining stocks, brokerage firms have launched precious metals certificate programs, and investment services have initiated new and innovative ways to purchase and sell precious metals.

One reason for the popularity of gold and silver is their potential for rapid price appreciation. In recent memory, silver appreciated from a few cents to more than $50 per ounce, and gold grew from $35 to more than $800 per ounce. Even during the equally dramatic price declines that brought silver to an early 1985 price below $7 and gold to $300, intermediate market moves made it possible for investors to realize short-term gains of many percent as metals prices fluctuated.

Another reason for precious metals' popularity is long-term capital growth. At a price of $300, investors who bought gold at $800 aren't too happy, but those who bought at $35 still have gains to their credit.

In addition, gold and silver have enjoyed favor for what you might call insurance value. Historically, investors have regarded precious metals as survival holdings. Even those who aren't doomsday survivalists recognize that gold and silver are likely to be valued in an economic collapse, and they purchase metals against the possibility of that day. Many investors regard precious metals as a hedge against inflation. Also, many investors buy precious metals as a hedge against losses elsewhere in their portfolio, for the price of gold and silver tends, though not inevitably, to move opposite to prices of paper investments.

Just as there are many reasons why investors might be drawn to precious metals, so are there many forms in which they can invest in metals.

As we've seen, investors can participate in price rises— and declines—through commodities trading and commodities pools. Investors can buy and sell, personally or indirectly as pool participants, contracts for delivery of gold and silver. Commodities trading offers the chance for capital gains, but only institutional traders or highly capitalized individuals buy metals through commodity markets with the intention to take delivery. Futures markets give investors gains from price moves in metals, but they aren't the investment of choice for those who want to own the metal itself.

In addition, investors can also buy and sell options on futures contracts, a recent financial innovation that makes one investment—a futures contract that's already based upon a second investment, namely gold or silver—the underlying medium for a third investment—the option. As we discussed in the chapter on publicly traded stock options, options on futures contracts provide investors the opportunity to profit from upward and downward moves in prices of underlying metals and also offer downside protection as well as current income from the sale of puts and calls.

Options on futures contracts are of use to life cycle investors who wish to profit from price moves with less risk than trading futures contracts. Unlike trading futures contracts themselves, the most that investors dealing with options on futures contracts can lose is the price of the option. Conversely, of course, profit potential is frequently less than with futures trading, although still potentially substantial.

For further information about options on futures contracts, one source is COMEX, a major market-maker. Write Commodity Exchange, Inc. at Four World Trade Center, New York, NY 10048. The phone number is (212) 938–2900.

Another derivative—that is, second-hand—means of achieving investment gains from precious metals is the purchase of stock in mining companies and shares in mutual funds that concentrate in such companies. Shares in such companies and mutual funds react to the price of the metals they mine, just as stock in any company reacts to the fortunes of the company's product. Again, derivative investment offers the opportunity for capital gains, but not the actual possession of the metals.

(Note: One mutual fund offers subscribers the option of taking quarterly dividends in gold coins. It is International Investors, Inc. at 122 East 42d Street, New York, NY 10168. The phone number is (800) 221–2220. For bond buyers, The Sunshine Mining Company has issued debentures redeemable in silver.)

Investors who prefer to participate in gold and silver as owners of mining shares are often attracted to penny mining shares, so named because of their very low prices, often literally pennies per share. These cheap stocks, not all of which are shares of metals mining companies, offer the chance for exceptional percentage gains and reduced downside risks: an investment of a few hundred dollars produces attractive gains if prices move and represents minimal exposure if prices turn sour.

Investors who purchase penny mining shares directly often follow specialized advisory services. One service is The Penny Stock Journal at P.O. Box 2009, Mahopac, NY 10541. Those who prefer indirect investment in gold and silver shares—not necessarily penny stocks—are attracted to the Fidelity Precious Metals and Minerals Portfolio from the Fidelity Investment Group at 82 Devonshire Street, Boston, MA 02109. The phone number is (800) 225–6190.

Investors interested in indirect holdings of penny shares—
not all of them mining companies—might be attracted to
Combined Penny Stock Fund, Inc., a new closed-end investment company traded in the over-the-counter market and
listed in *The Wall Street Journal* under "Additional OTC
Quotes." The address of Combined Penny Stock Fund is
P.O. Box 6429, Colorado Springs, CO 80934. The phone
number is (303) 636–1522.

Another popular form of investing in gold and silver is
the certificate program. Major brokerage firms and large
metals dealers collect small sums from many investors and
purchase bulk bullion with the accumulated funds, pro rating each investor's ownership according to his and her contribution. They then issue certificates testifying to ownership of a specific quantity of metal. Investors can add to
their holdings with additional contributions of small
amounts, often as little as $100. The brokerage maintains
liquidity, so you can cash your holdings with ease.

Certificate programs give life cycle investors ownership of
bullion, enabling them to participate in price advances, but
they do not give you possession, as the metal is held (with
storage fee) in a consolidated account. One certificate program sponsored by a reputable agency is the Citibank Gold
Purchase Plan. The address is Citibank Gold Center, 399
Park Avenue, New York, NY 10043. The phone number is
(800) 223–1080. The minimum initial investment is $1,000.

A related type of program for gold and silver is available
through USA Metals. USA permits investors to buy gold
and silver on margin but without margin calls or interest.
You secure your holdings with a down payment representing a fraction of the purchase price, and you can maintain
the account for three years, at which time you must sell out
or pay the remaining balance to take delivery. Write USA
Metals at 180 Newport Center Drive, Newport Beach, CA
92660. The phone number is (714) 640–4561.

As we've noted, though, none of these methods of investing in precious metals permits investors to hold gold or silver directly. For many reasons, including catastrophe value,
immediate cash liquidity, and foreign transportation, some
investors prefer to invest directly in metals bullion, either
coins or bars. Available in weights of one-tenth ounce to a

kilogram, gold and silver bullion give investors the opportunity to profit from price rises and, in the case of bullion coins, give investors some assurance that they'll have a presumably universally accepted medium of exchange in the event of wholesale economic collapse.

The easiest way to purchase bullion is through dealers, many of whom advertise nationally or are abundant in most cities. Investors merely walk in the dealer's door, buy the desired size coin or bar, and walk out with their metal in their pocket. One advantage to purchase through a local dealer is that he or she will usually buy metals back from you if you wish to sell, although in highly troubled markets sometimes local dealers will refuse to maintain liquidity.

Following the collapse of Bullion Reserve of North America that cost investors millions of dollars in a highly publicized scandal, many advisors insist that the only way to purchase bullion is for direct personal holding. If you're going to pay for something, they say, then take possession of it, even if you do business with dealers of unquestioned integrity.

Purchase of bullion gives investors the opportunity to participate in rising prices of metals, although costs associated with direct holdings, such as storage fees, minting premiums, dealer repurchase discounts, cut into gains, particularly for smaller holdings.

One criticism of holding gold and silver directly or through certificate programs is that metals offer no current income, unlike shares in dividend-paying mining companies and precious metals mutual funds. As we noted earlier, metals investors can receive current income as writers of options on futures contracts, but that isn't the same as receiving income directly from personal holdings of metals. There is, however, an alternative for income-oriented holders of metals, and that's the customer-granted option, which permits investors to write calls on their holdings and receive the premium as current income.

The distinction between options on futures contracts and customer-granted options is an important one. In the former case, investors purchase options on which the underlying investment is a futures contract—that is, the option represents one degree of abstraction beyond the abstraction of the futures contract. In the case of customer-granted options, investors who already hold metals buy and sell options backed by their holdings. By granting a call option, for example, investors who hold these metals can receive a cash premium just like those who write calls on their stocks. Of course, investors risk the possibility that their holdings will be called away from them by the purchaser of the call, and the minimum unit of optionable holdings is usually 1,000 ounces.

For information on how to receive current income from metals holdings through customer-granted options, contact MONEX International, Ltd. at 4910 Birch Street, Newport Beach, CA 92660. The phone number is (800) 854–3361.

Before moving on to discuss how life cycle investors might wish to view precious metals at different times of their lives, there's a final point we should cover. One problem in evaluating precious metals is the emotional amplitudes that surround them. An incredible number of investors and advisors are so single-mindedly enthusiastic about precious metals that they simply can't be trusted for an objective opinion. In their view, virtually every economic and political circumstance is abundant evidence favoring precious metals.

You may, for instance, have seen advertisements proclaiming, "Many advisors predict $2,000 per ounce gold by 1987. What if they're only half right?" To which the jaundiced investor might respond, "What if they're only half-witted?" The problem is that metals enthusiasts aren't half right or half wrong. Their predictions are either right—sometimes by good fortune and not good analysis—or wrong. Frequently they're wrong because they aren't critics of their own thinking. They endorse metals somewhat like the piano player who can only play "Chopsticks": urging people to buy metal is the only tune they know.

There's no question that precious metals can make money for investors. They have provided, and presumably can again provide, aggressive gains and long-term gains. Some evidence suggests that they can also reduce the overall volatility of your portfolio, and, depending upon your temperament, perhaps they can help you sleep better if the prospect of financial apocalypse gives you insomnia. But there's also no question about two other issues. First, any investment that routinely fluctuates 25 to 50 percent of its price cannot be said to have dependable value. Second, many investors have constructed very successful portfolios without metals at all.

That said, let's look at how precious metals might serve life cycle investors.

PRECIOUS METALS AND THE MINOR'S PORTFOLIO

There's something in the American psyche that seems to motivate grandparents to give coins to grandchildren, and when those coins have been gold and silver, capital gains have generally been the consequence. A little illegality may also have been the consequence, as Americans have been prohibited from owning gold at various times in our history.

You can still buy precious metals for your children, and if they hold them for many years some capital appreciation may be a likely result. However, the most reasonable choice for metals in the UGMA is probably stock in mining companies, shares of precious metals mutual funds, or penny stock funds weighted with mining shares. These derivative metals investments offer capital appreciation and reinvestable dividends, and therefore are better suited to the long-term orientation of the minor's portfolio.

In some cases, precious metals certificate programs will serve the custodian who feels that bullion is the preferred way to hold metals for the minor's account.

PRECIOUS METALS AND THE PORTFOLIO OF YOUNG ADULTHOOD

Again, shares of mining companies and mutual funds would seem to be the preferred way for investors in their 20s to participate in metals. Via mutual funds, these life cycle investors can use switch privileges to move out of metals when prices sour, and direct purchase of mining shares offers liquidity.

The cheapness of penny mining shares makes them particularly appropriate for these life cycle investors, who can buy thousands of penny shares with a modest investment.

For those who prefer to purchase metal for possession, coin dealers can fit the pocketbook of investors at this stage of life, and certificate programs that permit steady accumulation of gold or silver can serve long-term horizons.

Given that metals can serve both the aggressive gains and long-term growth objectives of the portfolio, these life cycle investors might have good reason to investigate precious metals.

PRECIOUS METALS AND THE ESTATE BUILDING PORTFOLIO

At this time of life, investors generally concentrate on long-term growth, and metals mining shares can meet that portfolio element. So, of course, can certificate programs and regular purchase of gold or silver bullion coins. Therefore, the appropriateness of metals for the estate building portfolio is generally the same as for the portfolio of young adulthood.

In addition, investors at the elder end of the 30 to 45 year old spectrum might be interested in futures, commodities pools, and the two types of metals options discussed earlier. They usually have the capital to withstand setbacks and to meet suitability requirements of commodities pools. If finances permit, some consideration of metals as aggressive growth vehicles is reasonable, and those types are the most accessible.

PRECIOUS METALS AND THE MATURE PORTFOLIO

Between ages 45 and 55, investors begin to become concerned with capital preservation, yet they also realize that some aggressive growth investments are suitable as a companion to capital growth investments. Precious metals and derivative investments can meet these portfolio needs.

The insurance value of metals is a consideration for these life cycle investors, who generally have accumulated stocks and bonds and wish to counterbalance paper investments with "hard assets." Therefore, many advisors argue that it's particularly important for this age group to have a modicum of holdings—10 to 15 percent of total portfolio value—in precious metals, either bullion or certificates. Of course, other advisors suggest that Treasury bills also serve the insurance cause, for they are short-term, highly liquid, and provide inflation-sensitive yields.

Those who wish to pursue long-term growth through metals investments might choose mining shares and mutual funds concentrating in mining stocks, as well as bullion and certificates. Those who seek aggressive gains consider futures, commodity pools, and options.

As we've noted in all our discussions of investments, these life cycle investors most certainly should be investing the maximum affordable amount in IRAs or Keogh Plans. Some investors like to include hard assets in their retirement portfolios, therefore they hold shares in metals mutual funds or eligible commodity pools.

PRECIOUS METALS AND THE SENIOR PORTFOLIO

In general, investors in the 55 to 65 age group prefer to apportion their portfolios away from riskier and more volatile investments, making precious metals unsuited for their needs. Conversely, many investors of this age pursue conservative preferences to the conclusion that they must own metals, gold particularly, as the most ultimately conservative investment possible.

Those whose conservative reasoning leads them away from risk usually prefer to avoid metals, except perhaps for certificate programs or metals mutual funds, both of which offer counterbalance to the paper investments that likely constitute the majority of their portfolios.

Those whose conservative reasoning inclines them in favor of metals generally prefer to hold bullion rather than its derivative investments. Nonetheless, holding a plurality of their portfolio in bullion presents two dilemmas: exceptional vulnerability to loss from price fluctuations and the absence of current income from metals. Accordingly, these senior life cycle investors who are devoted to metals must become more familiar with the price-protection and income-generating possibilities of put and call options on metals futures and of customer-granted options.

In either event, direct futures investment and indirect investment via commodities pools should, at this stage of life, generally be reserved for more affluent investors whose sizable income or portfolios permit pursuit of aggressive gains. As a course of intermediate aggressiveness, penny mining stocks and penny mining funds offer the prospect of potentially aggressive gains with minimal exposure.

PRECIOUS METALS AND THE RETIREMENT PORTFOLIO

As we've noted many times, capital stability and current income are usually the most important requirements for the retirement portfolio, and neither purpose is especially well-served by metals investments. The exceptions, of course, are dividends from mining shares or metals mutual funds and premium income from options. To some extent, even the usefulness of metals as insurance against losses in paper investments is lessened for these life cycle investors, for they can achieve capital stability, safety, current income, and inflation protection through short-term investments such as T-bills and near-term bonds.

SUMMARY

In short, the many types of direct and derivative investments possible with precious metals can offer aggressive gains, long-term capital accumulation, occasionally some current income, and, to some extent, balance for a portfolio. Many investment advisors regard precious metals as necessities, and equal numbers regard them as niceties. There is no doubt, however, that metals investors must be prepared to suffer above-average price fluctuations if they are to become involved in gold and silver. Further, if they choose to become serious metals investors, they must be willing to devote time to become sophisticated in their understanding of markets and investment vehicles. For the lucky, the bold, the patient, or the studious life cycle investor, however, precious metals can be a worthy addition to a portfolio.

CHAPTER 12

Annuities and the Life Cycle Investor

An annuity is a contract, usually with an insurance company or a financial institution affiliated with insurance companies, that permits life cycle investors to earn tax-deferred returns in anticipation of retirement. In years gone by, annuities were useful for any tax-deferred accumulation of capital, and many parents used them in place of the UGMA to gather funds for children's education. In 1984, however, Congress enacted legislation confirming annuities strictly as retirement-planning vehicles by imposing tax penalties on preretirement withdrawals from annuity contracts. Therefore, if life cycle investors contribute funds to annuities, they must be prepared to let their money grow until reaching age 59 years and 6 months or face a 5 percent tax penalty on withdrawals. Consequently, we'll discuss annuities as long-term growth investments set aside for retirement even though some life cycle investors could purchase an annuity and begin receiving proceeds immediately without penalty.

Disregarding private annuities, which involve dispositions of income-producing property through legal counsel, annuities are of two types: single premium and variable

142

premium. Single premium annuities require a large initial deposit, usually at least $5,000. Some contracts permit investors to contribute additional sums to a single premium annuity, and others do not. Variable premium annuities permit investors to contribute small sums, often $50 or less, at intermittent or regular periods for many years. The advantage to the former is immediate earning of higher tax-deferred returns, whereas the latter allow tax-deferred accumulations on a modest budget.

In either case, exceptional tax-deferred accumulations are possible. For example, a single deposit of $5,000 earning 8 percent compounded monthly would grow to more than $54,000 in 30 years. In the case of variable premium annuities, deposits of $50 monthly compounded at 8 percent would grow to more than $74,000 in 30 years. The amount you actually earn is determined by the size of contributions, the rate of interest paid (or, with some annuities, performance of stocks), and the length of accumulation period. As of mid-1985, annuity contracts yield 8 to 11 percent, although 8 percent is the consensus figure with which to estimate average lifetime yields from annuities. Typically, single premium annuities offer higher returns than the variable premium variety.

Although those tax-deferred yields are attractive, life cycle investors must consider several potential disadvantages when contemplating an investment in annuities.

First, annuities aren't liquid. They can be closed out prior to retirement, but investors must pay tax penalties. Some annuities, especially those sponsored by mutual funds, levy surrender charges for withdrawals prior to the annuity commencement date in addition to tax penalties imposed by Uncle Sam. Those charges can be as much as 5 percent of principal contributed, with a downward sliding scale usually applying. Further, some mutual fund-affiliated and brokerage-sponsored annuities have administrative fees for early withdrawals, usually $10 to $50. By withdrawing funds from your annuity prematurely you can lose both principal and interest.

Second, tax-deferred compounding is more advantageous to high-bracket investors. Therefore, younger and lesser-taxed investors might be better off in fully taxed invest-ments.

Third, annuities are tax-deferred investments, not tax-exempt investments. When you begin to receive payments from an annuity, you must declare some portion of pay-ments as fully taxable current income. In contrast, interme-diate-term and long-term municipal bonds pay federally untaxed interest of 8 to 10 percent as of mid-1985. Conse-quently, direct purchase of municipals or subscriptions to a municipal bond fund can provide higher untaxed returns than annuities offer. They're also liquid without penalty, although, as always, interest rates and market forces can depress prices of these investments, meaning a possible cap-ital loss if you need your money.

Fourth, it doesn't make sense to invest in annuities with untaxed income. For example, don't purchase an annuity with the proceeds from municipal bonds or municipal bond funds. By doing so, you convert federally untaxed income into income that eventually will be taxed.

Therefore, attractive as an annuity can be as a retire-ment-anticipation vehicle, life cycle investors need to exam-ine the investment in light of their need for liquidity, their tax situation, and the attractiveness of other investments. As we'll see in the next two chapters, annuities must also be examined as companions to two prominent types of re-tirement-anticipation investments, IRAs and employer-sponsored retirement programs.

Besides being long-term growth investments, annuities are also current income investments. During their accumu-lation phase annuities serve the former portfolio need, and during their payout phase they serve the latter. Just as an-nuities can be classified according to fixed and variable pre-miums, so can they be classified according to the kinds of payments they make.

A fixed payment annuity, as the term implies, pays the annuitant a fixed amount for a contracted period. The ad-vantage to such an arrangement is relative certainty and predictability of income. The disadvantage is that contrac-tual payments may not be sufficient for the annuitant's needs.

In an attempt to overcome this disadvantage, insurance companies and affiliated brokerages developed variable income annuities. Most annuities invest in fixed-income securities such as government and corporate bonds. This ensures stable, predictable returns and minimizes surprises. However, variable income annuities invest some portion of their funds in equity investments. Payments are in some measure determined by fluctuations in the value of stocks within the annuity's portfolio. "Some measure" is an important qualifier because, typically, a portion of the variable income annuity portfolio will remain in bonds, which provide a floor of predictable returns. Variable income annuities try to provide higher income to annuitants, the assumption being that stocks will outperform bonds, while also establishing a base level of returns from the bond element.

Deciding between fixed payment and variable payment annuities is something of a judgment call. Some advisors feel that stocks are likely to outperform bonds over extended periods and counsel variable income annuities for what they feel is their higher potential.

Many investment advisors argue that retirement planning should emphasize predictability above all other features. Therefore, they favor fixed payment annuities, arguing that stocks should be reserved for other sections of the portfolio. In addition, they point out that annuity receipts are taxed as current income, meaning that investors forfeit capital-gains taxation by choosing a variable income annuity.

Performance of the annuity's portfolio aside, the greatest determinant of an annuity's payments is your choice of a payment schedule. Typically, you have several choices:

1. Lump sum distribution—all accrued interest plus principal mailed to the annuitant in a single check.

2. Period certain—accumulated proceeds distributed over a set period, frequently 120 or 240 months.

3. Lifetime receipts—the "straight-life" annuity pays a certain amount for the life of the annuitant.

4. Joint and survivor payments—the annuity provides income for the life of the annuitant and a survivor of insurable interest.

5. Some combination of any above—for example, a large lump sum payment coupled with a period certain, or a period certain together with lifetime receipts.

The longer the period of payment is, the lower the promised amount of payment to you. Different annuities will offer some, but not all, of these choices, and investors must look carefully at payment options when investigating annuities. You usually need not specify the payment option when purchasing an annuity, but once you select an option you can scarcely ever change it.

Selecting a payout option is a difficult point on which to advise. Some of us fear outliving our income and are likely to choose the lifetime annuity in exchange for lower current income. Others of us find some satisfaction in providing for heirs after we're gone and want the survivor option. Still others who have additional income will prefer the higher payments of a period certain, relying upon other investments for support should they outlive their contract with the insurance company. And a few will want a lump sum payment in order to buy a retirement condo or a long-postponed world cruise.

Most investment advisors who deal frequently with annuitants advise a 10-year certain option. If it's an available choice, they suggest as an alternative that annuitants receive 10 percent of their annuity's accumulated value each year. The former choice provides predictable income from a fixed payment annuity. In the case of a variable payment annuity, the latter choice provides higher receipts during good markets for stocks and doesn't deplete capital in lackluster markets. However, the 10-percent choice does not provide constant receipts.

In deciding upon a choice of payment, three considerations prevail: anticipated tax status on the annuity commencement date, level of income provided by other investments as part of total income needed to maintain a desired standard of living, and intended use of the accumulated money.

Besides conventional deferred annuities, many mutual funds offer roll-over annuities, often called guaranteed return plans or something similar. Through these vehicles, life cycle investors can obtain a guaranteed rate of interest to accumulate tax-deferred for a specified time, usually a year, and that rate of interest is higher than interest for conventional deferred annuities. Advantages are three-fold: a high rate of return (around 11 percent in early 1985) guaranteed for a period, tax-deferred compounding of interest, and the security of interest and principal associated with conventional annuities. Typically, minimum initial investment is $5,000.

Guaranteed return plans are "rollovers" because at end of the contracted accumulation period the deposit plus deferred interest can be recontracted, or rolled over, extending tax-deferred accumulation. When rolling over the deposit, though, investors might receive a lower rate of guaranteed interest for the subsequent period.

Identical tax consequences and fees or charges that apply to standard annuities also pertain to guaranteed return plans. Even though these products are advertised as short-term, tax-deferred accumulation vehicles, you still have to treat them as long-term investments or pay the consequences if you make withdrawals before age 59½.

Guaranteed return plans can be useful to three categories of investors who can muster the relatively high minimum initial investment.

First, they can be useful to people within a few years of retirement. Say, for example, you've accumulated a sizable nugget from a lifetime of investing. You can place that sum into a guaranteed return plan and draw tax-deferred interest that's higher than prevailing rates on similar investments and protected from fluctuations in other markets. They're also useful receptacles for company pensions that aren't needed right away or for other lump sum disbursements from insurance. Proceeds can be withdrawn after retirement, when your tax bracket is often lower than during working years.

Second, guaranteed return plans can be of advantage to investors willing to accept higher accumulated interest now in exchange for the risk of falling interest rates later.

Third, guaranteed return plans are useful to investors who already have an annuity that isn't paying as much interest as the new guaranteed return plan. Section 1035 of the Internal Revenue Code allows untaxed exchanges from one annuity to another. Consult a tax advisor before switching, however, for the 1984 revisions to the tax code have made switching more complicated than it used to be.

In seeking further information about annuities, you can consult almost any insurance company or major brokerage firm. Nearly all full-service brokerages are now affiliated with insurance companies, so they can offer clients annuities in addition to other financial vehicles.

For further information about variable income annuities, one source is Connecticut Mutual Life Insurance Company. Write the company's Annuity Service Center at P.O. Box 2370, Boston, MA 02107. The phone number is (203) 727–6500.

In closing the discussion of annuities, we should be aware that many foreign insurance companies, particularly in Switzerland, also offer annuities. An advantage to investing outside the U.S. is that foreign currencies may appreciate against the dollar, thereby increasing returns to you when you reconvert the currency into dollars. Of course, a disadvantage is that premiums must be paid in the currency of the hosting country, meaning your premiums can increase substantially during the accumulation phase if that currency is appreciating against the dollar. One company accustomed to dealing with Americans offers fixed premium and variable premium annuities:

Assurex, S.A.
Volkmarstrasse 10
P.O. Box 209
8033 Zurich
Switzerland

Because an annuity is a long-term contract, check the strength of the sponsoring company. The company should be rated at least "A" in *Best's Insurance Report,* available at most libraries. If the volume is unavailable, write A.M. Best Company at A.M. Best Road, Oldwick, NJ 08858. The phone number is (201) 439–2200.

By this time, you've come to expect a summary of how annuities can fit into the portfolios of life cycle investors at different stages of life. However, retirement planning has become such a critically important issue to Americans that we need to take a broader look at this investment objective. Therefore, let's treat this chapter and the two following chapters—on employer-sponsored retirement plans and Individual Retirement Accounts—as an independent minisection of the book. Having covered annuities, employer-sponsored plans, and IRAs, we'll then have an extended summary that discusses all three retirement vehicles simultaneously. Investors who are conversant with each of these vehicles can go directly to that trichapter summary as a guide to structuring their retirement plans. Life cycle investors who are less familiar with annuities, employer-sponsored plans, and IRAs will then have time to digest the chapters on each before consuming the consolidated summary.

CHAPTER 13

Employee Investment Plans and the Life Cycle Investor

Every employee receives a paycheck for his or her labor, but you can make the nine-to-five grind more lucrative by letting the stock market pay you for working while your boss pays, too. In the parlance of finance that's called "market capitalization," and it works by your becoming a shareholder of the company you work for. If your employer's company stock is traded publicly, you can become an owner-employee by phoning your broker and buying shares of your company's stock in the open market. Or if yours is one of many companies that have one, you may be able to do something smarter: join your employee investment plan (EIP).

First, a definition. We'll use the term *EIP* in reference to any program sponsored by your employer that permits you to accumulate tax-deferred funds through a choice of investment alternatives. Accumulations in an EIP grow untaxed in whatever investments your company offers and you select until you retire. When you retire and begin receiving distributions, your cost basis will be recovered free of income tax. Even though the excess of distributions over cost would normally be taxed as current income, it may qualify for favorable tax treatment under certain conditions. For a discussion of those conditions, consult *Pension Planning* by Everett T. Allen, Jr., Joseph J. Melone, and Jerry S. Rosenbloom (Homewood, Ill.: Dow Jones-Irwin, 1984).

Employee investment programs are of two types: contributory and noncontributory, and the contributions in question are yours, not the company's. Contributory plans are of two types: those to which you contribute pretax dollars and those to which you contribute aftertax dollars. Noncontributory plans are those to which you contribute nothing, for they are totally company sponsored.

The most common type of contributory plan to which you may donate pretax dollars is the 401(k) Salary Reduction Plan, so named because of the section of the Internal Revenue Code that established it. As an example, a company may permit an average 401(k) contribution equaling 6 percent of base salary, although the law permits a higher maximum. The term "salary reduction" scares many employees, so companies rename 401(k) plans with a jaunty moniker.

The chief advantages to the 401(k) plan are that it allows you both to contribute before-tax dollars to your retirement account and to avoid current taxation on investment income. If, for instance, you earn $20,000 per year and are permitted to contribute 6 percent of earnings to the plan, you invest $1,200 before you're paid. Your federally taxable salary is then reduced by $1,200.

(Special note: Technically, the amount of salary that you contribute to a 401(k) plan is an employer contribution. Although the money is still yours, the contribution is treated for tax purposes as if it were an employer contribution to an EIP.)

In general, however, EIPs are funded with aftertax dollars, meaning, in our example, that if you're paid $20,000 and you contribute $1,200 yearly, your taxable income is not reduced, as it is with the 401(k) plan.

In both kinds of contributory plans your company generally will match some portion of your investment. Company matching can run from 25 to 100 percent of your contribution up to an established percentage of salary, with 6 percent being a standard maximum. So, in the case of a company with 25-percent matching, for each dollar you contribute to an EIP your company will add 25 cents.

Company matching is a great incentive for investing in your company's stock. If your company matches dollar-for-dollar, your contribution of $1 immediately generates $1 in matching, and earnings from both dollars accumulate untaxed until retirement. In addition, some companies will permit employees to contribute larger percentages of salary to an EIP, although company matching ceases beyond the permitted ceiling—again, commonly 6 percent of salary. Earnings from unmatched contributions also grow untaxed until you retire.

The problems, if they can be called that, with EIPs are *eligibility* and *vesting*—that is, the amount of time you must work before you're able to participate in an EIP and the amount of time you must be with your employer before company contributions and their earnings are yours. Your contributions and their earnings are always yours. Some companies may require you to work one year before you can participate in an EIP and could require five years of participation in the plan before vesting occurs, although sometimes vesting requires merely five years of service regardless of how long you've been in the EIP.

(Another note about 401(k) plans: Your contributions to a 401(k)—which, again, are technically employer contributions—are immediately vested once you begin participating in the plan.)

Similar restraints apply to noncontributory plans, those to which you contribute no money. One such plan is the "official" company-sponsored retirement program, whatever its name, which usually pays retirement benefits based upon a percentage formula of terminal salary times years of service.

Another type of noncontributory plan results from tax laws that permit companies to deduct certain types of expenditures if an equal amount is granted to employees in the form of stock ownership. Usually called TRASOP, PAYSOP, or something similar, this program gives you stock in your company merely for being an employee. The company typically computes your share of the eligible sum based upon your salary. That amount goes toward purchase of your company's shares, and those shares are put aside for you. Vesting occurs immediately, although many companies require you to work up to three years before you're eligible to participate.

There are many compelling reasons—tax deferral, company matching, enforced savings—why life cycle investors should regard EIPs as essential to their total portfolio. Add the tax breaks of 401(k) plans and the company-granted retirement or stock ownership plans, and it's clear that contributory and noncontributory plans can be important additions to a portfolio. But, as with any investment decision, you need to look at the broadest facts and consider many questions.

First, in the case of 401(k) plans, tax-reduction benefits are greatest for the highest-paid employees. For instance, if you're permitted to contribute 6 percent of earnings to the 401(k), the tax consequences of reducing $20,000 income to $18,800 are less than those of reducing $100,000 to $94,000.

Second, many employees cannot afford to contribute the maximum permitted amounts to contributory plans. Drains on current income may prohibit full participation, meaning you don't receive the full benefit of company matching. Still, something is better than nothing, although EIPs do favor employees who can afford to invest the maximum.

Third, the conventionality of EIP investment choices often prohibits seeking aggressive returns that are reasonable for younger investors. In short, they're not versatile investment vehicles, although many EIPs offer a variety of investment opportunities.

Fourth, having a notable portion of your long-term and retirement dollars invested in your company's stock makes your portfolio especially vulnerable to the fortunes of one company. As we've seen, life cycle investors can defend against losses in these holdings through purchase of put options on their company's stock, but not all stocks are listed in public options markets, and defending holdings with puts occasions frequent outlays of capital and capital losses if your company's stock goes up, which, of course, is what you want it to do.

Fifth, many people never work for one employer long enough to become vested in an EIP or retirement plan. Job mobility means that employees forfeit an employer's contributions to their EIP if they leave a company before becoming vested.

Because of these drawbacks, life cycle investors must manage EIPs as astutely as they manage other investments in their portfolio, and there are guidelines to follow in doing so. Chiefly, they deal with the amount of contributions and the disposition of contributions.

Many advisors counsel employees to set aside as much as possible into EIPs so as to take advantage of company matching and tax-deferred growth, particularly if your EIP is a 401(k) plan, which adds the advantage of reducing tax liability. They further counsel that people should, if at all possible, contribute unmatched portions of their salary to EIPs to take even greater advantage of tax-deferred growth. Following such advice may seem to be the obvious course, but it may not necessarily be the wisest for reasons cited about the disadvantages of EIPs.

As an alternative, employees could begin with minimum contributions to an EIP—say 1 percent of salary—and escalate contributions 1 percent each year they stay with their company. This 1-percent strategy offers a number of advantages. First, when participation in an EIP is a requirement for other retirement programs, you'd be foolish not to contribute something to the EIP, for you might spend your career with one employer. Second, the 1-percent strategy permits you to set aside something for long-term growth while still freeing salary for current needs and for other portfolio decisions. Third, by following this course you commit greater portions of income to the EIP after you're vested and all tax-deferred earnings are yours.

After you've decided how much to contribute, you may have a choice of where to place your money. This, too, is a subject on which there is divergent opinion among financial advisors.

Most counsel employees to invest totally in their company's stock. They argue that investing in your company's stock is the best way to multiply the value of your labor.

Also, what investment are you more familiar with than the stock of the company you work for?

Corporations often encourage this option by subsidizing employees' stock purchases with average price calculations and below-market discounts. That is, your company will credit your EIP stock purchases based upon the average monthly or quarterly price instead of the actual market price on the day of purchase. In addition, many corporations underwrite EIP stock purchases by offering discounts below average market price, giving you even more shares for your contributions.

The combination of company matching, average pricing, and subsidized discounts makes purchase of your company's stock a very attractive investment choice for your EIP. The disadvantage, as we've noted, is that the accumulated value of your EIP is totally dependent upon your company's stock price. Consequently, you may wish to consider other investments your company makes available for your EIP.

Purchase of government bonds is frequently an alternative offered by company-sponsored investment programs, and for many life cycle investors this option is a wise choice. U.S. government bonds offer the ultimate in assurance against default, and their returns can provide attractive long-term accumulations. As a further advantage, an EIP permits investors to accumulate government securities gradually with modest monthly sums, much like participating in a government bond mutual fund.

However, your company probably will not subsidize investment in bonds with average price calculations and below-market discounts as it will with investment in company stock. Also, your company stock could outperform government bonds, causing you to forsake greater growth for assurance against default.

If your EIP offers a mutual fund option, that could be a means of receiving returns from a portfolio of professionally managed stocks and government bonds, for many funds have a portion of their assets in T-bills. Growth-oriented funds provide an additional degree of diversification for your EIP, and they can serve employees at any stage of the life cycle.

Another frequently available EIP investment is the guaranteed return plan, which pays an established rate of return for a fixed period. Guaranteed return plans generally offer a higher rate of return than the government bond component of an EIP, but sometimes access to them is restricted to employees over age 55. After age 55, investors generally look more favorably upon less variable returns, making guaranteed return plans more attractive than fluctuating company stock and mutual fund shares.

If their companies provide more contemporary investments as part of their EIPs, life cycle investors will want to consider those in the context of their total portfolio. Such vehicles as aggressive growth mutual funds, option income funds, and perhaps even commodity pools can provide spectacular returns when combined with company matching. However, few EIPs offer these alternatives, and many advisors counsel against employees' choosing them if they are available, arguing that pursuit of aggressive gains doesn't serve the long-term growth emphasis for which EIPs are best suited.

Of course, most company-sponsored plans permit employees to apportion their contributions among competing alternatives. Therefore, you could have part of an EIP in company stock and part in other investments. Dividing contributions is an excellent way to balance EIP holdings among various alternatives and to achieve diversification in tax-deferred investments.

Further, most companies will permit employees to alter composition of investments in their EIPs, albeit at distant intervals, sometimes as infrequently as every two years. The ability to alter composition of investments is different from the ability to alter disposition of contributions. In the former case, you completely change the accumulated investments in your EIP—for example, switching your holdings from company stock to government bonds by selling the stock and redirecting the proceeds into bonds. In the latter case, you merely deposit your contributions into another investment medium—for example, you had been buying company stock and you direct your subsequent contributions into government bonds. In this latter instance you still hold your company's stock, and your future contributions go toward purchase of bonds. The ability to switch holdings from one vehicle to another enables employees to abandon an investment that's not performing as well as an alternative.

In today's mobile society, many employees change companies frequently, both before and after they're vested in an EIP. When you leave, your employer may close your EIP and pay you a lump sum distribution. In the case of unvested employees, the lump sum will represent the amount of your contributions plus tax-deferred earnings from your contributions. Unvested employees have two choices for disposing of lump sum distributions from a previous employer's EIP.

If your previous company's plan was a 401(k) and your new employer also sponsors a 401(k), you can place all or part of a lump sum from your preceeding employer's plan into your new employer's 401(k). You may also place all or part in an IRA rollover, discussed in the next chapter. If your previous employer sponsored a 401(k) and your new employer does not, you may place all or part of your lump sum distribution into an IRA rollover.

If your previous EIP was not a 401(k) and you leave your company before being vested, you cannot reinvest your contributions in another tax-deferred investment, except, of course, that you can purchase an annuity. You may, however, place the tax-deferred earnings from your contributions into an IRA rollover. You'll have been taxed already on the amount of your contributions, but not on their earnings. That's why you cannot place your contributions in a rollover, but you may place tax-deferred earnings from those contributions in a rollover.

Vested employees face similar choices. If you are vested in your employer's EIP, your lump sum distribution will represent all contributions and tax-deferred returns, yours and your employer's.

If the former plan was a 401(k), you may transfer all or a portion of the lump sum to a new employer's 401(k) or into an IRA rollover. You may also place all or a portion of a lump sum in an IRA rollover if your new employer does not sponsor a 401(k).

If you're vested in a previous employer's plan that was not a 401(k), you can reinvest, in total or in part, only your employer's matching, the returns on your employer's matching, and the returns on your contributions. You can reinvest in a 401(k) if your new employer sponsors one, or you can reinvest in an IRA rollover. You may not reinvest amounts you contributed to the previous employer's EIP. Those are yours to keep, and you owe no tax because you've already been taxed on contributions you made to an EIP that was not a 401(k).

After receiving a retirement distribution from a former employer, you have 60 days in which to deposit the *employer's* contribution in a rollover. And remember: Technically your contributions to a 401(k) plan are employer contributions. If you fail to meet the 60-day deadline, the employer's contribution becomes fully taxable current income. Under some circumstances, that might not be so bad.

Employees who participated at least five years in a qualified retirement program are eligible to reduce the tax liability of the employer's contribution [all contributions in the case of a 401(k)] through a special IRS provision called "10-year averaging." Ten-year averaging permits taxpayers to treat the employer's contribution as if it had been received in equal installments over 10 years and was the only income received. This provision can significantly reduce tax liability on distributions not deposited in an IRA rollover, with the consequence that the recipient may be better-advised to average out the employer's contribution and use it for current income rather than future needs. For information about this technique, call the Internal Revenue Service and ask for free publications about lump sum distributions and 10-year averaging.

In the case of distributions from noncontributory sources, such as PAYSOP, you'll receive stock certificates representing the amount of your accumulated ownership when you leave the company. Because you're vested immediately, the stock is yours. The stock is fully taxable as current income in the year you receive the shares, but unrealized capital appreciation isn't taxed until you sell the shares. Your tax liability will be indicated on the form your company mails you along with your shares. You may not place these distributions in a rollover.

The final issue that many employees confront is converting holdings from contributory and noncontributory plans into current-income vehicles upon retirement. In the case of the "official" retirement plan, arranging retirement income benefits is unnecessary because your current income will be established by the company's formula. [If you leave your company before being vested in the "official" retirement plan, you'll usually forfeit all benefits, but if you leave after being vested, you may be eligible for retirement income even though you've changed employers. For more detailed study about these matters, consult *The Handbook of Employee Benefits* edited by Jerry S. Rosenbloom (Homewood, Ill.: Dow Jones-Irwin, 1984.)] However, converting accumulations in an EIP into income-producing investments requires some active decisions.

Most companies give employees two alternatives for converting accumulated proceeds of an EIP into current-income investments: purchase of an annuity or receipt of a lump sum distribution. The annuity is the easiest but probably the less-wise course, for the income stream that you and your heirs receive could easily be far less than you'd receive by taking the proceeds in a lump sum and reinvesting for current income.

The problem with the lump sum choice is tax. If you take receipt of your EIP funds at one time, all of it becomes current income. Receiving the accumulated proceeds of a working lifetime's contributions all at once can easily put employees in the highest tax brackets, even after reducing their income with 10-year averaging.

To avoid this dilemma, advisors counsel employees to take their EIP in a lump sum and place all of it in an IRA rollover within 60 days so there's no tax. Place the proceeds into income-producing investments and then arrange to have yourself paid regular monthly or quarterly checks of interest and dividends plus principal, if necessary. Thus, you avoid a big tax bill and the reduced income often associated with annuities while assuring yourself and your heirs a source of continuing payments. You do lose the benefits of 10-year averaging in this case, however.

When choosing a disposition of retirement income, it's particularly important to consult a tax advisor. Rules change constantly concerning these matters, and you'll want to arrange your affairs not only with regard to the tax code but also in consideration of other retirement income such as social security and other investment returns.

Contributory and noncontributory company-sponsored investment programs are often an investor's single greatest source of long-term growth and retirement income. They can be the most significant parts of life cycle investor's portfolio, and they deserve the utmost consideration. Of all the investments we'll cover in *Life Cycle Investing,* EIPs are probably the most useful and most appropriate to adult investors. Combined with other tax-deferred accumulations like annuities and Individual Retirement Accounts, employee investment plans can provide the ample retirement income that investors deserve for decades of service to employers and to society. EIPs are the second element in our minisection on retirement-anticipation investments, and now it's time to examine the third, namely, IRAs and Keogh Plans.

CHAPTER 14

Individual Retirement Accounts and the Life Cycle Investor

In the preceeding two chapters we discussed annuities and employee investment programs as two vehicles with which life cycle investors can accumulate tax-deferred funds in anticipation of retirement. Now it's time to discuss the third in our trilogy of retirement-anticipation investments, the Individual Retirement Account, or IRA.

As its name suggests, an IRA is an account established by individuals who want to invest for their retirement. IRAs are offered by depositaries, brokerages, mutual funds, and other money management institutions that act as custodian for annual contributions. Any American below age 70 years and 6 months who has job income—wages, salaries, tips, commissions—may contribute to an IRA.

Requirements are simple: each year you may deposit 100 percent of earned income to a maximum of $2,000 in an IRA; you must begin receiving distributions from your IRA prior to reaching age 70½ years; unless you're willing to pay tax penalties, you may not receive distributions from an IRA before reaching age 59½ years unless you become permanently disabled.

As was true of 401(k) plans, contributions to an IRA are

credited against taxable income. For example, if you have earned income of $12,000 and contribute $2,000 to an IRA, your taxable income immediately becomes $10,000 before computing any other deductions and credits. You have until April 15th of the following tax year in which to make an IRA contribution for a previous year. That is, you have until April 15, 1986, in which to make an IRA contribution for 1985.

As was the case with annuities and EIPs, no dividends, interest, or capital gains generated by your IRA are taxable until you begin receiving payments upon your retirement or upon incurring permanent disability. Should you die before receiving payments, accumulations in your IRA are distributed to your heirs.

There are three misconceptions about IRAs that need to be clarified.

First, the prohibition against depositing unearned income into an IRA has caused many investors not to open accounts, mistakenly believing that they can't place money from investment income in an IRA. Congress merely requires that investors have earned income before they can open an IRA. If *all* your income derives from investments— and that's true of very few people—you may not open an IRA. However, if you have a single dollar in earned income, you can take money from savings or sell securities in order to contribute to an IRA.

Second, you need not contribute a full $2,000 each year to an IRA, nor must you keep contributing to an IRA in years after you opened it. Most banks will open IRAs for $250, and most mutual funds or brokerages have established $500 minimums for Individual Retirement Accounts. Of course, you may not make up a year of whole or partial contributions if you missed the April 15 filing deadline.

Third, you can borrow money to open IRA, and it might pay you to do so. Let's say that you're in the 40 percent tax bracket and borrow $2,000 at 15 percent interest for one year. The $2,000 contribution will give you about $800 in tax savings because it is a direct offset against other taxable income. The interest on $2,000 for a year would be about $166. If you itemize deductions, the government will underwrite about $66 of that fully deductable interest expense in the 40 percent bracket. All things considered, your $2,000 loan would cost you about $100 for a year, and that's a small price for an $800 tax savings.

Besides conventional IRAs of the type we've been examining, there are two other types: the spousal IRA and the IRA rollover.

The spousal IRA is designed for the increasingly rare case of households in which only one spouse works outside the home. The employed spouse may contribute up to $2,250 in IRA accounts, the only restriction being that no more than $2,000 may be deposited in any single account. Institutions accepting IRA deposits are familiar with requirements for spousals and can provide you with necessary forms.

When both spouses have wages from employment, both may have individual IRAs, each contributing 100 percent of earned income to a maximum of $2,000 each. The operative consideration is "100 percent of earned income." Should one spouse have income of $3,000 and the second have income of $1,000, the former may deposit $2,000 and the latter $1,000 into IRAs.

As the previous chapter indicated, the IRA rollover account accommodates a transfer of funds from EIPs. Workers vested in employer-sponsored retirement programs may transfer amounts contributed by their employer, tax-deferred earnings on employer contributions, and tax-deferred earnings on their own contributions to a rollover if they change jobs. IRA rollovers are similar to conventional IRAs, with two exceptions: (1) the rollover is a one-time deposit which cannot be added to; (2) amounts contributed by *employees* may not be deposited in the rollover.

A reminder: you'll recall that your contributions to a previous employer's 401(k) plan are technically employer contributions. You are immediately vested in these "employer" contributions, and they can be placed in a rollover.

A rollover may also be used to transfer IRA funds from one custodian to another. You can, for example, take IRA funds from a maturing certificate of deposit and place them in a mutual fund. As was the case in transfering funds from an EIP, you have 60 days after receipt in which to effect a transfer of funds from one IRA custodian to another.

For the self-employed, the tax code provides additional retirement incentive in a Keogh Retirement Plan. The self-employed may have an IRA and a Keogh, just as employees can have an EIP and an IRA—and a Keogh, too, if they also have self-employment income. You may contribute the lesser of 20 percent of earned net income or $30,000.

Despite their many commendations, IRAs—and now we're using that term to include spousals, rollovers, and Keoghs—have some drawbacks.

IRA contributions must be regarded as lifetime investments. Once you make a contribution, you must regard that money as gone until you retire or become disabled. You can retrieve IRA contributions before retirement, but you must pay substantial tax penalties for the withdrawal, and the withdrawal is immediately and fully taxable. You must not open an IRA believing you can withdraw the money if you need it.

IRAs may not be used as collateral. Losses from IRA investments aren't tax-deductible. Establishment and yearly maintenance fees are usually, but not always, charged for IRAs, and amounts vary with institutions. Commissions are included in the maximum you can contribute to IRAs and Keoghs.

If you contribute more than $2,000 to an IRA, the overage is subject to continuing tax penalties. (Even in the case of spousal IRAs, in which the maximum investment is $2,250, remember that no more than $2,000 can be invested in any one account each year.)

Finally, life cycle investors should realize that other investments carry some advantages of an IRA while overcoming some of the IRA's disadvantages. For instance, municipal bond funds pay interest exempt from federal tax, and they are liquid if needed. Annuities can also defer taxation for many years. Neither, of course, provides tax off-sets of the IRA.

Many financial advisors claim that every working American should open an IRA and contribute the maximum

$2,000 each year, and every working American is certainly eligible to do so. There seems to be nothing in the tax code to prevent your preteen daughter from putting $2,000 of baby sitting money into an IRA. Silly as the example may seem, it does point to some legitimate considerations to assess in deciding to contribute to an IRA.

If typical life cycle investors begin working full-time at age 22, receiving four decades of untaxed growth is a powerful incentive to open an IRA as soon as you start working. However, the $2,000 tax offset and tax-deferral on earnings from IRAs are most rewarding for investors in higher tax brackets, and most younger life cycle investors don't occupy them. As a very general rule, age 30 seems to be the optimum time to begin maximum contributions to an IRA. Given a typical working lifetime, life cycle investors would have 35 years in which to permit tax-deferred contributions and earnings to grow.

By all means, workers in their 40s should give increasing consideration to opening an IRA, for it is an integral part of the estate building portfolio. By age 45, the importance of contributing to an IRA approaches an imperative, and by age 50 life cycle investors should do everything possible to contribute the maximum permitted amount to an IRA.

Considerations other than age and tax bracket influence the decision to contribute to an IRA. Life cycle investors should have liquid reserves for emergencies. Depending upon the investor's age, indebtedness, and personal circumstances, that reserve may total 10 to 50 percent of net yearly income. Without this reserve readily available, investors should consider less than a maximum IRA contribution.

In addition, investors should evaluate other economic circumstances before contributing to an IRA. A 40 year-old steel worker would be well-advised to contemplate the tenuousness of his or her employment before making an investment as inaccessible as an IRA.

Finally, investors should examine an IRA in company with other long-term investments or retirement programs offered by employers. The wage earner whose employer offers meager retirement benefits will give greater consideration to an IRA. Conversely, investors who are pleased with their EIP might consider lesser contributions to an IRA.

Once life cycle investors decide to contribute to an IRA, they must choose the financial intermediary best suited to receive their deposits. There are two ways to invest IRA funds: a self-directed account and indirect investment.

Self-directed IRAs are sponsored by brokerage firms. Depository institutions may also offer this service soon. As the term *self-directed* implies, you are the manager of your IRA, picking the investments you want for your IRA and directing a broker to buy or sell for your account. You pay normal commissions and probably start-up and maintenance fees also.

All major full-service brokerage firms offer self-directed IRAs. The advantages to a self-directed account with a full-service broker are the advice and recommendations you can receive as a customer. In addition, many full-service brokerages offer IRA-approved investments, like real estate partnerships, that aren't available from any other institution. The disadvantage to self-directed accounts with full-service firms is higher commissions and maintenance fees than other institutions charge.

If you feel capable of picking securities for your IRA, you probably will prefer to use a discount brokerage firm, which charges lower commissions than full-service houses. Commissions, remember, are included in the maximum you may contribute to an IRA, so if you reduce commissions you increase the amount actually invested in your IRA. Whether you open an account with a full-service or a discount broker, you can trade securities in your self-directed IRA at will, giving you exceptional flexibility.

In addition to self-directed IRAs, life cycle investors can open IRAs with financial intermediaries like depository institutions and mutual funds. Virtually every bank, savings and loan, and mutual fund family offers IRA accounts, and maintenance fees are much less than those charged by full-service brokers.

We covered the advantages of investing in depositories and mutual funds in our earlier chapters, and those advantages apply as fully to IRAs as to conventional investments. The advantages of depository-type investments included federal insurance against default, the absence of fluctuation in constant-dollar deposits, and frequent compounding of interest. Advantages of the mutual fund included diversification and professional management. You will also remember that you can switch investments in fund families among their mutual funds as you see fit.

Besides depositories and mutual funds, other financial intermediaries, such as some real estate partnerships and commodities pools also offer IRA-approved investments.

Whether you choose direct or indirect investments, your IRA can be arranged to accommodate each of the five elements critical to the conventional life cycle portfolio and can be rearranged as desired. Bear in mind that you can transfer IRA monies form one custodian to another. There's no limit to the number of IRA accounts an investor may establish, so a retirement portfolio can be as comprehensive as the number of financial institutions offering IRAs.

Of course, the decision about where to place IRA funds is inseparable from the kinds of investments you want for your IRA. Of all the investments we've discussed thus far, only purchasing bullion, buying and writing puts, buying calls, and writing naked calls are strictly prohibited investments for IRAs. Direct investment in commodities and futures is also prohibited, although some commodity pools are approved for IRAs.

Many advisors argue that an IRA is intended to provide long-term capital growth and, therefore, investors should favor growth stocks and growth-oriented mutual funds for their IRAs. This preference can be accommodated with both self-directed and indirect IRAs, and mutual funds are often advised because of the $2,000 limit on yearly IRA contributions. With only $2,000 yearly to invest, many life cycle investors would have difficulty achieving portfolio diversification through direct investment in stocks via a self-directed IRA. Mutual fund contributions avoid the diversification problem.

As a companion to direct purchases of stocks, many advisors counsel IRA investors to write covered calls on their portfolio of stocks. As we noted in our chapter on options, covered calls provide tax-deferred additional income for the IRA portfolio. Of course, this strategy applies only to optionable stocks of which the investor owns at least 100 shares, the minimum optionable lot. Here again, mutual funds can be of value. Option income funds, most of which are IRA-approved, will serve this same strategy of providing current income on a diversified portfolio of growth stocks with a $2,000 yearly investment.

However, some advisors argue that investors should seek maximum capital gains in their IRAs. They point out that all distributions from an IRA are taxed as regular income, meaning that investors forfeit capital gains taxation on a long-term growth stock portfolio. Therefore, they say, investors should seek aggressive gains in a tax-deferred investment, leaving the tax advantages of long-term capital gains for the nonretirement portfolio.

Other advisors object to the aggressive gains strategy. They remind us that aggressive investments are, by definition, more volatile than long-term investments and that capital losses in IRAs are not tax-deductable. Therefore, they say, pursue aggressive gains elsewhere in your investment program, for you'll at least be able to deduct losses on your income tax.

Even the most aggressive advisors counsel against commodities pools as IRA investments. They are simply too volatile, and even if you have a long hot streak with your pool, you can lose everything if your pool manager makes a few inevitable bad trades.

In the investment climate of the mid-1980s, IRA advisors counsel investors to seek maximum interest and dividend income for IRAs—what's called the income reinvestment strategy. They argue that income investments benefit IRAs most by accumulating tax-deferred interest and dividends that otherwise would be fully taxed. In the present investment environment many good-quality stocks and bonds are yielding 10 to 13 percent. Over a lengthy period, high rates of dividends and interest can accumulate to impressive magnitudes, especially when they are permitted to compound without the tax bite that IRAs avoid. And when investors retire and begin receiving fully taxable distributions from their IRA, dividend and interest income would have been fully taxed anyway. By following the income reinvestment strategy, investors forfeit none of the tax advantages they would by choosing long-term growth investments.

Many advisors who favor the income reinvestment strategy for IRAs suggest that investors place substantial portions of their yearly contributions in certificates of deposit and money market funds. They point out that these investments feature market-level rates of interest, frequent compounding, and deferral of otherwise taxable returns. They add that these constant-dollar investments also offer invulnerability to price fluctuations, an advantage not available in stocks and bonds. In addition, custodial fees associated with these investments are minimal, and they don't require extensive familiarity with investments.

However, the prominent choices among those who advocate the income reinvestment strategy for IRAs are corporate and government bonds. Novice investors can pick bonds with more assurance than stocks, and to the extent that anything is certain in the investment world, bonds offer safety, income, and capital appreciation. Do not, however, purchase municipal bonds for your IRA, for interest which otherwise would be federally tax-exempt will be taxed fully when you retire.

Another advantage to the IRA account holding bonds is that investors can stagger maturity schedules to coincide with retirement. Investors retiring in 10 years can easily find bonds maturing in 10 years, and the present crop of bonds available to the public offers maturities ranging out to 2015.

Among the most favored bond investments for IRAs are zero-coupon bonds and bond-like zero-coupon certificates of deposit. As you'll recall from our chapter on bonds and the life cycle investor, zeros pay interest only upon maturity even though the Internal Revenue Service expects you to declare phantom interest as it accrues. Zeros held in IRAs avoid yearly interest declarations, so they're the ultimate in tax-deferral for investments that otherwise would be taxable. Both types of zeros offer other advantages for IRA accounts.

They can be purchased without commissions if you compare brokers. They often are designed expressly for IRA accounts, meaning you can buy them in even multiples totaling $2,000. Zeros lock in a known interest rate if held to par, unlike money funds with fluctuating rates, so you know exactly how much you'll have when they mature. Zero CDs and government bonds assembled by brokerages as zeros are highly safe investments.

Bearing in mind that life cycle investors can contribute to IRAs for 30 years or more, the issue of managing the IRA portfolio becomes exceptionally important. Strategies for managing IRAs can be as intricate and active or as straightforward and passive as investors care to make them. For example, investors could simply toss $2,000 every year into a money market fund and let returns compound, or they could find a series of bonds maturing in their year of retirement and buy those every year. On the other hand, investors could purchase common stocks, take gains every few months, and reinvest elsewhere. They could purchase mutual fund shares and utilize switch privileges, riding markets and the wisdom of fund managers. At various times they could invest actively for aggressive gains. If plagued by lassitude or indecipherable markets, they could relax their investment activity. Investors can diversify their holdings, or they can concentrate their holdings. When it comes to managing IRAs, investors can be guided by time, temperament, commissions, or markets.

From the point of view that we're working with in *Life Cycle Investing* we need to ask ourselves whether the IRA portfolio should parallel the investor's stage of life, counterbalance other elements of the life cycle portfolio at various stages of life, or be based entirely upon investments appropriate to the retirement portfolio, regardless of our present position in the life cycle. To illustrate, let's look at the case of a 30 year old investor trying to decide where to invest IRA funds.

Suppose this investor decides his or her IRA should parallel other portfolio elements. As we noted in our earlier chapter, life cycle investors during the estate building phase tend to emphasize long-term accumulations, although some element of aggressive gains is appropriate for this time of life. Consequently, this investor may decide that the IRA should also feature long-term growth investments with a bit of aggressive gains. In that case, this investor's IRA may contain long-term growth stocks, similarly oriented mutual fund shares, and a modicum of aggressive growth investments such as high-growth mutual funds, junk bonds, or speculative stocks.

However, what if this investor decides his or her IRA should counterbalance the total portfolio? In that case, the IRA portfolio might be weighted with income-producing investments because those aren't prominently featured elsewhere in the portfolio, or a greater percentage of aggressive growth investments might be appropriate as counterpoint to a concentration in long-term growth investments.

As a third possibility, this investor may ask, "What investments will I need when I'm retired?" As we noted earlier, retirees tend to emphasize income-producing investments with high degrees of safety and capital stability. Therefore, this investor would look ahead 30 years and would begin today to acquire the kinds of investments that would be necessary three decades from now. Accordingly, this IRA might feature zero-coupon securities with retirement year maturities or government bonds.

None of these three strategies is really disputable. Some advisors, of course, would counsel one over the other, but it's the investor who lays the money on the line. As we've seen, every form of investment entails advantages and disadvantages, and no one escapes that reality by putting funds in an IRA. There will always be one investment that in any given context is "better" than another, but that doesn't mean it's the best investment at the time. Regardless of your strategy for selecting IRA investments, two issues you'll have to deal with are fees and diversification.

As we noted, most IRA custodians charge a maintenance fee, some charge a start-up fee, and self-directed IRAs require you to pay brokerage commissions. These fees may appear to be modest, but over many years they can represent a sizable chunk out of your invested capital. Say, for instance, that you have a self-directed IRA and your yearly commissions are $100. Over 30 years, you'd pay $3,000 in commissions, and if you'd been able to invest that $100 yearly at 10 percent for 30 years your IRA would be $16,000 richer. So if you're an active trader paying frequent commissions, your IRA had better be making generous gains to compensate for the time value of that money.

The issue of fees ties in with the issue of diversification. In the early years after you open an IRA, you're not likely to have sufficient funds with which to diversify your IRA portfolio. You can achieve diversification by placing your contributions into one or several mutual funds, which usually charge modest yearly maintenance fees, often as little as $10 yearly. However, some funds are load funds, which in effect have built-in commissions, and they charge loads in addition to maintenance fees. Given that loads range from 2 to 8 percent, diversification can cost you some compounded returns, even through mutual funds.

Take the case of an investor deciding between a no-load money market fund paying 10 percent and a stock fund with an 8 percent load. For an investment of $2,000, the money fund will probably charge a $10 maintenance fee, whereas the stock fund will charge $160 in loads as well as the $10 yearly maintenance fee. The stock fund will have to achieve an 18 percent return to equal the 10 percent offered by the money fund.

To overcome some of the returns you lose through the time value of commissions and fees, some advisors counsel a naive buy-and-hold strategy for IRAs. That is, they urge you to pick one investment and stay with it. In effect, these advisors are saying it may cost you too much in foregone returns to be a diversified IRA investor. In some cases, investors repeatedly buy government bonds of a single year's maturity. They reason that they minimize commissions in a high-yielding investment of maximum safety. If they ever wish to alter composition of their portfolio, they have their investment in one place and don't pay multiple commissions to realign holdings.

The problem of commissions and fees is more acute for investors with self-directed IRAs. Even through a discount broker, you'll pay at least $25 for purchase of stocks or bonds. To maintain a minimally diversified portfolio of four stocks, you'll pay at least $100 in commissions, whereas you'd get by with $25 for a one-stock portfolio. If you're an active trader, commissions will cost you a great deal to support diversification.

The main issue with diversification is, "How diversified is diversified?" The answer depends upon the time investors can devote to monitoring their IRA portfolio as well as how much they're willing to spend in commissions and fees. As a generality, few investors can track more than 10 securities with any reliability, so that's probably the outer limit in numbers for a self-directed IRA. For investors seeking diversity through mutual funds, three or four funds is probably an adequate number. Investors can apportion indirect IRA investments among, for example, a growth stock fund, an aggressive income fund, and a bond fund, and that would make them a partial owner of hundreds of securities.

The advantages to a consolidated IRA portfolio include reduced fees and greater ease in monitoring investments. In addition, experienced investors may be able to generate greater returns by putting their money into a single stock or mutual fund and then trading the account actively. The chief problem with consolidating IRA holdings in one or two investments is fallibility. Every investor and every portfolio manager will make costly mistakes, and losing money is something you don't want to do with your IRA. Therefore, many investors who prefer to consolidate their IRA holdings do so strictly in portfolios of bonds or constant-dollar vehicles.

The advantage to a bond portfolio is that the obligations will mature to par, assuming no default, even if their value will fluctuate with interest rates. Therefore, bond holders don't have to lose money in an absolute sense (disregarding erosion of purchasing power through inflation) if they don't sell their bonds before maturity. The buy-and-hold strategy with bonds also reduces commissions. Of course, through instruments like CDs and money funds, price fluctuations are no consideration. In addition, consolidating holdings in bonds, CDs, and money funds also follows the maxim of putting IRA money where tax-deferral is optimum, for otherwise taxable interest accumulates tax-deferred.

Apart from commissions and fees, other matters influencing diversification of your IRA portfolio are your other investments, including annuities, EIPs, and conventional investments. If you have diversified stock holdings elsewhere, you might wish to favor bonds in your IRA. If your annuity is largely in fixed-income securities, perhaps a stock component for your IRA would produce a favorable balance. Through similar reasoning and examination of your total portfolio, you could conclude that a range of investments might be suitable for your IRA, including aggressive growth funds, penny stocks, junk bonds, gold mining shares, or virtually anything else that is approved for IRAs.

Whatever your choices, most advisors agree that you'll want your IRA to minimize fees, maximize returns, and guard capital. Consequently, most Americans favor four vehicles for IRAs: certificates of deposit, zero-coupon bonds, money market funds, and growth-oriented mutual funds. As we saw in chapters devoted to each of these investments, each offers singular advantages, and those advantages apply well for IRAs.

In conclusion, though, no IRA investment has to be forever. If you're troubled by the performance—or nonperformance—of one type of investment in your IRA, you can select another at any time. All the issues we've covered in reference to IRAs are important, but none has to be incapacitating. All life cycle investors need to do is choose among the alternatives available to them, and those alternatives are formidable in number.

Individual Retirement Accounts, spousal IRAs, rollovers, and Keogh plans can be handsome additions to the portfolio for life cycle investors. Singly, they permit tax write-offs, tax-deferred compounding, and ample opportunity to prepare for retirement. In companion with untaxed investments and other tax-deferred investments, they can be compelling investment choices. In the case of fortunate investors who can have all three of the tax-deferred investments that we've discussed, substantial retirement-anticipation accumulations are possible. In the hope that all of us can fit into that fortunate group, it's time to summarize our three retirement-anticipation investments in the promised tri-chapter summary.

Tri-Chapter Summary: Life Cycle Investors and Retirement-Anticipation Investments

In the preceeding three chapters we've examined annuities, employee investment programs, and Individual Retirement Accounts as three vehicles exceedingly well-suited for life cycle investors who wish to plan for their retirement. We noted that all three permit tax-deferred accumulations that may be converted to taxable income upon retirement. In addition, 401(k) plans and IRAs, including spousals, roll-overs, and Keogh Plans, offer immediate off-sets against other taxable income, making them tax-reducing as well as tax-deferred investments. We also noted the immense flexibility offered by IRAs. But mostly we noted that the great advantage to all three retirement-anticipation investments is their overwhelming accessibility. Finally, we noted the disadvantages to each of these forms of investment: the need to leave sums untouched for lengthy periods, the tax penalties for preretirement withdrawals from annuities and IRAs, and the frequently conventional choices offered by EIPs. Let's compare these three investments with each other in several categories.

SIZE OF CONTRIBUTIONS

All three are available in very modest amounts. Variable premium annuities can be purchased with as little as $50 per deposit, whereas IRAs are generally available in minimums of $250. Most EIPs require only 1 percent of gross annual salary as minimum participation. The fixed premium annuity, which usually requires a minimum investment of $5,000, has the highest minimum investment floor.

When it comes to maximum contributions, you can put as much as you'd like into an annuity, and when transferring funds from an EIP upon retirement there's no limit to the size of contributions to an IRA rollover, providing you meet the constraints outlined. For Keogh Plans, the maximum deposit is 20 percent of net income or $30,000, whichever is less. For EIPs, the maximum contribution is determined by your company's guidelines and your salary, but the typical ceiling is 16 percent of salary. Next in order of magnitude is the spousal IRA with a maximum of $2,250, providing you place no more than $2,000 in any single account, ending with the standard IRA, which, at no more than $2,000 per year, has the lowest investment ceiling.

Accordingly, all three allow considerable latitude for life cycle investors who wish to place the minimum or the maximum amount in tax-deferred investments. The choice for investors seeking minimum or maximum tax-deferred contributions is the variable premium annuity, followed, in most investors' circumstances, by EIPs. Keoghs permit the maximum for tax-deferred investors who are self-employed, and rollovers accept the largest sums for the newly retired and for other investors leaving company EIPs. Conventional IRAs have the smallest maximum.

DIVERSITY AND CONTROL OF INVESTMENT OPTIONS

Here the award goes hands down to IRAs, for almost any investment is eligible for IRAs, even some that shouldn't be, and through self-directed IRAs you can manage a tax-deferred portfolio yourself. IRAs through mutual funds permit versatility via switch privileges. Variable income annuities, comprised largely of stocks, are the next most diverse, although you have no voice in selecting securities. As we've seen, EIPs generally offer the fewest investment choices, although you retain some ability to move investments from one available vehicle to another.

Therefore, the life cycle investor seeking the greatest control over a diversified tax-deferred portfolio will opt for self-directed IRAs, followed by indirect IRA investment with mutual funds, followed by annuities and EIPs, which trade off in diversity and control.

GREATEST POTENTIAL GROWTH

Other things being equal—such as the amount of time funds are left to compound and the amount invested—IRAs (spousals, rollovers, Keoghs) offer the greatest potential for growth because of their high marks for diversity and control. When you can buy almost anything you want and trade it at will in a tax-deferred account, the successful investor can produce fine returns.

In theory, although not in practice, the variable income annuity, with its component of professionally managed stocks, should be the next greatest potential performer. During the lackluster markets that dominated most of the recent past, however, variable income annuities haven't done so well. In practice, although not in theory, employee investment programs have done very well for long-term investors, largely because of company matching and company-sponsored discounts on the purchase of company stock.

With their relatively staid but predictable returns, single premium and variable premium annuities offer the least potential for tax-deferred growth, although obviously they can accumulate to princely sums over many years.

Therefore, life cycle investors after the greatest potential growth favor IRAs first and (always preferring practice over theory) EIPs second.

But the plain and happy fact is that life cycle investors don't have to exclude one of these three investments in favor of another. Even on modest salaries and strained budgets, we can have all three. The question, as always throughout *Life Cycle Investing,* is appropriateness and proportion in selecting among these three alternatives. With that in mind, it's time to summarize the preceeding three chapters by looking at life cycle investors and retirement-anticipation portfolios. For reasons we covered earlier, we'll assume that life cycle investors begin to anticipate retirement at age 30, and we'll start with retirement-anticipation investments and the estate building portfolio.

RETIREMENT-ANTICIPATION INVESTMENTS AND THE ESTATE BUILDING PORTFOLIO

For life cycle investors in their early 30s, retirement is distant enough to permit minimal investment in retirement-anticipation vehicles and to allow sums contributed to appreciate to comfortable amounts. Therefore, investors at the beginning of this age group need not feel compelled to contribute the maximum to retirement-anticipation investments, although it can be to their advantage to set aside as much as possible. (Once investors enter their 40s, however, they should make greater efforts to approach maximum investment in tax-deferred vehicles.) For the most part, these investors will decide between contributions to employee investment programs and IRAs as their preferred choice.

The flexibility and tax-reduction advantages of IRAs may promote these life cycle investors to emphasize IRAs over their EIP, particularly if it isn't a 401(k). On the other hand, the inducement of company matching, especially if it's dollar-for-dollar, may direct them toward larger contributions in an EIP, particularly if they believe they'll remain with an employer long enough to be vested.

In either case, investors in their early 30s must decide on the type of investment suited for their retirement-anticipation dollars. If concentrating on the EIP in building funds for retirement, these life cycle investors will probably look more favorably upon investments in their employer's company stock, as average pricing and below-market discounts provide more shares for the dollar.

Investors preferring the IRA will select securities that endorse their strategy for retirement planning. As we've seen, that strategy can complement or counterbalance their other investments, or it can emphasize the accumulation of securities appropriate for retirees. Generally, life cycle investors beginning their IRAs will favor one of three types of investments.

First, stock or bond mutual funds will permit diversification in a portfolio of securities for a minimal investment. As we noted, diversification is difficult to achieve when investments are restricted to $2,000 yearly. However, an investment of growing popularity for IRAs is the option income fund, which provides diversification in stocks and reinvests income from writing calls.

Second, many younger investors place the first few years of IRA contributions into a money market fund until they assemble an account large enough to afford diversification. Investors who intend to pursue a mutual fund strategy open their money fund with a mutual fund family, and those who expect to manage a self-directed IRA open accounts with a brokerage. After a few years, they use switch privileges to realign holdings among several mutual funds, or they direct the brokerage to purchase securities with the balance in their broker's money fund.

Third, younger life cycle investors have been increasingly drawn to zero-coupon securities purchased through self-directed IRAs. Zeros provide known returns to maturity, giving a high degree of reliability to retirement planning. They are suited for a buy-and-hold investment strategy, which limits commissions. Zero-coupon bonds backed by U.S. government securities are safe against default, so investors can select even the most distant maturities with relative confidence that their investment is safe, and they're easy to choose because a wide assortment of maturities is available.

Investors approaching the middle and far end of this stage of their life cycle will re-evaluate their retirement-anticipation investments in light of their growing careers. Their generally increasing tax burdens, however, will cause them to look more favorably upon retirement vehicles that provide offsets against income. If they feel they've settled in with one employer, they may wish to increase contributions to an EIP, particularly if it's a 401(k). Conversely, if their careers require great mobility among employers, they will want to emphasize IRAs as their retirement nestegg.

Investments these middle-year estate builders select will generally be the same as when they were younger members of this age group. If they're concentrating on a career with a single employer, their EIP will likely contain increasing holdings of their corporation's stock. For those emphasizing the IRA, mutual funds and self-directed accounts are still appropriate receptacles for retirement funds. For the most part, however, these life cycle investors will seek aggressive gains though their conventional portfolios, for capital losses associated with volatile investments are not tax deductable within EIPs and IRAs.

Annuities are not generally suited for these life cycle investors. With their highly conservative returns and illiquidity, annuities force younger investors to keep funds locked away for 20 years or more. In the case of a single premium annuity requiring a minimum of $5,000, investors would be better off contributing to an IRA, which provides tax offsets as well as tax-deferred returns. In the case of variable premium annuities, which can be purchased for modest regular payments, investors would probably be better off contributing an extra percent of salary to a EIP, which features company matching and which can be transferred to an IRA rollover upon leaving their employer.

Of course, many advisors disagree that annuities are less appropriate for younger investors. They point out that a single premium annuity is a consolidated investment independent of an EIP, meaning you don't have to transfer it if you change jobs. In addition, they say, professional management makes annuities competitive with mutual funds. They further argue that variable premium annuities are an ideal way to set aside unmissed amounts from regular pay and are an excellent supplement to other investments. Further, they point out that inaccessibility of annuities is no greater than for EIPs and IRAs. Their arguments are worth considering.

RETIREMENT-ANTICIPATION INVESTMENTS AND THE MATURE PORTFOLIO

Between ages 45 and 55, investors must plan seriously for their retirement, and that means they must give EIPs and IRAs greater importance in their investment program. If at all possible, these life cycle investors should be contributing substantially to both.

Their generally growing incomes will require maximum tax offsets. If their company EIP is a 401(k), it could be their preferred retirement-anticipation investment, for the 401(k) permits employees to reduce taxable income by more than the $2,000 per year permitted by IRAs. If their EIP is not a 401(k), these life cycle investors will want to make sure they contribute the full amount to tax-reducing IRAs.

One hopes that these life cycle investors will have been contributing to retirement-anticipation vehicles for 15 years or more, and if that's the case they'll have hefty amounts set aside, perhaps $30,000 to $50,000. Consequently, investors at this stage of life will need to review their retirement-anticipation portfolios with an eye toward any necessary restructuring of investments. The general issue in realigning a tax-deferred portfolio is whether to consolidate or diversify holdings.

The issues of diversification and concentration also apply as these life cycle investors examine holdings in their EIP. The decision to diversify away from holdings of company stock will be based upon their company's prospects and the professional status of being a shareholder. Where both are formidable, it may be wise to continue buying and holding the company's stock, seeking diversification, if desired, through an IRA.

Given that most EIPs offer few investment alternatives, diversification will be difficult to achieve, anyway. Nonetheless, if an EIP does offer a wider array of alternatives than is customary, it should be considered for its benefits in rounding out the retirement-anticipation portfolio.

Annuities can be more beneficial for these life cycle investors than for those who are younger. Presumably, these investors are approaching the highest marginal tax brackets in their careers, making the tax-deferred returns of annuities as appealing as fully taxable investments paying greater pretax returns. For investors in their mid-50s the maturity horizon of annuities is no more distant than for intermediate-term bonds. The single premium annuity is preferable to the variable-premium annuity for these investors because the initial deposit of $5,000 will accumulate greater value than a variable premium annuity.

RETIREMENT-ANTICIPATION INVESTMENTS AND THE SENIOR PORTFOLIO

After age 55, investors are well-advised to take fewer risks in their portfolios, and that counsel holds for retirement-anticipation investments as well as for general holdings. As we noted earlier, investors at this age should be setting aside the maximum permitted in retirement-anticipation investments, and it might be worthwhile for them to borrow, if need be, in order to do so.

Although some diversification with growth investments is necessary, portfolio concentration in fixed-income securities is more the rule for these investors. These life cycle investors will generally want to consolidate their IRAs into stable, high-yielding securities for predictability and compounded returns. In general, government and top-grade corporate bonds maturing within 10 years are suited for the retirement-anticipation investments at this stage, as are certificates of deposit. Because investors are working with a known investment horizon, probably 10 years, lump sum investments like zero-coupon securities that compound to predictable sums become highly appealing.

Generally speaking, the best way to obtain safety, predictability, and high returns in a fixed-income portfolio is for investors to transfer funds to a self-directed IRA. The unfortunate reality about bond mutual funds is that their net asset value will fluctuate indefinitely, whereas individual selections of directly held bonds will appreciate to par. Therefore, bond buyers have greater assurance than bond fund investors from indefinite capital losses.

In the growth component of the senior investor's retirement-anticipation portfolio, mutual fund holdings might be advisable, for they offer diversification and professional management. Unless investors are wise pickers of stocks, it might be best to leave the growth component of an IRA to indirect investment vehicles.

Common stocks with generous dividends might be included in the self-directed IRA, and indirect investors will wish to investigate income-oriented mutual funds or funds seeking a combination of growth and income. Depending upon the investor's total portfolio, especially stocks in the EIP, around 30 percent of the IRA might be in growth stocks.

While reconsidering disposition of their retirement-anticipation portfolios, investors will want to take another look at their EIPs. We noticed that after age 55 employees often can convert EIP contributions and accumulated holdings into a guaranteed insurance contract. Exercising that prerogative may be advisable, depending upon performance of company stock and other investments.

After age 55, annuities become especially attractive, bearing in mind that federally tax-exempt securities like municipal bonds can compete as a favorable alternative when investors enter what are probably the highest marginal tax rates of their career.

In addition, these life cycle investors may want to consider an additional option: contributing unmatched amounts to their EIP's guaranteed insurance contract. Remember that most companies permit employees to contribute unmatched portions of salary to an EIP. If their company is one of them, life cycle investors in their 50s should investigate guaranteed insurance plans as an alternative to annuities, for their returns are often higher.

RETIREMENT-ANTICIPATION INVESTMENTS AND THE RETIREMENT PORTFOLIO

Until reaching age 70½ years, Americans with earned income can contribute to an IRA, even if they're simultaneously making withdrawals. Many people work part-time after "retirement," either because they want to or have to, so it's important to remember that they can still contribute to an IRA.

For the most part, however, the issue of retirement investments is one of drawing down capital, not contributing further to a portfolio. Therefore, we'll discuss converting retirement-anticipation investments into current income investments in the final section of *Life Cycle Investing*, where we'll display sample portfolios for each stage of an investor's life.

PART III

The Tools, Techniques, and Methods of Life Cycle Investing

Thus far, we've talked about the stages of an investor's life, the elements of a portfolio, how a number of investment alternatives provide those portfolio elements, and how life cycle investors will select among those investments as their circumstances cause them to emphasize one element over another. Now it's time to look at how life cycle investors can manage their portfolios, making the alterations necessary in their holdings to accommodate a growing and evolving life.

Obviously, the most important thing that any investor wants to know is how to pick *the* stock, *the* mutual fund, *the* commodity pool among the hundreds and thousands available that will provide the top returns for each portfolio element. It's one thing to realize that an investor of a certain age should tilt a portfolio toward long-term growth stocks, but it's quite another to tell investors how to pick the growth stock that will offer the maximum in long-term growth.

Regrettably, no one can give investors that information with absolute assurance. An infallible, or even highly reliable, technique for picking individual securities hasn't been discovered, and there's little likelihood that it could exist. Markets change constantly, and no system serves long.

The outlook for individual stocks changes not only with the profitability of their companies but also with the seeming whims of securities analysts and institutional buyers. Thousands of investors have awakened to discover that overnight their investments in solid bonds (Washington State Public Power Supply System, New York City), deposits in large banks (Continental Illinois, Franklin National), and A-rated annuities (Baldwin United) are on the verge of vanishing.

What was first falls from grace (Xerox, AT&T), and what has fallen from favor rises again (Penn Central, Chrysler). Industries that enjoyed their moment in the sun (oil, banking, real estate) were eclipsed by those in the shade (metals mining, regional phone companies), and those currently out of favor may well rise anew (steel? airlines? nuclear utilities?).

Investment techniques that prevailed throughout the securities industry, like those in Benjamin Graham's *Security Analysis,* now seem antiquated by computerized valuation models. Some highly respected professionals, such as Fidelity's Edward C. Johnson III, have cast aside automated sophistication and applied Zen to investing, perhaps with success, as Fidelity has an impressive investment record. Philosophies that seem arcane or even ridiculous—the stock market moves inversely to women's hemlines, for example—seem to have credence in some investment climates. There's even a theory that investors should pick stocks according to the quality of a company's annual report, but not in a way you'd imagine: if the annual is the customary four-color, high-gloss affair, the theory says you shouldn't go near the stock.

Between the complicated techniques of professionals and the anecdotal wisdom of talented amateurs there's considerable divergence among approaches to picking specific securities. Any one of them will be fine for a time, perhaps even a long time, but none will assure investors of repeatedly picking profitable securities because no one investment is obligated to behave as analysis predicts it should.

However, there are some generally agreed-upon guidelines for managing a portfolio, whatever the particular method of selecting specific securities, and life cycle investors need to be familiar with them.

CHAPTER 15

Managing the Five Portfolio Elements

MANAGING THE STABILITY ELEMENT OF THE PORTFOLIO

The fortunate quality about investments offering capital stability is that they do not require a great deal of active management. However, like all investments, money funds, certificates of deposit, and other constant-dollar accounts cannot be left inert, gathering moss along with interest. If life cycle investors have too little in constant-dollar investments, they've built their portfolio upon an uncertain foundation; if too much, they're leaving funds in vehicles that generally offer only market-level returns, thereby forfeiting the possibility of above-market gains from other investments.

We noted early on that constant-dollar investments, representing sums subject to little market risk, are generally thought of as the savings component of a portfolio. Many advisors counsel investors to hold between 10 and 25 percent of their total portfolio value in these vehicles, depending upon the investor's age and life circumstances. At present, the standard requires investors to hold the equivalent of three to six months net salary in constant-dollar investments, regardless of their portfolio value.

With the wider availability of lines of credit, these ratios may decline, for investors can draw upon other sources for short-term emergency funds, assuming they are able to repay borrowings. Nonetheless, it's necessary for life cycle investors to have an accessible source of ready cash as defense against life's proverbial slings and arrows.

To acquire an adequate quantity of savings-type investments, most advisors are unanimous in recommending the self-tithe, that is, setting aside 10 percent of net income every payday before you can get your hands on it. The advantages to the self-tithe are ease of figuring (multiply take-home pay by one tenth) and its small dent in consumption.

The best way to implement the self-tithe is to participate in automatic deposit programs offered by depository institutions and money market funds. These intermediaries generally will make arrangements to withdraw a specified amount from your checking account at regular intervals, often the 1st and/or 15th of the month. The funds are deposited electronically, and your checking account shows the amount withdrawn as it does any other debit. Even those surviving on the most modest of salaries can probably afford $25 per month to buy a savings bond through bond-a-month plans offered at work or through their bank.

The key to effective management of the stability element of the portfolio is concentration—having all of your constant-dollar investments in one place—for two reasons. First, if you need to draw down savings, having them in one vehicle facilitates accessibility. That vehicle might be a customary savings account in a bank, S&L, or credit union, a NOW account, or a money market fund. Second, having your constant-dollar investments in one place makes it easier to move them to higher-paying investments that offer capital stability.

Moving the savings component from one investment to another is an important part of managing the stability element of the portfolio. We noted that many investments offer capital stability but that they require differing minimums

for participation and that the higher the minimum investment the greater is interest accrued. Therefore, as life cycle
investors build up the stability element of their portfolio,
they'll want to and be able to move their holdings into
higher-yielding vehicles. Let's take the case of a young investor just beginning to accumulate a portfolio.

In its most rudimentary form, the self-tithe involves placing a portion of monthly pay into a conventional savings
account paying 5½ to 7 percent and requiring no investment minimum. If our young investor saves 10 percent of
net salary each month, he or she will save three months'
salary in slightly under three years. By that time, the savings account will likely be large enough to move into a
money market fund, paying several percent more interest
and generally requiring $1,000 as a minimum investment.
As sums equaling three to six months' net income increase,
the investor will move the constant-dollar investment into a
higher-paying certificate of deposit, say, one with a $5,000
minimum, and after that will likely favor Treasury bills,
beginning with $10,000 minimums, or larger denomina-
tion CDs.

Obviously, more aggressive strategies are possible for the
constant-dollar element of the portfolio, just as other accommodations may serve the needs of different life cycle investors. For example, investors could move from savings accounts to money funds as soon as they've accumulated the
minimum investment rather than waiting until they've
gathered three months' net salary, or tax considerations
may compel investors to keep the savings element in tax-
free money funds rather than CDs or T-bills.

In pursuing consolidation and maximum returns, investors must not forget liquidity. Keep maturities on CDs
short, even if it means sacrificing interest. The shorter the
maturity, the more frequently you can get your hands on
the money—and add to the CD as your need for greater
savings increases. In general, today's constant-dollar investments are uniformly safe, but maximum safety is available
in U.S. government obligations and government bond
money funds. Investors with substantial sums in the stability element of the portfolio might wish to invest in govern-

ment or municipal bonds with near-term maturities, but they must be wary of commissions, time-consuming paperwork, and slight delays in converting investments to cash.

We also noted that another use of constant-dollar investments is as a temporary parking lot for capital normally invested in another portfolio element. If investors have just sold a security and are awaiting another investment opportunity, or if securities markets are in disarray and no investment seems particularly attractive, constant-dollar investments are temporary repositories. In this case, money funds will be the preferred medium of stability, for they're convenient, feature checking privileges for easy reinvestment elsewhere, and have no fees or delays.

MANAGING THE INCOME COMPONENT OF THE PORTFOLIO

Income-oriented investors are of two types: those needing current income to meet current expenses and those who prefer income investments because their strategy is to reinvest interest and dividends for compounded growth. Both types of investors will seek to acquire current receipts from the highest quality sources. In addition, frequency of receipts is an important consideration in managing the income component of the portfolio. Life cycle investors who need current income to live will need it as often as possible, and those intending to reinvest current receipts will want them as often as possible in order to maximize compounding.

Investors seeking current income have several alternatives from which to choose—stocks, bonds, mutual funds, money funds, and certificates of deposit—the advantages of which we've reviewed in their chapters. As a practical matter, income-oriented investors are extending the stability component of their portfolio, for it does little good to invest for current income if the value of investments fluctuates widely. Even if investments maintain their interest or dividend payments, losses from capital fluctuation can wipe out the compounded gains from reinvestment and deplete capital that could be reinvested elsewhere for higher current income.

Therefore, the income element of the portfolio often minimizes holdings of stocks and stock mutual fund shares. Although many investors hold common and preferred stocks as "dividend plays," they frequently do so in an equity-income strategy that combines capital gains with dividend payments. Equity-income investors are not strictly income investors, for they seek capital gains in addition to current income. We'll discuss that use of equities under "Managing the Growth Component of the Portfolio" later in this chapter.

In the high interest rate climate of the past few years, many income investors have been attracted to money funds and certificates of deposit, both of which provide high current returns, capital stability, and frequent payments. They are also available without commissions and fees that subtract from current receipts. These are excellent income-generating investments, and they serve the income component of the portfolio well.

Money funds generally win out over CDs as the preferred income investment. With their low initial minimums, checking features, and diversification, money funds are excellent income-generating investments that pay market-level returns. Highly liquid, deposits in money funds can be easily restructured when other income investments provide higher returns. In erratic interest rate environments, money funds couple high returns with capital stability.

CDs are less liquid, and their highest interest is paid by the longest-maturing instruments. In addition, investors can add to money funds at discretion, whereas additional deposits to CDs can be made only upon rolling them over at maturity, unless subsequent investments are large enough to open another certificate. Nonetheless, CDs can serve investors who need current income for expenses or for reinvestment, as investors can arrange to have interest paid in cash or compounded.

In general, however, income investors are bond buyers, and when one speaks of managing the income component, one is generally speaking about managing a portfolio of debtor-creditor securities. Most commonly, interest from bonds is higher than interest from money funds and from all but the longest-maturing CDs. In addition, bonds are more liquid than CDs, for they may be sold without penalty, albeit with commissions. Unlike stock dividends, which must be declared to be paid, interest from bonds is an obligation of the issuer. The requirement to meet interest payments is the principal attraction of bonds to income investors.

In managing the bond portfolio, the first issue confronting investors is quality. The conventional income investor will seek investment-grade instruments, those rated BBB or better by rating agencies. The higher assurance of interest and repayment by investment-grade obligations attracts the investor who needs dependable receipts for current needs and the investor who seeks compound growth. Therefore, picking highly rated bonds is the first imperative in managing the income element of the portfolio.

Related to the first, the second issue in managing the bond portfolio is selecting interest rate differentials, the difference in yield among types of obligations. As a general guide, government obligations are preferable to corporate obligations unless corporate yields are at least 2 percent higher than yields on governments, and some advisors would say 3 percent is the threshold for preferring corporates to USGs. Given that government obligations are thought to be immune from default and also that their interest payments are exempt from state and local taxation, an interest differential of 2 or 3 percent is the minimum needed to compensate for default risk and tax consequences.

Taxation is another consideration for income investors. As we noted in the chapter on "Bonds and the Life Cycle Investor," municipal obligations often pay higher post-tax yields than corporates or governments. Consequently, high-bracket investors may prefer municipals. Here again, quality is the watchword. Even among municipal obligations, the interest differential between highly rated bonds and lower-rated bonds is often insufficient to compensate for greater default risk. Therefore, income investors should stay

with higher-rated municipals, preferably those insured by
MBIA or a similar backer. The key to a portfolio of municipals is to manage the quality of investments first and the
returns second. As a general rule, investors will prefer municipals when their yields are at least 2 percent higher
than the post-tax yield on corporate or government obligations, assuming, of course, that safety is accommodated.

The third issue in managing a bond component is length
of maturity. Fixed-income investments follow what is called
a "yield curve." Typically, the longer-running maturities
pay higher interest as compensation for uncertainties associated with long-term investments. Under these circumstances, the yield curve is said to have a positive slope with
respect to maturity.

During the mid-1980s the interest differential between
intermediate-term maturities and long-term maturities has
not been sufficient inducement to choose long-term maturities. The fixed-income market of the recent past has had a
"gentle elbow" in its yield curve, meaning that yields have
flattened out over maturity schedules rather than presenting a sharp difference between near-term and long-term
rates. When the differential between maturities is less than
1½ or 2 percent interest, investors are better off to keep
maturities short, within five years at the outside. Shorter
maturities will enable investors to reinvest more frequently
and will reduce capital fluctuations.

Thus far, we've discussed direct investment in bonds and
have slighted opportunities for indirect investment represented by bond mutual funds and municipal income trusts.
You'll recall that bond mutual funds and investment trusts
offer diversification in a single investment ranging from
minimums of $1,000 to $5,000. Accordingly, they're well-
suited for investors who lack the capital to achieve diversification in directly held portfolios. Interest and gains from
the diversified portfolio are reapportioned to investors, who
may opt to receive current income payments or have gains
reinvested in the portfolio.

At this point, we need to make a clear distinction between income investors who need current receipts for expenses and income investors who seek reinvestment of re-

ceipts. Investors wishing to reinvest current income for many years may be better off placing their income investments in mutual funds, which offer professional management, diversification, and frequent compounding. These investors can acquire a portfolio for small initial investments and can add to their holdings at regular intervals in modest minimums for subsequent investment. However, income investors who need current receipts for current expenses may be well-advised to avoid bond funds and trusts because direct investment offers greater advantages, particularly investment in USGs.

First, loads charged by some funds may be greater than commissions from direct purchase of bonds. Loads reduce the amount invested and reduce yields. Consider the case of an investor contemplating a $10,000 investment in a government bond fund with an 8 percent load. In this case, the investor pays $800 in loads and $9,200 goes to work generating current returns. In contrast, through a discount broker this investor could purchase $10,000 in bonds for about $100—one percent of investment instead of 8 percent, putting $9,900 to work earning interest.

Second, distributions from bond funds are usually legally interpreted as dividends instead of interest. Therefore, if our investor had purchased government obligations directly, interest payments would be exempt from state and local tax, whereas through the bond fund he or she receives fully taxable dividend income. State and local taxation can reduce returns by 1 to 10 percent if the income investor chooses funds over direct investment in this case, and that's in addition to reductions in investment from paying loads.

Third, bond funds feature indefinitely fluctuating net asset value, whereas directly held bonds will appreciate to par upon maturity. If, for instance, a bond fund invests with a 10-year horizon, its portfolio will be constantly renewed with bonds averaging 10 years' duration. This means that the net asset value will constantly fluctuate with changes in interest rates. In contrast, if investors purchase a 10-year bond directly, its price will stabilize as the bond approaches maturity. Thus, fund investors are forever subject to capital fluctuation, and direct investors are assured of maintaining the absolute value of their investment upon maturity.

However, some bond funds don't charge loads. In the case of corporate bond funds, there is no tax difference between interest from directly held obligations and dividends from indirect bond investment, just as interest from municipal bonds and returns from municipal funds are exempt from federal taxation. Also, target funds are subject to less fluctuation in net asset value than conventional bond funds, and they still offer cash distributions. In addition, funds will usually pay distributions monthly, whereas bonds pay semi-annually. Consequently, income investors needing current receipts may be served well by a bond fund if they choose carefully.

Those who buy income-generating stocks and bonds for reinvestment purposes face the problem of what to do with regular dividend and interest payments. There is only one reasonable choice: reinvest them before you can spend them. It's advisable for life cycle investors to establish a money market account with the broker from whom they purchase their securities, directing all interest and dividends to be reinvested upon receipt. This policy works admirably for stocks and bonds, but not all brokers deal in municipal obligations. Therefore, direct holders of municipal securities will be responsible for investing municipal interest payments themselves. They should be very disciplined in doing so, for otherwise their interest payments will be attenuated unproductively.

It's wise to invest taxed-to-taxed and untaxed-to-untaxed. That is, place proceeds from fully taxed investments into money funds, stock funds, or bond funds providing fully taxed returns, and place proceeds from untaxed municipal investments into tax-exempt municipal bond funds or municipal money market funds. This preserves the integrity of tax considerations and enhances returns from your income investments. It makes little sense, for example, to place interest from municipal bonds into fully taxed vehicles, for you're converting federally untaxed returns into fully taxed returns. It makes slightly more sense to place fully taxed interest payments into municipal bond funds or tax-exempt money funds, but if your tax bracket is such as to make this strategy rewarding, you should probably have income investments in municipal obligations in the first place.

MANAGING THE GROWTH COMPONENT OF THE PORTFOLIO

Life cycle investors seeking long-term growth will generally be inclined toward stocks and growth-oriented stock mutual funds as their preferred investments. The chief features that favor the portfolio's growth component are time and the exceptional variety of investment alternatives available for meeting the growth objective: time, because growth investments by definition must be left to mature; variety, because this permits diversification among investment choices and accessibility to profitable investments.

Investors who seek long-term growth through directly held common stocks may have their own methods for culling among the thousands of public equities, yet picking *the* stock for purchase is generally the final step in managing the long-term growth component of the portfolio. Investment analysis involves working from the general to the specific, and the first step in selecting stocks is to examine the prevailing and emerging economic climates.

Economic analysis alone is a subject requiring exhaustive education and attention for any kind of detailed comprehension, yet it is a necessary first step. Most securities analysts agree that about half the variation in a given security's price, up or down, is attributable to broad economic influences. Therefore, investing with the economic trend is the first step in picking a profitable stock, and as we'll see in a moment, that doesn't always mean betting on a robust economy.

Becoming intimately familiar with the trillion dollar American economy is a task defying even those who spend full time following it. The average life cycle investor cannot hope to become fully conversant with the indexes the professionals follow, but he or she can benefit from professionals' observations by subscribing to services like Chase Econometrics or Merrill Lynch Econometrics. These publications track economic data and report on trends, and if they're not available where you work, you can probably receive similar economic reports from a broker. In addition, most major business publications print economic data in regular features for each issue.

After economic analysis as a first step in selecting a potential investment, examination of industrial trends is the second. According to financial specialists, influences acting upon the industry in which a company does business account for about 16 percent of variations in a given stock's price. Therefore, if investors can accurately predict economic trends and locate industrial categories promising to profit from them, they're about 70 percent on their way to picking money-making equities.

Although there are hundreds, perhaps thousands, of industries, investors generally classify them in a cyclical rather than competitive context. That is, they tend to classify industries according to economic patterns rather than commercial categories, unlike the Standard Industrial Classification Codes published by the government. In the investor's system, there are three general types of industries: growth industries, cyclical industries, and countercyclical industries.

Growth industries are those associated with major technological changes and innovations, and at one time or another almost every industry has been a growth industry. In their respective seasons, automobile, aerospace, photochemical, and television companies were considered growth industries because of their technological revolutions. Today's high-tech darlings are considered the major growth industries of the mid-1980s for much the same reason.

However, technological enhancements are not the sole criterion for classification as a growth industry, for changing consumer tastes and innovations in marketing may also create a growth industry. For instance, in the mid-1980s one of the major growth industries is knapsacks—not the kind that Boy Scouts or a draftees used to carry, but the kind that thousands of college students carry books and paraphernalia in and those soft-sided canvas briefcases that trendy ad execs tote around.

It goes without saying that what once was a growth industry may no longer be and that mature industries can enjoy a revival of vigorous growth. Witness the decline of mobile homes, once considered a promising growth industry, and the revival of roller skates, once thought confined to the bandage-on-the-knee stage of childhood.

Cyclical industries are those associated with amplitudes in the general economy. They are industries most likely to blossom with good economic times and wither in bad. Steel, consumer durables like refrigerators and televisions, and automobiles are common cyclical industries. These industries tend to manufacture products that are purchased during booming economies and postponed during stagnant economies. However, what was once a cyclical industry may not always be so. For instance, home repair and the do-it-yourself industrial categories used to be considered cyclical, because people would buy drill presses and such when economic conditions were on the upswing. Now they are considered countercyclical, for during poor economic times people have returned to self-sufficiency.

Countercyclical industries, also called defensive industries, are those that tend to hold their own during slack economies. Traditionally, companies dealing in food, clothing, and shelter tend to suffer least during recessions, and perhaps even outperform other industries under economic adversity. As you'd expect, fortunate economic conditions sometimes, but not always, cause contractions in the earnings of firms within this industrial category.

The growth-oriented investor will, of course, be interested in the so-called growth industries, whatever they might be during any period of marketing or technological innovation. However, he or she isn't confined to growth industries in order to achieve long-term growth from a portfolio of stocks. Growth-oriented investors can also select securities from industries promising to benefit from economic circumstances—that is, industries benefitting from the economic cycle rather than changes in technology or consumer tastes. They might, for instance, pick companies in food processing over automotives when economic trends are down and vice versa when the trend is up.

The American economic cycle is more erratic than it used to be. The cycles of recession and recovery seem to be sharper and briefer in duration than has been the case for much of our economic history. They are more inclined to last around 18 months than several years. Nonetheless, that is ample time to profit from economic cycles if growth-oriented investors are astute at recognizing them.

But better than recognizing economic cycles is anticipating them, for the greatest long-term growth comes from buying into industry groups when they're most battered by economic cycles and holding their stocks until recovery boosts their prices. Countertrend analysis, as this technique is called, requires as much courage as economic incisiveness, but time—the friend of the long-term investor—will bear it out, providing one picks the right stock within the industry group.

If economic trends and industry category account for close to 70 percent of variation in stock prices, it's that unaccounted-for 30 percent that growth investors seek through analysis of individual firms. There are as many techniques for analyzing stocks as there are analyzers of stocks, but in general they fall into two categories: fundamental analysis and technical analysis.

Fundamental analysts examine the economic and industrial factors that we've discussed, and to them they add evaluations of a firm's management, balance sheet, and competitive position, as well as other factors within management's control that influence growth and profitability. Most formally trained analysts are fundamentalists, and the fundamentalist philosophy dominates academic preparation and the preponderant population of professional money managers.

The tools of fundamental analysis require a rigorous accounting and financial background for proper use, but life cycle investors can tutor themselves successfully in the tools' application. There are many excellent texts covering this particular type of securities analysis, and one of the more prominent is *Security Analysis and Portfolio Manage-*

ment by Donald E. Fischer and Ronald J. Jordan (Englewood Cliffs, N.J.: Prentice-Hall, 1975). In addition, the evergreen of the phylum is *The Intelligent Investor* by Benjamin Graham (New York: Harper & Row, 1973).

The principal intent of fundamental analysis is to compare a particular company's anticipated growth rate with an individual investor's estimation of its growth rate. The formal technique through which comparisons are made is regression analysis, a somewhat complicated mathematical procedure that attempts to determine the market's anticipation of future price growth by calculating the rate at which the stock price has grown.

A somewhat simpler and more accessible figure that many analysts regard as a proxy for growth is the price-earnings ratio, or P-E. Mathematically, the P-E is a company's share price divided by its earnings per share. For instance, if a company is selling at $100 per share and earns $10 per share, its P-E is 10. To look at the problem another way, investors pay $10 in share price for each $1 of earnings per share.

Analysts regard the P-E as a proxy for growth because it reveals a multiple on which investors can base estimates of share price. In our example of a company earning $10 per share and selling at a P-E of 10, what would become of the share price if earnings increased to $11 per share? If the P-E analysis is correct, the share price would increase to $110 ($11 in earnings times the P-E of 10).

Many analysts regard the P-E as the single most important piece of information available about a stock. They consider an increase or decrease in the P-E of a given stock to be highly significant, for it registers the market's estimation— that is, the estimation of other investors—of a firm's potential share price. Investors generally compare a specific stock's P-E with the price-earnings ratio of other stocks in the same industry. Other things being equal, if a stock carries a price-earnings ratio greater than the average for its industry, it indicates that investors hold higher prospects for the stock.

Consequently, if everything works out right, growth-oriented investors can pick the accurate economic cycle, the industry most likely to profit from the economic cycle, and the firm most likely to benefit most from the trend. They can be assisted in doing so by The Value Line Investment Survey, one of the most useful resources for direct investors in managing a portfolio of growth stocks.

Value Line is a comprehensive investment resource that provides investors not only detailed information about a firm's business and financial status but also summary opinions, recommendations, and timing advice. In addition, Value Line publishes outlooks for selected industries at regular intervals and updates its recommendations about particular companies.

In its major publication, a thick, black loose-leaf binder containing discussions of the major stock exchange issues, Value Line rates stocks for safety and timeliness. Safety is Value Line's assessment of the stock's downside risk, and timeliness is its advice about purchasing a particular stock right away.

Value Line also publishes the beta coefficient for each stock. Beta is a record of a stock's movement in relation to the total market. A beta of one indicates that a stock generally moves up or down in near-identity with the general market. A beta greater than one indicates that a stock is more volatile, up and down, than the market in general. A beta smaller than one indicates that the stock is less volatile than the general market.

Value Line can be highly useful for growth-oriented investors, for it takes the place of independent research and encapsulates needed data. For example, let's say an investor believes the general market is headed upward. He or she can consult Value Line for the industrial outlook, and then for selected companies within desirable industries. It could provide comparisons of the financial data and investment recommendations for three or four promising stocks, with particular attention to timeliness and safety. Finally, he or she could examine the beta coefficients, presumably selecting stocks with above-average beta, indicating the likelihood of above-market gains if the stock market produces the expected upturn.

Conversely, investors anticipating a declining general

market could consult Value Line for industries likely to hold ground or profit in a declining market. Again, they could consult listings for individual securities, select firms with a high safety rating, and confirm their examination by selecting stocks with below-average betas, which generally don't relinquish as much ground in a declining market.

A personal subscription to Value Line is rather expensive, but its issues are available in most libraries and in nearly all business college libraries.

There's only one problem, and we've mentioned it before: stocks don't have to behave as analysis says they should behave. That's where technical analysts enter the picture.

The general premise of technical analysis is that every other investor in the market has done his or her fundamental analysis. Therefore, every bit of known information is already accommodated, *discounted* is the technician's term, in the stated price of a stock. If the price of a stock reflects all available information, price movement is proof that information is being processed about a particular stock. To the technician the nature of the information is irrelevant. Maybe a company's CEO just had a heart attack, or the economy became more bullish, or a firm's laboratory wizards pulled off a competitive miracle—no matter. What counts is that the stock is behaving a certain way. The technician would counsel investors to examine how a stock is actually behaving and to make investment decisions based upon the stock's behavior.

Although there are many denominations of technical analysts, some more akin to fundamental analysts and others unyieldingly orthodox in their technical dogma, the two general deities of technical analysis are price and volume. Price reflects all available information; volume reflects the desirability of owning a stock. Accordingly, price and volume represent a supply-demand relationship for a stock. Like most supply-demand relationships, those pertinent to a particular stock, or a whole market, tend to remain in force, gathering momentum until some event brings the trend to a halt.

For the most part, however, technicians seldom rely upon a single indicator or two. Instead, they seek other indicators to confirm the behavior of a single stock or market of stocks.

One other indicator is insider trading, the accumulation or selling of stock by officers of a corporation. Corporate officers are thought to be more sagacious judges of their company's future performance, so if insiders are buying or selling their company's stock then other investors should be buying or selling that stock, too.

Another indicator is the odd-lot index, or the number of trades occuring in fewer than hundred-share increments. The idea behind the odd-lot index is that small money is dumb money. If the preponderance of trades in a stock is in odd-lot purchases, technicians regard that as a sell signal.

Technical analysts also examine mutual fund indicators. If the funds are laden with cash, that indicates pent-up demand for securities. If the funds are relatively fully invested, that indicates diminishing momentum for securities. In addition, technicians examine mutual fund redemptions and purchases in much the same fashion as the odd-lot index, apparently feeling that mutual fund transactions represent the assessments of unsophisticated investors and are an excellent contrary indicator. If purchases of fund shares are on the increase, that indicates a declining market and vice versa for redemptions.

But the most relied-upon tools of the technical analyst are point-and-figure charts, bar charts, and moving averages. These technical indicators trace the behavior of a stock or market over a period of time, usually three months to two years. Technical analysts believe that stocks develop a trading pattern that repeats itself. This pattern establishes a basis for determining whether a security should be bought or sold at a particular time.

Technical analysis is far too complicated for explanation in a single chapter, but the Fischer and Jordan book offers an excellent discussion. Life cycle investors need not confine themselves to fundamental analysis or technical analysis, and many investors use both, not only for selecting individual stocks but also for timing purchases and sales. Whether life cycle investors select one or a combination of both, market analysis is a critical tool in managing the growth element of the portfolio.

Fortunately, life cycle investors interested in managing long-term growth aren't confined to directly held common stocks. They may also achieve the same objective as indirect investors in growth-oriented mutual funds. We've already discussed the main advantages of mutual funds—professional management, ease of purchase and sale, switch privileges among other funds in a family. In order to profit as a growth-oriented mutual fund investor, life cycle investors need to pick the right fund and invest at the right time.

Picking the right mutual fund is somewhat easier than picking the right stock. The prospectus of a mutual fund will identify its orientation as a long-term growth fund, and that fund's record in providing returns for investors is published in many places other than the prospectus. Each year, *Money* magazine publishes the performance record of nearly all the major funds, as do several other national publications. The most comprehensive record of fund performance is *Lipper's Analytical Service,* which is available in most libraries. By checking these publications, life cycle investors can receive ample information in choosing among the hundreds of growth-oriented mutual funds. As always, past performance is no indication of future performance, but it is one readily accessible clue on which to base an investment decision.

Deciding upon which fund or funds to participate in is half the solution to achieving long-term growth as an indirect investor. The second half of the solution is market timing—knowing when to invest. Later in this section of *Life Cycle Investing* we'll talk about dollar-cost averaging as an exceptional investment technique to use with mutual funds and other investments. But right now, we need to look at one timing technique that's been useful for generations of investors: the Dow Theory.

Around the turn of the century, Charles H. Dow, father of the Dow Jones Industrial Average, suggested that the stock market behaves in cyclical trends that point to a general direction for the market. He divided those trends into three elements: the primary, secondary, and tertiary.

He argued that the primary trend is the general long-term direction, up or down, of the market as a whole, usually lasting a year or two. The secondary trend represents counterdirectional movements within the primary trend—slight deviations downward within a generally rising market, and deviations upward within a generally declining market—usually lasting for several weeks or months. Tertiary trends are day-to-day fluctuations within markets, usually lasting a few hours or days and lacking predictive significance.

Dow studied movements in the 30 stocks comprising the industrial average in order to discover whether they would reveal a predictive pattern about the future direction of the market. He postulated that a bull market was in effect when the secondary lows in the industrial average were higher than the previous lows in the secondary pattern and when secondary highs were above the previous secondary high. A bear market was in progress when the secondary highs and lows were lower than the preceding secondary highs and lows.

Here is an illustration of the Dow Theory in process.

Illustration of Dow Theory Bull Market

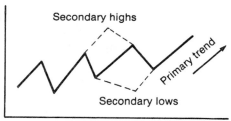

Illustration of Dow Theory Bear Market

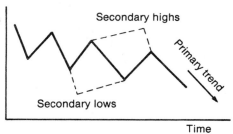

In full practice, advocates of the Dow Theory require that secondary corrections be of shorter duration than the preceding secondary corrections. In addition, they also look to the Dow Jones Transportation Average to confirm the pattern in the industrial average. When both averages are moving in similar primary and secondary directions, Dow practitioners regard that as evidence of a full-fledged bull or bear market, and they base securities purchases accordingly.

More recently, investors have sought other patterns of confirmation. One technique is to compare movements in the industrial and transportation averages with movements in the broader market indexes, such as the Standard & Poor's 500 Stock Index. These cautious analysts argue that the industrial and transportation averages represent a very small number of the stocks listed on public exchanges and that greater confirmation is required before identifying a market as being in a bona fide bull or bear pattern. They are particularly alerted when the industrial and transportation averages are moving in one direction and the broader market averages are moving opposite.

Many long-term growth investors also study movements in indexes of other exchanges, such as the American Exchange Stock Index and the Over-the-Counter Stock Index. Analysts feel that movements in indexes of other exchanges follow movements in the New York Stock Exchange. Up to a point, they regard movements in these other indexes as confirmation of the primary trend on the New York Stock Exchange, but "up to a point" is a major qualifier. American Exchange and OTC securities are regarded, rightly or wrongly, as more speculative and volatile than securities on "The Big Board." When securities on these exchanges follow the Dow trend in a relatively modulated way, analysts tend to regard that as confirmation of the major Dow trend. However, analysts tend to be suspicious when movements amplify those of the Dow averages, apparently feeling that speculative excesses may signal the crest of a bull market or that excessive selling may falsely confirm downward trends in the Dow averages.

The Dow Theory offers investors the opportunity to confirm their economic, industrial, and company analysis, and it's also a useful tool with technical analysis. It can be used by the direct investor to pick specific securities, but it is an even more useful guide for managing long-term growth through mutual funds.

Indirect investors, remember, participate in a whole portfolio of stocks representing many industries. By holding a broad portfolio they are in a better position to participate in market upswings. Holding more securities, they have more bets covered. Therefore, when the Dow Theory indicates a bull market, mutual fund investors are more broadly situated to participate in movements of many stocks.

However, the Dow Theory doesn't tell mutual fund investors how to manage portfolios during declining markets. Obviously, when confirming patterns suggest a bear market, growth-oriented investors might be tempted to get out of stocks. That may not be the wisest advice, for we recall from our discussion of defensive industries that some stocks perform their best in declining markets. Consequently, a bear market can present long-term investors with a chance for continuing capital gains.

When signals indicate a bear market, direct and indirect investors have two choices. First, they can take their capital out of growth stocks and growth mutual funds and place it elsewhere—in a money fund, in short-term bonds or a short-term bond fund, in CDs, or in defensive securities. Indirect investors can use switch privileges to transfer into mutual funds that typically, but not always, perform favorably in down markets. Gold funds are an example, as are government bond funds. Second, indirect investors can trust the wisdom of fund managers and leave capital where it is, hoping that fund managers will rearrange portfolios into countercyclical investments.

This is a difficult call, but growth-oriented investors need to be aware of the importance of not fighting the basic market trend in managing their investments. Time is the ally of the growth-oriented investor. Wise and responsible life cycle investors will not insist upon getting what the market isn't giving.

What the market often gives is very favorable long-term growth from fixed-income securities. You'll recall from our chapter on bonds that many government, corporate, and municipal bonds sell at deep discounts from par. When bonds mature, investors receive capital gains in addition to the semi-annual interest payments, adding a dimension of capital growth to the income-generating portfolio.

The decision to manage long-term growth through purchase of deeply discounted bonds is one of the safer ways to meet this portfolio need. Assuming life cycle investors select highly rated issues, they can be relatively well-assured that long-term gains are in hand. However, several issues must be considered in pursuing long-term growth in this fashion.

The first is taxes. As we noted, stocks and other financial assets held for six months and one day qualify as tax-favored capital gains. Under the 1984 laws, part or all of the discount from bonds is taxable as current income for bonds issued after July 18, 1984. The exception is discounts on municipal bonds, which are taxed as capital gains—long-term gains if held for the qualifying period. Therefore, if taxes are a critical investment consideration, the fixed-income investor will wish to remain with municipal securities, will be sure that the fixed-income portfolio contains bonds issued before the 1984 tax laws, or will give greater consideration to long-term holdings of stocks.

The second issue is maturities. Again, as we noted in our discussion of managing income investments, bonds selling at the greatest discounts are those with the longest-running maturities. This means that in order to receive maximum capital growth, investors must be prepared to hold discount bonds to maturity, or they must be prepared to trade bonds when declines in interest rates boost prices. Doing so will tie up capital that otherwise might be invested for long-term growth elsewhere.

The third issue is inflation, although this doesn't concern many investors as much as it seems to concern many investment advisors, particularly those selling inflation-hedge investments. Fixed-income securities, excepting variable-rate bonds and variable preferred stocks, do not alter their payments. By the same token, the matured discounts on bonds may not represent the kind of postinflation gains that investors had anticipated. We'll look further at inflation later.

In addition, many life cycle investors manage long-term growth through convertible bonds and preferreds. These hybrid securities offer growth-oriented investors the opportunity to receive current (reinvestable) interest and dividends, to obtain capital growth through discounts from par, and to participate in the growth of the underlying stock. They are very attractive to growth-oriented investors for these reasons, and they represent an excellent compromise among growth strictly from stocks, strictly from bonds, and strictly from an income reinvestment strategy, as discussed in the previous chapter.

Investors who manage long-term growth through selections of convertible securities are one type of equity-income investor. A second type is the investor who selects stocks and mutual funds because they offer a balance of capital growth and dividend payments. Many stocks and mutual funds fall into this category. Equity-income investors feel that dividends and interest are more predictable than capital gains, and their examination of compound interest tables reveals that reinvested dividends and interest can accumulate handsomely. They regard capital appreciation as an added plus in an equity-income strategy. Equity-income investors are increasing in numbers, particularly in the investment climate of the past few years. While their counterparts are striving for growth from an erratic stock market, they're taking a more measured and balanced approach.

The problems with managing capital growth through equity-income investments are two-fold. First, as growth securities they're subject to the normal vagaries of markets and the fortunes of firms; as income securities they're sensitive to interest rates and the capital fluctuations interest rates cause. Second, the income stream from dividends and interest is generally fixed.

With the exception of variable-rate securities, the payments by bonds are specified by the coupon. Boards of directors can increase stock dividends, of course, and many companies have a long history of regular dividend increases, but raising dividends is becoming more difficult to justify in an environment of high interest rates. Businesses need re-invested income to grow, and money paid out in dividends restricts capital available for expanding the business. If companies increase dividends, they may be forced into credit markets, where they'll pay doublt-digit interest on borrowings. Consequently, many boards have chosen to maintain dividend levels rather than increase them, and they may continue to do so in the future.

Finally, many investors regard precious metals as ideal long-term growth investments. They argue that the inevitable trend of the U.S. and international economies is toward escalating inflation that will debase all paper receipts. Whether they are right is an emotional as much as a rational question, but for long-term investors the only reasonable way to manage precious metals as growth investments is through dollar-cost averaging, which we'll discuss shortly.

MANAGING THE AGGRESSIVE GAINS COMPONENT OF THE PORTFOLIO

The aggressive gains component of the portfolio is the most volatile and potentially the most profitable, but in no other part of the portfolio are the issues of appropriateness and discipline more important. Let's look first at aggressive capital gains investments and then examine aggressive income investments.

"Appropriate" has two definitions in the context of aggressive capital gains: appropriate in the sense of acceptability to younger and better-heeled investors and appropriate with respect to an investor's temperament. Regardless of age, earning prospects, or wealth, some investors simply don't have the temperament to place capital in the volatile investments that produce aggressive gains. Their personal chemistry doesn't permit concentration in the aggressive gains component of the portfolio, and they shouldn't be in aggressive investments even if their financial situation permits. Many life cycle investors construct very rewarding portfolios without an aggressive gains component at all.

By the same token, "discipline" has two meanings in the aggressive capital gains context. First, there's investment discipline evidenced by self-restraint. Life cycle investors must be prepared to lose much or all of what they invest for aggressive capital gains, disciplining themselves so as not to let the prospect of great gains jeopardize their finances. What's more important, they must be prepared to accept capital as gone if it's lost and not reinvest further in an attempt to salvage a dead profit. Second, there's the intellectual discipline needed to evaluate the risks and returns of aggressive investments.

The first issue in managing aggressive capital gains is determining how much you can afford to invest. Most advisors will suggest you set aside a portion of total liquid assets for aggressive purposes. For investors in the young adulthood stage of their life cycle, advisors suggest a quarter of liquid assets. For those in the estate building part of the cycle, they say 10 to 20 percent is an appropriate range. For the mature and senior portfolios, advisors counsel 5 percent unless the investor is relatively well-off.

This book departs from that counsel. We'll use The Antacid Index of Aggressive Gains Management. Regardless of your age, income, wealth, or portfolio size, if you're chewing Rolaids in the middle of the night because you're worried about your investments, you have too much money in aggressive capital gains vehicles.

The second issue in managing the aggressive capital gains component of the portfolio is assessing a risk-reward relationship. By and large, this is something that only the fully tutored and experienced life cycle investor can do with precision, and that's one reason why most life cycle investors prefer to have the aggressive component of the portfolio under professional management.

In an investment context, risk is the calculated reduction of uncertainty, and in general it means accepting the possibility that an investment will not pay the return its risk structure declares possible. Given our constraints of space and purpose, we will have to assume that a stockbroker or advisor assesses the possibilities of risk and likelihood of return and informs us of them.

All investors are risk-averse, which is to say that at some point they will decline an investment opportunity because its possible returns are less than its possible risks. Obviously, some of us are less risk-averse than others, although there are many types of risk and most of us would be surprised at the risks we're taking with our portfolios. It is possible for investors to chart a formal risk/return frontier curve, complete with probability distributions and variance deviations and Greek letters inside square root signs. Almost any modestly sophisticated investment text can provide instruction in doing so with only rudimentary algebra required. There is, however, a somewhat less difficult, if less precise and more emotional, way to evaluate risk as we're using the term.

The economy offers a so-called "risk-free rate," and that's the rate of interest paid by U.S. government bonds. (Government bonds are not totally free of risk, as we've seen, but their interest payments are as close to guaranteed as is possible in this life.) As of mid-1985, Treasury bills and government bonds are paying a zero-risk rate of 11 to 12 percent. This interest rate return forms the basis from which to compare the return from other investments.

Let's say that a stockbroker advises you that an investment has the possibility of providing a median return of 15 percent. In most cases, "median" means about 6 chances in 20, assuming equal distribution of likelihoods greater or less than a 15 percent return. If we're able to make that assumption, then the chances of making more than 15 percent are equal to the chances of making less than 15 percent, and we have a 30 percent likelihood of earning 15 percent. Our comparison looks like this:

Possible Return	Likelihood of Achieving Return
12 percent	1 chance in 20
13 percent	2 chances in 20
14 percent	4 chances in 20
15 percent	6 chances in 20
16 percent	4 chances in 20
17 percent	2 chances in 20
18 percent	1 chance in 20

At this point, we break out the antacid tablets. If the risk analysis is correct (investments don't have to behave as analysis says they should behave), we have 20 chances in 20 of making more than the 11 percent return on T-bills and 19 chances in 20 of making more than the 12 percent available from government bonds. Analytically, the odds seem to favor this investment. Excluding considerations such as taxes and commissions and faulty analysis of minimum return, there's not much chance we'll be worse off in this investment than in the risk-free investment.

But what if the risk-free return were 15 percent? Would you accept 7 chances in 20 of making less than 15 percent for the equal prospect of making more than 15 percent? Would you accept only 6 chances in 20 of making the risk-free return of 15 percent? Some of us would, and some of us wouldn't. All of us must ask ourselves two questions when confronted with these decisions: "What return do I demand for a stated level of risk?" and "What risk am I willing to accept for a stated possibility of return?"

The problem with aggressive capital gains analysis is that risk and return evaluations aren't presented to most of us. Instead, investors receive sales pitches emphasizing the "enormous profit potential" of a particular investment. Chances are good that these salespeople wouldn't know what you were talking about if you asked them for a formal risk-return analysis, and chances are better that they wouldn't want you to see it if it were available. Life cycle investors must have information in order to manage the aggressive capital gains component of the portfolio, and the kind of information needed is usually cloaked in ambiguity and surmise. Therefore, most of us are asked to gauge risk emotionally and viscerally rather than intellectually, and most of us let our emotions run away when the subject is money.

The third consideration in managing aggressive capital gains is time. Time, by definition, is one consideration that separates aggressive capital gains from long-term gains. The chief question to ask in assessing a prospective return is, "Over what period?" Five dollars at the trifecta window and $5 at the teller's cage will both double, only the bet on the ponies is going to double right away or not at all. As we can see, time is the ally of the long-term investor, but not necessarily of the aggressive capital gains investor.

Yield over the "holding period," what investors call time, is the critical variable in assessing aggressive gains. The investor's holding period is an integral part of the volatility that aggressive gains feature, and the estimated time required to produce a desired return is something that investors must demand to know from an advisor or salesperson. Unfortunately, the "investment horizon," another term investors use to describe time, has been distorted by changes in law and in financial markets. Now that 181 days is the legal definition of long-term in measuring capital gain, an investment producing a desired return in fewer days would seem to be, by default, an aggressive gain, or at least a short-term gain.

Measuring aggressive capital gains by legal and tax definitions is a mistake, but it's one that is forced upon us. As a practical matter, six months constitutes the time horizon for an aggressive investment. Again, the reasoning for that conclusion is related to the risk-free characteristics of government securities. Government securities provide not only a so-called risk-free rate, but they also establish the risk-free time horizon. The purchase of a T-bill through noncompetitive tender will provide a return in a few weeks, and government bonds or notes will provide a risk-free rate within six months because they pay semi-annual interest. Therefore, aggressive investors should consider six months as a general frame in which to expect returns from an investment.

The aggressive investor's response to the time factor is liquidity. Given that an aggressive gains investment is supposed to produce a return within a relatively brief period, investors must be able to withdraw their investment promptly if it doesn't produce the desired return. The buy-and-hold strategy is truly naive when it comes to aggressive gains.

The emphasis on liquidity is important for investors seeking aggressive capital gains as indirect investors as well as for direct investors. We've examined a number of indirect aggressive gains investments—commodity pools, aggressive mutual funds, certain types of corporate stocks. The important feature of all these investments is their liquidity, but some of these investments have less of it than others.

Some types of stocks, particularly the penny shares, have "thin" markets, meaning they may be difficult to sell if you want to reduce losses. Some commodity pools require investors to leave funds on deposit for at least one year. Investments with these constraints are too illiquid for aggressive investors. Avoiding them is an important part of managing for aggressive capital gains.

As we noted earlier, professional management can be an important advantage for the aggressive capital gains investor. Professional money managers can make mistakes as disasterous as any novice, but some modest checking of credentials can help avoid the incompetent, leaving you at the whims of the merely unlucky. As a generality, it's probably best for most life cycle investors to entrust the aggressive capital gains component of their portfolio to professional managers. In so doing, they restrict their decisions to how much they can invest and to what form of aggressive investment suits them. They let their managers make the other decisions, possibly with profitable results.

However, one decision that indirect investors must make—and direct investors, too, for that matter—is whether to take gains or let them accumulate. Many investors favor accumulated gains, reasoning that their initial investment produces multiplied returns when reinvested. They argue that they've decided to commit a certain sum to aggressive growth and to take distributions in cash reduces the growth from their investment. They regard returns from aggressive growth as a source of further aggressive growth.

Other investors prefer to keep a fixed dollar amount in aggressive growth investments. They reason that contributions to aggressive growth investments represent a known level of at-risk capital and take gains in cash so as to stabilize the aggressive growth element of the portfolio. They regard returns from aggressive growth investments as precisely that—returns, not additional capital to be exposed to further volatility.

There is some credence in both points of view. Obviously, the former is a more assertive portfolio management strategy, and the latter is a more moderate way of managing for aggressive gains. In deciding whether to reinvest or take distributions in cash, life cycle investors should be guided by their temperament and by alternate uses for funds. If watching high-risk capital grow makes investors uneasy, then they should minimize their distress by taking distributions in cash. Also, reinvesting for consistent returns may be more attractive if alternate uses for distributions are presenting high, predictable returns, as money market funds do in many investment markets. Where neither emotional distress nor economic opportunity inclines investors toward a clear decision, letting aggressive gains compound may be the preferred course.

Along with the decision to let gains accumulate goes the decision to prevent losses from compounding. Every investor should establish a stop-loss point beyond which he or she won't endure further capital losses. A high stop-loss point means you get out of an investment before it declines too far; a low stop-loss point means you're willing to accept deeper losses in the hope an investment will turn around and produce a gain. Thus, the greater your willingness to accept a loss, the lower is your stop-loss point.

No one can advise you on where, exactly, to draw the line against accepting further investment losses, for it will vary with age, income, and the nature of the investment. As a norm, accepting no more than a 15 percent decline in investment value is a high stop-loss point, indicating great unwillingness to accept losses. A 50 percent stop-loss point is quite low, indicating ready willingness to hold an investment for eventual gain. For aggressive investments, a 25 to 35 percent decline in value is an average range for establishing a stop-loss point.

As a generality, younger investors can afford to accept greater losses and wait out price declines with the hope that an investment will turn around. Just as they have time to recoup losses, so they have time to hold on to a losing investment. Their stop-loss point will be lower than that established by older investors, other things being equal.

The higher an investor's earned income from a job, the lower can be his or her stop-loss levels. If investment losses hamper any investor's style of living, he or she shouldn't be entering into aggressive investments in the first place. Therefore, wealthier investors can generally afford to lose more money with investments, and that means their stop-loss levels can be lower.

Investing for greater returns inherently involves greater volatility, but some types of aggressive investments are inherently more volatile than others. The more volatile an investment, the greater the likelihod that it can turn around and convert a loss to a gain, just as there is a greater chance that gains can become losses more quickly. Therefore, patience is a necessary virtue, necessary evil, and necessary folly in aggressive gains investing.

Liquidity is exceedingly important in setting a stop-loss point for aggressive investments. If, for example, you're involved with a commodities fund that prevents your cashing in the account for a certain period of time, you effectively have no stop-loss point for that investment. The same holds true for infrequently traded stocks and bonds, although aggressive equities and fixed-income mutual funds provide great liquidity.

When investing for aggressive capital gains, remember that when you lose money you're not only losing money, you're losing the returns that could be accruing if your money were invested more conservatively. Perhaps losing $100 per month doesn't sound like much, particularly when you can deduct capital losses from your federally taxable income. But $100 monthly invested in a 5½ percent passbook compounding monthly will be worth almost $16,000 in 10 years.

Investing for aggressive income is another option for the aggressive component of the portfolio. In our sections on fixed-income securities and managing the income component of the portfolio we noted that aggressive income investors frequently are drawn to lower-rated debt instruments and common or preferred stocks paying above-market returns. These investors are willing to accept higher risk of default in exchange for higher potential interest and dividend payments.

(Strictly speaking, the term *default* applies only to debtor instruments, for companies don't really default on dividends; they merely don't declare them. Accordingly, we need to modify our use of default to include payments that are less than anticipated and not restrict the term to mean unpaid interest.)

Just as regular income investors check rating agencies to determine the soundness of obligations, so do aggressive income investors consult Moody's and Standard & Poor's indexes to identify potential aggressive income investments. Rating agencies confirm the speculative status of municipal obligations, corporate debentures, preferred stock, and common stock, although the rating on common stock is generally inconsequential.

Life cycle investors could, of course, undertake their own analysis of these instruments, measuring asset coverage, cash flow, and other ratios pertaining to the likelihood of an issuer's meeting interest and dividend payments. Most basic investment texts can provide instruction in doing so, and the exercise can be entertaining. For the most part, however, detailed study is rendered unnecessary by rating agencies and by quotations from the financial pages of *The Wall Street Journal*.

Just as ratings BBB and above indicate investment grade securities, ratings below BBB identify more speculative obligations. In addition, the current yield quotations annotated next to stock and bond entries in the *Journal* indicate the speculative nature of securities. If the yield on a stock or bond is notably higher than for firms in the same industry, or if it is notably higher than the overall prevailing rate, the market has announced the investment's speculative nature.

Generally speaking, the aggressive income investor will prefer notes, bonds, and debentures over stocks, for interest is an obligation whereas dividends may be discontinued. Even for the aggressive income portfolio, the relative assurance of receiving interest makes creditor securities more appealing than owner-equity securities.

There is one type of stock play that might reward aggressive income investors, and that's offered by cumulative preferreds which have deferred dividends for a few quarters. Unlike common stock dividends, unpaid dividends from cumulative preferreds remain an obligation of the issuer. If the issuer resumes dividend payments, all cumulative dividends in arrears must be paid to the current owner of the shares. Accordingly, aggressive income investors could purchase these preferreds and perhaps eventually receive all back dividends.

The issues in managing an aggressive income portfolio are similar to those discussed in managing the standard income portfolio—yield, maturity, investment rating—only the investor evaluates those considerations with a willingness to accept higher risk. There are, however, two considerations that the aggressive income investor must weigh.

The first is deciding between new issues of lower-rated obligations and already existing issues actively traded on public exchanges. Other things being equal, investors should prefer already outstanding securities, largely because they've been "seasoned" through public trading and their prices will reflect the market's estimate of their attractiveness. In addition, outstanding issues will likely be selling below par, adding some capital growth to the current yield. New issues don't have the benefit of extensive market testing, although investment banking syndicates will have looked them over and incorporated their assessment in the rating, price, and yield indicated in the offering circular.

Still, there are two reasons why aggressive income investors might prefer new issues of lower-rated securities. First, they are available without commissions. Second, new issues of debt may be senior to outstanding issues, meaning that holders of newly issued obligations are first in line for interest and principal payments.

The second issue that aggressive income investors confront is whether to invest for aggressive income at all. In the market climate of mid-1985, for instance, tax-advantaged government bonds of intermediate-term maturities were yielding nearly 11 percent and investment grade corporate obligations were yielding 13 percent. Given the relative safety of these obligations, is it really worthwhile for investors to accept the higher risk associated with more speculative obligations offering 14 or 15 percent?

Most investors would say no, and probably for good reason. When interest rate differentials are so slight, it makes little sense to manage for aggressive income. Unless investors are willing to accept the far greater risks with obligations of potentially insolvent issuers, offering 18 to 22 percent in mid-1985, there's little reward in investing for aggressive income.

Just as there are mutual funds emphasizing aggressive capital gains, there are funds emphasizing aggressive income. As we noted, these mutual funds invest in obligations of lower-rated issuers and pass on higher yields to shareholders of the fund. In addition to higher yields, they offer the customary advantages we've learned to associate with mutual funds. For many aggressive income investors, mutual funds can be the favored means of pursuing aggressive interest and dividend returns.

As we also noted, managing for aggressive returns can be achieved through selected investment techniques as well as by selected investments. One of the aggressive techniques we've covered is buying securities on margin—borrowing money with which to purchase investments.

The decision to borrow to finance securities purchases is prompted by one of two events. The first is an anticipation of a sudden and dramatic decline in overall interest rates, driving prices of fixed-income investments and high-dividend stocks upward. The second is anticipation of a dramatic increase in the price of selected stocks or in the entire market; the former being occasioned by a new product, higher than anticipated earnings, or a takeover; the latter by more general forces such as good economic news.

The advantage to borrowing money for securities purchases is leverage. Investors use someone else's funds to finance securities, and if all works out well, they make a profit, repay the loan, and walk off with what's left, all without using their own resources extensively. The disadvantages are obvious. If developments don't appear as anticipated, investors end up with a losing position and a loan to repay.

The record shows that only the most sophisticated investors, or the luckiest, win with leverage. As an investment tool, leverage is the proverbial two-edged sword, and too often the unprofessional investor gets sliced up. Life cycle investors who wish to take advantage of leverage would best do so through extremely aggressive mutual funds that utilize borrowed capital. Relying upon these funds minimizes downside risk while providing opportunity to profit from the borrowings by professionals.

Much of the same advice holds for another of the aggressive techniques we've mentioned, short selling. The most aggressive mutual funds will sell securities short, and, again, the record shows that unprofessional investors usually lose by selling short based on their own assessments. In addition, the purchase of put options has generally made short selling an outdated investment technique.

MANAGING THE LUMP SUM ACCUMULATION PORTFOLIO

We've looked at lump sum accumulations primarily with reference to zero-coupon bonds and certificates of deposit. We noted that these investments are particularly useful in setting aside funds for a known period—in anticipation of retirement, perhaps, or of a child's starting college. The fixed-dollar price, fixed compounding, fixed period, and fixed maturity date make zeros ideal for investments requiring a high degree of specificity and known returns. Therefore, zeros are preferred investments for the lump sum accumulation element of the portfolio, and we'll concentrate on them in this section. Still, we should note that three other investments offer some characteristics of lump sum portfolio management.

First, conventional bonds paying coupon interest do provide a fixed maturity date and a fixed par value of $1,000.

They are stable, at least among near-term maturities, and predictable, assuming investors select high-quality issues. However, they aren't exactly lump sum accumulation investments, for their total return depends upon the rate at which semi-annual coupon payments are reinvested.

Second, conventional CDs offer high predictability as one of their advantages. They can be used in managing the lump sum component of the portfolio, but they are useful only if their maturities coincide with the time for which the investor is accumulating lump sum capital. At present, the longest-running CDs are 12 years. Investors planning for periods longer than 12 years will have to renew their certificates at then-prevailing rates, and that detracts from their predictability.

Third, variable premium annuities have some characteristics of a lump sum accumulation investment. Assuming that investors contribute fixed amounts at fixed intervals for a fixed period, they can calculate with relative certainty the amount they'll have when the annuity is ready for withdrawals. Again, however, variable premium annuities aren't exactly lump sum accumulation investments, for their ultimate return depends upon rates paid by the annuity sponsor, and those will vary over the years.

Nonetheless, life cycle investors may wish to have conventional fixed-income investments and annuities in their lump sum accumulation portfolio. However, given the purpose of this portfolio element and its requirements of highly predictable accumulations, it's best to use the investment best-suited for the purpose. That brings us back to zero-coupon bonds.

In general, the issues governing other fixed-income investments also pertain to managing a portfolio of zeros: quality, maturity, and interest rate. Let's deal with these issues in turn as they apply to zeros.

Quality is the easy part. Without doubt, the most favored zero-coupon bonds are those assembled from conventional government bonds by brokerage houses that take USGs and reconfigure them as zeros. These securities go by many names—the Merrill Lynch Treasury Investment Growth Receipts (TIGRs), the Salomon Bros. Certificates of Accrual on Treasury Securities (CATS), the Dean Witter Easy Treasury Receipts (ETRs), and the E.F. Hutton COUGRs.

Their backing by U.S. government obligations makes them highly secure. Although many corporations issue zero-coupon bonds, there seems little reason to select them over government-backed zeros offering similar yields and greater safety. Zero-coupon CDs also are highly safe, although their illiquidity and minimal selection of maturity dates place them an overall second behind zero bonds. Therefore, the quality issue is rather easily resolved.

Maturity is a slightly more difficult problem. Many investors follow the buy-and-hold strategy in managing their portfolio of zeros. They select issues maturing in the year they'll need the money and hold them. Other investors, particularly those accumulating zeros for retirement, prefer to refrain from selecting maturities 20 or 30 years distant, arguing that they can better benefit from changes in interest rates by keeping maturities short and reinvesting accumulations.

Interest rate is a problem affiliated with maturities. In our section on managing the current income element of the portfolio we noted that there's little reason to invest over the long term unless distant maturities are paying rates notably higher than short- and mid-term obligations. In some respects, that counsel might also hold for zeros, but in other respects it might not.

Investors can adopt three general attitudes about their investments in zeros. First, they can opt for the highest interest rate for the shortest time. Second, they can opt for

CATS	zr88	. .	6	66⅜	66⅜	66⅜	. .
CATS	zr91	. .	4	43⅞	43⅞	43⅞	− ¼
CATS	zr95	. .	5	35	35	35	. .
CATS	zr97	. .	5	26⅜	26⅜	26⅜	+ ⅝
CATS	zr98	. .	19	26	24¼	26	+1¾
CATS	zr99	. .	5	22½	22½	22½	−1
CATS	zr01	. .	11	18½	18½	18½	− ¼
CATS	zr02	. .	6	16¾	16¾	16¾	. .
CATS	zr03	. .	25	15¾	15½	15¾	+ ¼
CATS	zr06–11	. .	20	8¾	8¾	8¾	. .

the highest rate for the longest time. Third, they can opt for the maximum quantity of ultimate accumulations, regardless of interest rate. Let's look at an actual selection of zeros from the New York Bond Exchange and examine how investors with each of these orientations might choose to manage a portfolio of zeros.

The securities in question are Certificates of Accrual on Treasury Securities issued by Salomon Bros. The interest rates on these issues are computed from present-value tables. It so happens that these CATS mature in May of the indicated year, so for mathematical simplicity let's assume that in May of 1984 an investor wishes to place about $2,000 in a Keogh Plan Account and expects to retire in 30 years, or approximately 2014. We'll look at CATS serving each of the three orientations we discussed, and the issues under consideration are the CATS of 1988, 2003, and 2006–11.

The investor who seeks the highest yield in the shortest time will opt for the 1988 CATS, maturing in four years. Its discount from par places its yield at slightly below 10.5 percent on a price of $663.75 per $1,000. For approximately $2,000, this investor can purchase $3,000 in par value of securities.

The investor who seeks the highest rate for the longest period will select the CATS of 2003, priced at $157.50 per $1,000 par for a yield also slightly below 10.5 percent. For approximately $2,000, this investor will purchase CATS maturing in 19 years with a par value of $13,000.

The investor who seeks the greatest ultimate accumulation will prefer the CATS of 2006–11, maturing in 27 years. Assuming these securities aren't called in 2006 and are left to mature in 2011, their price of $87.50 per $1,000 par value yields slightly below 9.5 percent. For approximately $2,000, this investor can purchase CATS with a maturity value of $23,000.

Accordingly, for an outlay of about $2,000 this life cycle investor can select an interest rate of about 9.5 to 10.5 percent, or he or she can select among accumulated face amounts of $3,000, $13,000, or $23,000. Which is the better strategy—managing for rates or managing for ultimate accumulations? The answer, of course, is, "It depends."

On the surface, it would seem foolish to sacrifice nearly a full point in interest by selecting the securities maturing in 2006–11. Their yield of 9.5 percent is clearly less than the four-year yield of 10.5 percent, although why this issue should present a declining yield curve is unclear. The yield-conscious investor would argue that the four-year issue presents a higher interest rate and greater reinvestment opportunity. Therefore, he or she would accept the 10.5 percent offered by the CATS of 1988, hold the issue to maturity, and re-examine investment opportunities in four years. This is certainly a reasonable management strategy, for it follows our canon about preferring shorter to longer maturities when rates are undifferentiated.

However, there is also some rationality behind preferring the 10.5 percent offered by the CATS of 2003. An investor could reason that the course of interest rates is unknown. His or her reasoning might be confirmed by the atypical interest rate structure of these CATS, which, as we've noted, perversely declines over time. Therefore, this investor is likely to prefer the highest available rate for the longest period of time. He or she is willing to sacrifice the chance that rates may increase in exchange for protection against their decline and to lock in 10.5 percent until 2003.

And, as you might well have guessed, there is also some logic in preferring the longest-running issue, despite its perverse yield curve. First, a $2,000 investment increases 10-fold. Second, it is the most predictable among all the choices, for investors selecting briefer maturities are at the mercy of rates prevailing every few years when they must reinvest matured securities. Predictability, remember, is highly desirable in managing the lump sum component of the portfolio, Third, this investment minimizes commissions.

Managing commissions is especially important in managing zero-coupon securities because zeros generate no current income to counterbalance commissions. Therefore, commissions paid for zeros detract from capital, for they can't be paid from interest. Commissions are important for another reason: compounding.

With the CATS of 2006–11 selling at $87.50, every $87.50 that an investor pays in commissions today denies him $1,000 in 2011. The more frequently his portfolio of CATS matures, the more frequently he must reinvest; the more frequently he must reinvest, the more frequently he must pay commissions; the more commissions he pays, the greater the compounding he denies himself for not selecting the longer maturity. Consequently, the long-term CATSnapper may actually end up with more retirement cash even though he receives a full point less in interest. The so-called "naive buy-and-hold strategy" might not be so naive after all.

There is, however, a way to have high rates and low commissions, and that's by purchasing zeros when they're initially issued by a managing broker. The CATS we've been looking at are traded in public exchanges, and brokers will charge a commission for purchasing them on the open market. However, when these securities are initially offered to the public, issuing brokers make their profit from basis pricing, and they cannot charge purchasers a commission. Original issues of zeros offer a wide range of maturities. Investors may pick and choose among them, managing yields or managing maturities as they are inclined.

CHAPTER 16

Managing Inflation

For much of the recent financial past, inflation has been one of the major concerns of all investors, if not the preeminent consideration, in managing a portfolio. It has been a concern to young investors seeking real (inflation-discounted) returns from the growth portfolio, to estate building investors who find that high prices reduce investable income, to senior investors anticipating the time when they will live off their investments, and to retired investors whose portfolio might not be producing the income needed for dignified retirement.

Inflation has also been a source of income for investment advisors and securities salespeople who've profited from investors' fears about inflation. Sometimes they've profited more from selling investments than investors have by purchasing them. Fear of inflation may be worse than inflation itself, for the reality is that inflation may not be as damaging as many people would have us believe. Accordingly, the very first step in managing a portfolio to avoid the depletions of inflation is to manage the fear of inflation.

When formally trained economists talk about inflation, they generally discuss one of two events. First, by "inflation" they may mean "any increase in the supply of money." You've heard the definition of inflation as "too much money chasing too few goods," with the consequence that prices of goods rise when confronted with all that money chasing them. This leads to the economists' second definition of inflation as "any sustained increase in the general price level."

When economists speak of "the general price level," they are referring to an index said to represent a standard market basket of goods and services. When you read in the newspaper that the CPI rose or fell, you are being told that the prices of goods and services comprising the index rose or fell, and from those movements comes a blanket statement about inflation.

Both definitions are generalities that do not necessarily pertain to individual investors and consumers. To some extent, we each have our own inflation rate, which may be greater or less than the norm. Peculiarities of region, personal tastes, position in the life cycle, and personal lifestyle influence our personal rate of inflation, and they may make it considerably less than the measured norm. Of course, these considerations may elevate our personal rate of inflation above the average.

In addition, discussions of inflation fail to consider higher income and reduced consumption. Most of us will make more money as we age, and often wages are tied to an inflation index. And we do spend less at different times in our lives. Therefore, inflation may not be as ravaging in personal and investment consequences as we're led to believe. There is a further possibility presented by inflation, and that is that it can make you rich, or at least better off than you used to be.

Typically, and we should emphasize "typically" as opposed to "inevitably," certain types of investments perform well in an environment of high inflation. These investments are generally asset plays in that they are financial instruments dealing with property, irreplaceable goods, goods with inelastic demand, and commodity-type produce such as petroleum. These investments are denominated in assets, and their assets will usually increase in price as the rate of inflation increases. Real estate, art and related tangibles, interest rate futures, gold, domestic oil stocks, and some commodities have traditionally performed well in inflationary times because they are investments backed by assets, and they've come to be called "inflation hedges" as a consequence of their past behavior.

Whether they are truly inflation hedges or whether they behave profitably in inflation because people think they are is a circular issue, but it's important because past patterns of behavior don't have to establish future patterns. This is particularly true in the case of real estate, which has proven highly respondent to interest rates. Now that the average American family can no longer afford the $95,000 price of the average American home, there's some question whether real estate will be the inflation hedge it has been in the past. Nonetheless, to the extent that understanding the past enables investors to profit in the future, an important aspect to managing inflation is understanding that asset-type investments can produce above-market returns during an inflationary cycle.

Many advisors still insist that common stocks are the greatest hedge against inflation, and they refer to any other investment, especially bonds and CDs, as "certificates of confiscation" because their returns allegedly don't meet inflation. Most people no longer believe that a general portfolio of common stocks is their best inflation hedge, and there's considerable evidence to suggest they're correct. Some types of stocks, yes. But common stocks in general are not the inflation-proof investment that many advisors still believe they are.

Investors who would like to read further about stock market prices and inflation might like to consult *The Stock Market and Inflation* edited by J. Anthony Boeckh and Richard T. Coghlan (Homewood, Ill.: Dow Jones-Irwin, 1982).

Conventional wisdom holds that the greatest sufferer from inflation is the fixed-income investor, the buyer of bonds and CDs, because inflation erodes the purchasing power of an income stream. That can be true, but not necessarily.

Convention asserts that high interest rates do not pro-

duce exceptional real returns because "nominal" rates—
coupon interest on newly-issued debt, current yield on existing debt, and, to some extent, dividend yield on
stocks—have two components: the inflation adjustment and
the "real" interest rate. Convention argues that investors
demand real yields of about 3 percent. If nominal inflation
is 10 percent, nominal interest will be 13 percent—10 percent for inflation and a real interest rate of 3 percent. Conventional wisdom further argues that the inflation component of interest rates is consumed by inflation and provides
no real returns. The conclusion is that whatever the rate of
inflation, only the real interest rate of about 3 percent is
paid on fixed-income securities.

Life cycle investors need not be bound by doctrinaire
thinking. We need to establish some counterconsiderations:
(1) Income investors can always at least keep abreast of
inflation; (2) Fixed-income investments can be managed to
maximize real returns; and (3) The inflation component of
interest rates might produce real returns.

By definition, inflation produces higher prices, but it also
produces higher interest rates. Inflation creates two types of
higher interest rates. First, inflation tends to increase the
rates paid by newly issued fixed-income investments. Second, it tends to increase rates paid by existing fixed-income
securities through declines in prices of long-term bonds and
interest-sensitive dividend stocks.

Newly issued debt, including not only bonds but also
short-term debts comprising the portfolio of money market
funds, must pay rates of interest competitive with the
known rate of inflation. If they don't, they can't be sold, for
investors will insist upon market-level returns. Therefore,
one strategy for managing inflation is to remain liquid. Invest in short-term securities that respond to high interest
rates, such as T-bills and money funds. Variable rate preferred stocks and debentures are also suited to inflationary
cycles. Avoid long-term certificates of deposit that have
fixed interest rates.

At some point in the inflationary cycle, investors can
profit from inflation by moving into long-term bonds and
high-dividend stocks. Yields on long-term investments, par-

ticularly bonds, will reflect today's demonstrated rate of inflation and expectations for future inflation through price declines of securities. The greater the present and anticipated inflation rates, the lower will be prices of long-term securities in order to produce higher yields. Buying these inflation-ravaged securities can produce capital gains, either by holding bonds to maturity or by holding stocks and bonds until diminished inflation causes capital gains by increases in their prices.

Keep maturities short until inflation has taken its toll on prices of income securities. Then, by moving into long-term bonds and interest-sensitive stocks when their prices are suppressed by inflation, investors can receive capital gains from price increases.

If investors can't precisely estimate the known and anticipated rate of inflation for the general economy, they can be more precise in judging their personal rate of inflation. If your personal rate of inflation is less than the general rate of inflation on which yields are based, the inflation component of interest rates will provide real personal returns.

The best way to manage one's personal rate of inflation is to keep expenses fixed and income variable. Keeping expenses fixed while arranging variable income may not be as difficult as it seems. For one thing, many major expenses are fixed. More frequently of late, fixed-rate mortgages are difficult to find, but many homeowner-investors still have them and at single-digit interest rates besides. Other major expenses, like automobile loans, are still commonly fixed-rate loans on which payments don't vary. Practicing household economies helps with managing variable expenses on the home front, and awareness of tax breaks helps investors avoid some of the double whammy of "taxflation."

Nor is it always difficult to increase income while holding down expenses. Wage income generally increases with inflation during a working lifetime, what with cost of living adjustments and inflation premiums being part of many yearly salary adjustments, and many retirement benefits are also indexed to inflation. Income from investments can be arranged to increase with inflation. Fixed-income investments can be managed by keeping maturities short, holding inflation-sensitive instruments like T-bills and money funds, and moving into long-term investments when inflationary psychology dominates expectations. Adjustable rate preferred stocks and debentures indexed to the consumer price index will increase dividends and interest payments during inflationary cycles. Investments in asset plays can produce capital gains.

Managing our personal rate of inflation along with our portfolios is the best response to the inflationary cycle. Increases in the cost of home heating oil are of greater consequence to the Midwesterner than to the Floridian, and less so to the Midwesterner who heats with electricity, especially if he has oil stocks in his portfolio. Increases in the cost of meat have minimal influence upon the budget of a vegetarian who has a commodity pool in his or her portfolio. The increasing cost of the American home doesn't much bother the renter, and it's likely to please the current homeowner greatly. A 10-fold increase in college tuition within 20 years is of less concern to retirees than to new parents, and even they have the UGMA on their side.

To put the issue succinctly, the general rate of inflation is comprised of many elements, many of which may not affect all of us. What counts is our personal rate of inflation, and when that's less than the norm we can benefit financially from the effects of general inflation through higher interest rates, depressed prices on long-term securities, and assets representing inflation hedges. It is highly important that life cycle investors invest with regard to their personal circumstances and not in the name of blanket generalities. That is the single most significant fact overlooked or ignored by nearly all investment advisors who present you with inflation hedge investments.

The problem with this point of view is that it's heresy. You'll not find many investors defending the idea that inflation can make people prosperous in real terms. During the past few years, investors have been instructed to regard inflation in the same way that college students of the 1960s regarded the CIA: something indigenously evil, forever threatening ruin, moving on silent feet to undermine us all. How easily we forget the 17 to 20 percent yields on money funds, the capital gains that inflation brings to home values, the extra tax write-offs on Schedule A from higher interest charges, the eroded real value of repaid loans, and all of those fantastic investment opportunities in inflation-battered long-term bonds. Inflation can be a wretched thing. But in the rules inflation makes there is the prospect of winning if you play by them. Life cycle investors can manage inflation, and they can manage it profitably.

CHAPTER 17

Dollar-Cost Averaging and Income Reinvestment

Some of the most powerful investment tools available to life cycle investors require little capital, reduce extensive research, and minimize analysis of markets. They can be used in purchasing many types of investments, and they actually help investors profit from declining markets. We'll look at several such techniques, but one of the foremost is dollar-cost averaging.

Dollar-cost averaging is a simple procedure that involves investing a fixed amount at a fixed interval in a single investment. Although that's similar to the self-tithe we discussed in managing the stability component of the portfolio, dollar-cost averaging works most effectively when used for investments that fluctuate in price, particularly precious metals, stocks, and mutual fund shares.

To illustrate dollar-cost averaging at its most straightforward, let's assume that an investor decides to purchase shares of a common stock mutual fund in amounts of $100 each month. Over a period of six months, our investor's purchase record might look like this:

Month	Purchase Price Per Share	Shares Purchased	Portfolio Value
January	$25	4	$100
February	20	5	180
March	30	3.333	370
April	25	4	408
May	27.50	3.636	549
June	35	2.857	799

As we see, this investor ended the six-month period with a portfolio value of $799 (22.826 total shares times $35 per share on the closing date) on an investment of $600. He or she was able to achieve that gain because dollar-cost averaging buys more shares when prices are lower and fewer shares at higher prices. The disciplined, elegant simplicity of this method helps investors shun two emotional mistakes: avoiding investment when prices are depressed and investing more when prices are rising.

However, dollar-cost averaging doesn't assure continual gains because prices fluctuate. Note the month of February in the example. Two months into the dollar-cost technique, our investor had placed $200 into a portfolio valued only at $180 (nine shares at $20 per share). Had he or she redeemed the mutual fund shares, 10 percent of the portfolio value would have been lost. By continuing the dollar-cost strategy, this investor purchased a greater number of shares at the temporarily depressed price of $20 per share and thus benefitted when prices improved by having purchased more shares.

Dollar-cost averaging is especially useful for mutual funds because funds permit investors to buy fractional shares. The strategy would be similarly useful for direct purchases of stocks, although commissions and inability to buy partial shares reduce maximum gains. Many advisors wisely counsel that dollar-cost averaging is the only intelligent way to invest in precious metals, for their prices fluctuate widely and their emotional attraction draws investors to them at the wrong times.

With a bit of intuitive understanding we can see how dollar-cost averaging helps investors to reduce the complexity of investment decisions. Once investors have made the decision to undertake a particular investment, a growth mutual fund in this case, dollar-cost averaging eliminates timing decisions. Investors are no longer compelled to examine every turn in the market, for they know that dollar-cost averaging helps them to profit through purchasing more of an investment when its price is depressed.

In addition, investors establish the amount they wish to invest per period. Through dollar-cost averaging it's possible for life cycle investors to pursue many portfolio elements simultaneously. For instance, they might decide to contribute $100 per month to the growth component, $200 per quarter to the stability component, and $500 semi-annually to the lump sum component. Whatever budgets permit and investment needs direct, dollar-cost averaging can serve.

Dollar-cost averaging is part of many investment programs, either actively, when investors direct that choice, or passively when dollar-cost averaging is built into other investments. Employee investment programs use dollar-cost averaging, for employers and employees contribute fixed amounts at fixed periods to an EIP. Payments to variable premium annuities also employ dollar-cost averaging, and it's the key principle behind reinvestment of distributions from mutual funds and dividend reinvestment programs.

In fact, reinvesting mutual fund distributions and dividends from stock are ideal uses for dollar-cost averaging, and that's an excellent passive adjunct to an active decision to use dollar-cost averaging. Let's say that you own common stock in a company that sponsors a dividend reinvestment program. Most public utilities offer dividend reinvestment, as do many industrial companies, and if your employer has a stock purchase plan apart from an EIP, it's probably eligible for dividend reinvestment.

As the name implies, dividend reinvestment programs permit investors to receive dividend payments in the form of additional purchases of stock. Instead of paying cash dividends directly to you by check, the company's transfer agent purchases additional shares of the company's stock and credits an account in your name. Dividend reinvestment programs typically permit shareholders to contribute additional sums, usually from $25 to $1,000 monthly, for additional share purchases (and without commissions, too).

Let's say that we subscribed to AT&T's dividend reinvestment program when we bought its stock back in our chapter on options. Every quarter, AT&T's transfer agent credits our account with shares purchased from redirected dividends, so over a few periods our record might look like this, given holdings of 100 shares producing a dividend of $120 per year, or $30 per quarter.

Quarter	Dividend	Share Price	Shares Bought	Portfolio Value
1st	$30	$15	2	$ 30
2d	30	16	1.875	62
3d	30	14	2.143	84.252
4th	30	15	2	120.27
5th	30	13	2.308	134.238
6th	30	16	1.875	195.216

As the numbers reveal, reinvested dividends use the principle of dollar-cost averaging to produce gains from temporary declines in share price. Over six quarters, share price fluctuated between $13 and $16. With a constant quarterly investment of $30, our average purchase price was $14.833, as dividend-reinvestment programs usually round purchases to three decimals. On an investment of $180 over six quarters, we purchased additional shares valued at $195 by the end of the period.

Dollar-cost averaging can't guarantee a profit, for nothing prohibits share prices from falling indefinitely. However, over time and a normal course of events, the average price of shares purchased through dollar-cost averaging will be less than their terminal price, producing a capital gain of some amount.

Note also that we've assumed no dividend increase in our example, nor have we considered that additional shares purchased from dividend reinvestment will also produce additional dividends to be reinvested, nor have we included the effects of continually contributing additional sums while dividends are being reinvested. Those are three very important omissions. By including them, our gain would have been more impressive.

To illustrate the magnitude of possible gains, let's take this actual example from the T. Rowe Price New Horizons Fund, which was printed in the summer 1984 edition of "The Price Report," the newsletter for investors in the T. Rowe Price family of mutual funds. The hypothetical investor in this example set aside $100 per month for 10 years, directing all capital gains and dividends to be reinvested in additional shares of the fund.

The editors of "The Price Report" summarized the results convincingly:

> The table shows that the investor's cumulative cost of monthly investments was $12,000. The total dollar amounts of dividend and capital gain distributions reinvested in additional shares were $1,702 and $7,051, respectively, bringing the total investment cost to $20,753. *By dollar-cost averaging, the investor's average cost per share each year was usually well below the Fund's peak that year.*
>
> Based upon an ending net asset value of $17.90, the total market value of the account as of December 30, 1983, was $34,357, or $13,604 more than the total amount invested. The ending market value consists of $22,742 in shares acquired through monthly investments, $2,464 in shares acquired through dividend reinvestments, and $9,151 in shares acquired through reinvestment of capital gain distributions.

The reinvested distributions aren't exactly dollar-costed, for they do vary with the performance of the fund's portfolio. Nonetheless, the principle remains intact. An investment program of dollar-cost averaging coupled with reinvestment of distributions can be a powerful generator of returns.

With the exception of bond funds, dollar-cost averaging is somewhat less effective for direct purchases of bonds, largely because investors have to set aside substantial amounts to cover the cost of these instruments. Given that conventional bonds will cost from $500 to $1,000 or more, life cycle investors would have to be well-capitalized in or-

Illustration of Dollar-Cost Averaging Program: Investments in T. Rowe Price's New Horizons Fund

Year Ended 12/31	Total of $100 Monthly Investments	Dividends	Capital Gain Distributions	Shares Purchased	Cumulative Market Value of All Shares Owned (Reflects Reinvestment of Dividend and Capital Gain Distributions)	Average Cost Per Share	Fund's Price Range Low	Fund's Price Range High
1974	$ 1,200	$ 0	$ 0	200.454	$ 974	$ 5.98	$ 4.51	$ 8.27
1975	1,200	18.32	0	185.918	2,573	6.55	4.91	7.72
1976	1,200	28.67	0	170.576	4,077	7.20	6.66	7.73
1977	1,200	39.38	0	171.225	5,949	7.24	6.68	8.17
1978	1,200	71.00	0	139.293	8,458	9.12	7.38	11.61
1979	1,200	136.28	0	122.721	12,882	10.89	9.65	13.01
1980	1,200	229.92	363.99	132.070	21,918	13.58	10.62	19.94
1981	1,200	359.68	1,883.37	207.450	21,355	16.60	14.07	19.60
1982	1,200	469.92	3,480.64	416.062	27,758	12.38	10.11	16.74
1983	1,200	349.15	1,323.29	173.615	34,357	16.54	15.17	21.35
Totals	$12,000	$1,702.32	$7,051.29	1,919.384	$34,357	$10.81	$ 4.51	$21.35

der to buy bonds at regular intervals, presumably investing at least $5,000 per interval.

In addition, dollar-cost averaging works most effectively with investments that fluctuate noticeably, meaning that dollar-cost averaging bonds requires investors to choose long-term maturities, for they produce greater price fluctuations. Unless investors are dollar-costing long-term bonds monthly (or at least quarterly) and are prepared to hold them for several years, dollar-cost averaging won't produce good capital returns as it will with stocks, mutual funds, and precious metals.

There is one exception, however, and we glossed over it earlier. Zero-coupon bonds can be acquired profitably through dollar-cost averaging. These instruments are low enough in price, present a range of maturities, and generally fluctuate enough in price to be acquired through dollar-costing. Life cycle investors who buy zeros for their IRA might wish to consider dollar-cost averaging.

There is a strategy similar to dollar-cost averaging that serves well in acquiring conventional bonds, and that's averaging down. Under dollar-cost averaging, we invest a fixed amount at a fixed period. Under averaging down, investors purchase a desired bond and then add to their holdings whenever prices are favorable. When interest rates are erratic, and, therefore, long-term bond prices volatile, investors can acquire bonds at reduced prices. If they intend to hold a particular bond to maturity, they can reduce the average price per bond by buying when prices fall. Held to maturity, these bonds produce greater capital gains.

Averaging down can be applied to stocks or any other investment that is temporarily (one hopes) suppressed in price. If investors are long-term holders of a stock—or precious metals, collectibles, or mutual funds—they can reduce the average cost of that investment by adding to holdings when prices fall.

For example, suppose an investor bought 50 ounces of gold at $400 per ounce for a total outlay of $20,000. Let us say the price fell to $200 per ounce. If the investor closes out the position, his or her loss is $200 per ounce or $10,000 because the average cost of holdings is $400 per ounce. If the investor holds fast, he can break even only if gold returns to $400 per ounce.

However, if this investor buys an additional 50 ounces at $200 per ounce, he or she holds 100 ounces of gold for a total outlay of $30,000, reducing the average cost to $300 per ounce. If the price of gold improves to, say, $300 per ounce, the investor breaks even. By not averaging down, break-even was $400 per ounce.

In this case, averaging down is the difference between a $10,000 capital loss and a break-even position. And if gold rebounds to $400 per ounce—the initial break-even point—then this investor will have made $10,000 instead of breaking even, having paid $30,000 for gold now worth $40,000.

The decision to average down requires life cycle investors to be patient, disciplined, and convinced of the long-term merit of an investment. For those who have these qualities, coupled with correct judgment, averaging down can be as profitable an investment strategy as dollar-cost averaging.

Similar to averaging down is averaging up, but it's generally a technique to be avoided unless an investor is exceptionally disciplined, savvy, and lucky, all at the same time and almost all of the time. It takes no semantic wizard to guess that averaging up is the opposite of averaging down: instead of buying when prices fall, you buy when prices rise.

Let's say that an investor buys one share of stock at $50 per share. The price rises to $60, and he buys another share. He now holds two shares valued at $120 for a total investment of $110 and an average cost of $55 per share. So long as the price keeps going up and our investor suffers no intemperate enthusiasm causing him to mortgage the house and put everything into the rising investment, everything will be fine. Each share he holds will be worth more than each additional share he buys.

The problem is that no investment works this way forever, or even for very long. Even in the case of our two meager shares, all it takes is a price fluctuation of 10 percent—$12—for our investor to be a loser. What he paid $110 for would then be worth only $108. Unless investors are rigidly disciplined to sell after a price run, which assumes they understand a particular investment exactly and that they time purchases and sales precisely, averaging up is going to cost them considerable profits.

Through dollar-cost averaging we took the bad with the good, permitting downward price fluctuations to reposition us for upward price fluctuations. By averaging down we did much the same thing, expecting upward price movements to reward our nerves. In other words, dollar-cost averaging and averaging down reward temporary suppression in prices by lowering average purchase price. Averaging up increases average purchase price, rewards only increasing prices, and devastates holdings if prices fall, as inevitably they must.

As you might guess, averaging up works for very, very few investors, and not even indefinitely for them. It's important to understand the pitfalls of averaging up because when prices are rising investment advisors will counsel you to add to your holdings. Your own instincts and greed will counsel you to agree. Unless you are one of the exceptionally disciplined and knowledgeable few, don't.

CHAPTER 18

The Mathematical Tools of Life Cycle Investing

During the past decade, investing has become a mathematically complex monster. The Markowitz Portfolio Equation, the Sharpe Index Model, and the multiple regression analysis of formal investment evaluation are enough to drive investors into savings accounts—assuming they could compute compound interest from stated interest.

Fortunately, investment isn't simply a matter of mathematics. Equally fortunate, the mathematics of investment can be simplified. A few relatively easy-to-master equations and mathematical procedures can aid life cycle investors greatly in their investment decisions.

THE MATHEMATICS OF THE STABILITY COMPONENT

The purpose of the stability component is to avoid capital fluctuation while earning a market-level rate of interest. We've noted that two types of investments are particularly suited for that purpose: depository accounts (savings accounts and certificates of deposit) and money market funds.

These investments are suited for the stability component because they do not fluctuate in value and because they produce a stated rate of interest. We also noted that the self-tithe is an excellent way to contribute to the stability component of the portfolio. Therefore, we confront two problems concerning the mathematics of the stability component.

The first issue is to determine how much a single investment of a fixed amount will compound to in specified period of time. We'll call this the certificate of deposit problem, named after one type of security that raises the question. The CD problem is also known as a future value problem, a compound interest problem, and a future worth of $1 problem. Whatever its name, the issue is the same: life cycle investors want to know how much $1 deposited today will be worth at a stated rate of interest for a stated period.

There obviously is a formula that will declare the answer, but there's an easier way to find it, and that is by consulting a compound interest and annuity table. These tables are nothing more than rows of numbers by which you multiply the amount of the deposit over a stated time. Let's say that you place $1,000 in a CD paying 10 percent interest compounded monthly and maturing in six months. The appropriate table will look like this:

Months	10 Percent Nominal Annual Rate
1	1.0083
2	1.0167
3	1.0252
4	1.0337
5	1.0423
6	1.0510

Through the effects of monthly compounding, your total return will derive from the payment of interest upon interest. The tables compute the effective yield from the nominal 10 percent annual yield. All you do is multiply the amount of your single deposit ($1,000) by the appropriate figure under the nominal interest rate for six months (1.0510). The answer is $1,051. For a deposit of $500, the answer would be $500 × 1.0510, or $525.50. That is the amount your deposit will grow to in six months.

The second problem related to the stability component is determining the growth of continuing deposits into a constant-dollar investment. We execute a similar procedure, but using a different table, to determine the growth of a series of deposits into the stability component. Let's say that an investor wishes to contribute $100 per month for two years to a money fund with an anticipated annual yield of 10 percent (yields on money funds vary with current market conditions, so we have to estimate a projected yield).

The money fund problem, as we'll call this issue, involves making a series of deposits rather than a single deposit. It is also called an accumulation of $1 per period problem, a future worth of $1 deposited per period problem, and a compound amount of $1 per period problem. In this case, our table would look like this:

Years	10 Percent Nominal Annual Rate
1	12.5655
2	26.3172

To find the answer, we merely multiply our monthly deposit ($100) by the appropriate figure under the interest rate column. The answer becomes $2,631.72. That's how much we'd have at the end of two years by depositing $100 monthly into a vehicle paying 10 percent nominal annual interest.

Dealing with compound interest and annuity problems is simpler than it would seem to be after gazing upon those formidable rows of tiny numbers. The most significant problem is making sure you've got the right table. But there are some more complicated considerations. For example, your answer will be different if you make a deposit at the beginning rather than the end of a period, if interest is paid daily rather than monthly, semi-annually, or annually, or if yields aren't constant.

However, for the most part these considerations have minimal importance. Most of us don't have to know with absolute exactness the amount of future compounding. What we're looking for is some way to figure compounding with high certainty and to be able to confirm what other people tell us.

The best source for life cycle investors seeking to become conversant with compounding is *Compound Interest and Annuity Tables* by Jack C. Estes (New York: McGraw-Hill, 1976). Don't be concerned because the book is almost 10 years old; the numbers haven't changed. Estes offers a comprehensive set of tables and sample instruction on how to use them. The tables are arranged in monthly, quarterly, semi-annual, and annual form. All you need is patience and a pocket calculator.

After you've become more adept at the procedure, you can improve your sophistication with *The Dow Jones-Irwin Guide to Interest* by Lawrence R. Rosen (Homewood, Ill.: Dow Jones-Irwin, 1981). Rosen takes his readers through some of the more complicated issues in the time value of money with actual examples gleaned from the financial pages.

THE MATHEMATICS OF THE INCOME COMPONENT

The math of the income component is related to that of the stability component, except here we're concerned with finding the yield in addition to calculating the accumulated value of an investment.

Calculating the yield on stocks—the dividend yield—is simple enough: divide the dividend payment by the amount paid for the stock. If you paid $10 for a share of stock and it pays $1 per share in dividends, the dividend yield is 10 percent.

To understand the complete yield from an income investment, however, investors must estimate the yield from reinvesting dividends. In our example, we'd receive the $1 in four quarterly installments of 25 cents. Presumably, life cycle investors would reinvest that 25 cents if they could. Consequently, we have another problem in calculating the compounding of an investment.

In this case, we deposit 25 cents every three months into, say, a money fund or savings account. This takes us back to the problem we just completed: What do we receive on a series of deposits at stated intervals and at stated interest rates? We consult the same table we consulted in The money fund problem, finding the appropriate interest rate and the appropriate time span.

The same issues prevail in computing the current yield on bonds. Current yield equals the coupon payment divided by the purchase price. If we paid $500 for a bond with a $50 coupon, current yield is 10 percent. We receive that $50 in twice-yearly payments of $25. If we place $25 in a money fund every six months, how much does the deposit grow to? That depends upon interest received from the money fund and upon how long we let the deposit grow. Consult the same table we consulted in the money fund problem, using semi-annual tables for the estimated interest rate and period.

As a consequence of their privileged tax status, munies provide a smaller absolute yield than fully taxed securities. Just to pick figures by way of illustration, munies may be offering 5 to 8 percent coupon yields when fully taxed bonds of similar quality are paying 10 percent.

Accordingly, munies are often evaluated according to "taxable equivalent yields," comparison of after-tax yield on one investment with the untaxed yield of munies.

There's a quick way to calculate whether you're better off with municipals or other securities by computing taxable equivalent yields. Look up your anticipated income and tax bracket in the middle of the tax booklets the IRS mails yearly. Then examine the yield from the municipal bond. Compare that with yields available from other investments.

Finally, plus those figures into the formula

$$TF = BT(1 - t).$$

TF is the tax-free return available from munies. *BT* is the before-tax return available from other investments. The *t* is your marginal tax rate from the IRS booklet.

Let's say that the tax-free yield on the municipal bond is 9 percent. The before-tax yield on other investments is 12 percent. Your tax bracket is 14 percent. Then:

$$TF = .12 \ (1 - .14)$$
$$TF = .12 \ (.86)$$
$$TF = .1032 \text{ or } 10.32 \text{ percent}$$

These calculations show the equivalent yield of the taxable investment is 10.32 percent. That means if you put your money into the fully taxed investment yielding 10 percent and pay your taxes, you're better off than by putting your money into the municipal bond paying 9 percent without taxation.

THE MATHEMATICS OF THE GROWTH COMPONENT

Calculating the growth of an investment can be an exceedingly complicated procedure. The key feature of the growth component is continual investment, and over time, with repeated purchases and reinvestment of dividends or interest, calculating an accurate return can be complex. In addition, growth investments involve some volatility, and with volatility comes unpredictability. Furthermore, determining the rate of estimated growth from an investment is a rather difficult mathematical process in itself, and unless you have some guide to calculating growth rates you may as well not bother to calculate them at all.

Nonetheless, there are some procedures that life cycle investors can follow. Let's assume a $1,000 investment in a common stock mutual fund in which all dividends and capital gains are reinvested for compound growth. In this case, total return is based upon capital growth and on growth in reinvested dividends. If this problem sounds familiar, it should: we're revisiting both the certificate of deposit problem and the mutual fund problem—and let's hope you also recognize that dollar-cost averaging is at work here via reinvested dividends.

In this case, we have a single deposit of $1,000 (the CD problem). That our total return is comprised of two elements is now inconsequential. Let's assume that we receive dividends of 5 percent (calculated as we calculated yield on stocks) and capital growth of 10 percent. Our total estimated, to say nothing of hoped-for, growth is 15 percent. But the important question is, "Over what period?"

Within that question lurk all of the issues of investment analysis we've discussed thus far: market timing, growth industries and growth firms, economic cyclicality, the wisdom of professional money managers, up-and-down price movements associated with dollar-cost averaging, and the estimates of other investors. We do know this: No investment grows at the same rate forever.

In estimating anticipated rate of growth from stocks, investors have three choices: (1) accept the implied rate of growth built into the current price of a stock, (2) estimate the future growth rate based upon the economy-industry-firm analysis covered under "Managing the Growth Component of the Portfolio" in Chapter 15, (3) use the historical growth rate established by an investment in the past. Each of those estimates implies a period of time. The first implies that growth will be indefinite. The second implies that growth will last through an economic cycle of some length. The third implies that future growth will equal an average of past growth for the same period.

For the sake of illustration, let's pursue the latter assumptions. We'll say that the historical return from our stock fund over the past five years has been 15 percent, 10 percent from capital growth and 5 percent from dividends, and that our anticipated return for the next five years equals the historical pattern.

What accumulations do we expect over five years if growth averages 15 percent annually from a single deposit in a stock fund? That's a certificate of deposit problem. We find the annual table for the future value of $1, trace our finger to the appropriate percentage amount, down to the appropriate year, locate the given figure, and multiply by $1,000. The resulting figure can only be approximate at best, for net asset values will fluctuate and growth will be irregular.

With a series of deposits into a stock fund (or stock, for that matter) we have a money fund problem—several deposits, regular intervals, estimated growth rate, estimated period of time. If we're depositing $1,000 per month into a money fund at an estimated growth rate of 15 percent yearly, we look for the "future worth of $1 deposited per period" table.

The mathematics of bonds are similar to those of the income component, except in managing bonds for capital growth we're concerned with more than the current yield. The first item of concern is determining the yield to maturity—the total return from interest payments plus capital appreciation. In calculating yield to maturity we know both the coupon rate and the amount of discount below par. We also know the maturity date of the bond. All we need is a formula with which to calculate yield to maturity—the average annual gain as a percentage of the average annual investment. Average annual gain is interest payments plus capital appreciation. Average annual investment is the midpoint between buyer's cost and maturity value. Here's the formula:

$$\frac{C + \dfrac{D}{YTM}}{\dfrac{PP + PV}{2}}$$

The C is the yearly coupon payment, D is the bond's discount from par, YTM is years to maturity, PP is the purchase price, and PV is the bond's par value. The 2 is necessary to make everything average out. The numerator reveals the average annual gain, which is interest payments plus capital appreciation. The denominator is average annual investment, the midpoint between purchase price and par value. The resulting figure is the yield to maturity, the total yield received by the holder of the bond.

We'll assume that a bond matures in 10 years and that we buy it at $500 five years before maturity. The coupon payment is $50 yearly. Figures enter the formula:

$$\frac{\$50 + \frac{\$500}{5}}{\frac{\$500 + \$1,000}{2}}$$

A bit of mathematical wizardry reveals:

$$\frac{\$50 + \$100}{\$750}$$

which further breaks down to:

$$\frac{\$150}{\$750}$$

which finally gives a yield to maturity of .2000, an even 20 percent.

A similar figure is yield to call. Yield to call is computed just like yield to maturity, substituting the call price for par value and the number of years until possible redemption for years to maturity. Obviously, bonds provide many different yields, and the pertinent yield is the one that coincides with the investor's intention to hold or sell.

In computing total return from conventional bonds, don't forget to compute the growth of reinvested interest payments, for this bond generates $25 every six months that can be reinvested into a money fund or depository account.

Another frequent calculation of use in managing the growth component is The Rule of 72. The mysteries of mathematics have seen fit to permit the number 72 special status in determining how long it takes to double your money. If you divide 72 by the expected interest rate or return on a particular investment, the resulting number tells you how long it will take your money to double. For instance, if the return is a steady 10 percent, your money will double in 7.2 years (72 divided by 10).

Conversely, The Rule of 72 will also reveal what return you need in order to double your money within a specified period. For example, let's say you want to double your money in five years. Divide 72 by 5 and discover that you'll need a return of 14.4 percent.

THE MATHEMATICS OF THE AGGRESSIVE GAINS COMPONENT

The mathematics of the aggressive gains component are essentially those of the growth component except, of course, that the time period is shortened in the case of aggressive capital gains. In the case of aggressive income, the calculations for current yield, yield to maturity, and reinvested interest or dividends are the same as for the income component of the portfolio.

In managing for aggressive capital gains, one important mathematical tool is the filter test. The filter test is a technical trading tool occasionally used in conjunction with fundamental analysis to determine whether investors should buy or sell a particular investment at a particular time. Filter tests can be used with any investment vehicle that fluctuates in price, but they have come to be recognized as especially useful in managing aggressive capital gains vehicles, which generally have above-average price fluctuations in relatively brief periods.

In its simpler form, a filter test is based upon the premise that movement in a security's price will generally proceed in an established direction once a price barrier is passed. Therefore, by tracing an investment's historical price performance investors can identify a trading range for the security. If the investment is behaving according to established pattern, then its price at a given time and its recent behavior may indicate the direction of movement up or down within the established pattern.

The filter test tells investors to buy a security if its price moves up a certain percentage from a previous level. Investors should hold the security until its price falls a certain percentage from an established high, at which time they should sell or sell short. Investors should remain out of the security (or hold the short position) until the price rebounds a certain percentage from an established low.

By following a filter test, investors are able to profit from price moves occurring between the established trading range for a security. On the buy side of the transaction, investors attempt to profit by establishing that a security is ascending in price. On the sell side of the transaction, investors attempt to curtail losses, hold on to gains, or—for the most speculative—achieve further gains by selling short. Presumably investors could also use filter tests in buying put and call options according to the movements of an underlying stock.

The obvious problem is in picking the percentage filter to use. If investors act on small percentage price moves, then they're likely to catch a security for the full run of its price movement. Also, they're more likely to act on false signals and to increase trading commissions. If investors use a larger percentage movement as their filter, they reduce transactions and the likelihood of reacting to false signals, but they also reduce potential profits from participating in the full direction of the price run.

As a very general, and perhaps outdated, rule, investors are advised to accept 10 percent price fluctuations for securities traded on the New York Stock exchange, 15 to 20 percent for securities traded on the American Exchange, and around 25 percent for securities traded on other exchanges. The general logic behind these filter percentages is that securities on the NYSE tend to be larger, more established companies with actively traded stock, whereas securities on the other exchanges are often less well-capitalized and traded in thinner markets.

The purpose of the filter is to filter out inconsequential price moves in order to identify a genuine trend. The assumption is that a fluctuation greater than 10 percent in the price of a NYSE issue intimates a real trend unfolding, whereas a 10 percent move in securities on other exchanges might merely represent a technical jiggle. Hence the counsel to set a larger percentage filter for issues on the AMEX,

OTC, and other exchanges in order to establish that price moves are genuine trends.

Filter tests are also occasionally used in trading commodities, in which trading ranges, movement patterns, and momentum also apply. There are two problems in applying filter tests to commodities, however. First, conditions that establish futures prices may replicate themselves generally, but often it's the extraordinary, unforeseen event that motivates commodities markets. Second, volatility is extraordinary, and commodities contracts are generally leveraged highly. Therefore, a sudden sharp price move can wipe out a position within minutes, prohibiting investors from applying filter tests and acting accordingly.

THE MATHEMATICS OF THE LUMP SUM COMPONENT

Given that the purpose of the lump sum component of the portfolio is to produce predictable gains within a known period, the mathematics of this component are, on the surface, relatively simple. When purchasing zero-coupon securities, the favored investment for this component, investors know that whatever they buy will be worth $1,000 when it matures, for $1,000 is the basic maturity value of zero bonds and CDs. There are, however, some subtleties to consider.

Zero-coupon securities have no current yield, nor do they offer problems in computing the reinvested growth of coupon interest. The mathematical problem with zeros is that purchase price and maturity value are known, but the rate of interested implied by the difference between them must be computed. To do that, we have to return to compound interest and annuity tables.

Let's say that an investor is perusing the zero-coupon bonds listed on the New York Bond Exchange and one particular issue maturing a year from now catches his or her eye. Let's say that the price quoted is exactly $890. Obviously, many different investments petition for our investor's attention, and he or she wants to select the most rewarding one within the elements of the portfolio appropriate to a life situation. Our investor needs to know the yield of this zero in order to make a comparison.

In establishing a price of $890, the market has, in effect, told us that $1,000 to be received one year from now is worth $890 today. In other words, the present value of $1,000 is $890. The question is, "$1,000 is worth $890 today at what rate of interest?" We turn to a present value table (also called present value of $1) in our book of compound interest and annuity tables and, through trial and error, scouring columns of figures for one-year maturities, we find these entries:

Years	11 Percent Nominal Annual Rate	11.5 Percent Nominal Annual Rate	12 Percent Nominal Annual Rate	12.5 Percent Nominal Annual Rate
1	0.9009	0.8968	0.8928	0.8888

These numbers tell us what the present value is today of $1 to be received one year from now. To find the present value of $1,000, we merely multiply these figures by 1,000. Accordingly, at an 11 percent nominal yield, $1,000 one year from now is worth $900.90. At an 11.5 percent nominal yield, $1,000 one year from now is worth $896.80.

We know that the market has established a price of $890. We see that $890 falls between $892.80, indicating a 12 percent yield, and $888.80, representing a 12.5 percent yield. By reasoning from price to yield we see that today's price of $890 represents a yield between 12 and 12.5 percent.

In this particular instance, we've used the present value table appropriate for an annual compounding schedule instead of a semi-annual schedule. This seems reasonable, as zeros are generally presumed to pay phantom annual interest. Nonetheless, some investors prefer to evaluate the present value of zeros using the semi-annual compounding tables appropriate to conventional bonds. As a practical matter, the answers derived from both tables will be very similar to one another, as they are in this case.

Compound interest is an important concept for life cycle investors to become familiar with. Nearly all investment problems deal with present value and compound interest. One doesn't have to master their formidable tables with the acumen of a professor of finance, but with a little bit of self-application, life cycle investors will find their study, particularly of the Rosen and Estes texts, well rewarded.

CHAPTER 19

Taxes and the
Life Cycle Investor

In each of our previous chapters we've covered some of the
tax consequences of investment income and some of the tax
advantages of varying types of investments. Managing a
total portfolio to receive maximum aftertax income is of
little importance to some life cycle investors and of considerable importance to others. We could easily agree, for instance, that taxes are of minimal significance for the portfolio of childhood and of greater consequence during the peak
earning years of the senior portfolio. Similarly, we could
agree that each of the five portfolio elements has its own
tax implications. At this point, we need to do two things:
review the tax situation of each portfolio element and discuss ways to reduce taxation, if possible.

Before getting into that review, however, there's one issue we need to raise, and, paradoxical as it sounds, that
issue is the possibility of paying too much attention to
taxes. Most advisors counsel investors to make tax implications their second priority in investing, with the first priority being to achieve maximum pretax gains. You'd think
that's awfully self-evident advice, but many investors have
such an aversion to paying a single penny more in taxes

than they have to that they allow tax considerations to dominate portfolio planning. Whenever life cycle investors become fixated with a single aspect of investing, regardless of what that fixation is, they make mistakes they shouldn't make. Here are some common examples:

Insisting upon purchasing municipal bonds because their interest is exempt from federal taxes even though fully taxable securities might provide greater aftertax yields.

Refusing to take short-term capital gains because they're taxable as current income, thereby risking erosion of gains from continued holding.

Investing in tax-advantaged partnerships strictly because their writeoffs offset tax liability instead of examining their income/risk considerations.

Deferring taxation via investments that eventually produce fully taxable returns instead of selecting investments that offer untaxed or lesser-taxed immediate returns.

Omitting zero-coupon securities from the conventional portfolio because they produce phantom interest that is taxable even though not received until the investment matures.

Single-minded dedication to tax reduction can lead life cycle investors into these errors. As a very general matter, the tax consequences of investment become greater as investors enter the 30 percent marginal federal tax bracket. After passing that tax threshhold, investors may find that securing post-tax returns is a more significant issue than it was when they occupied lower brackets. In addition, state and local taxation is becoming a more burdensome issue than it conventionally has been, with some states, cities, and municipalities taking upwards of 10 percent of an investor's current income. Nonetheless, wise investors put tax considerations into proper proportion and do not let them dominate investment decisions.

TAX CONSIDERATIONS OF THE STABILITY COMPONENT

We've noted that several investments are suitable for the stability component of the portfolio: money funds, CDs and depository accounts, and near-term bonds, particularly T-bills. These investments produce current income throughout their compounding periods, so they are taxed at current federal and state rates. Consequently, the stability component of the portfolio usually produces fully taxed returns.

Investors can, if it's appropriate for their tax situations, reduce some of the taxability of the stability component by selecting appropriate investments. We've already noted that tax-exempt money funds produce income exempt from federal taxation while providing the stability and liquidity associated with fully taxed conventional money funds. For investors in the 40 percent federal marginal bracket, a tax-exempt fund paying 6 percent is equal to a conventional fund paying 10 percent.

By the same token, municipal bonds and notes maturing within a year or two also provide capital stability and liquidity, as well as federally untaxed interest. Also, some states don't tax the interest from their own bonds, making returns from "double-dipper municipal bonds" fully tax-free. Capital gains from municipal securities are fully taxed as either short-term or long-term.

Interest from U.S. government securities is not taxable by states and municipal authorities. This makes T-bills and very-near-term USGs desirable for investors who seek maximum safety and some tax abatement in the stability element of their portfolio. Don't forget, though, that returns paid by government bond money market funds are taxable as dividends by federal and other tax authorities.

CDs and other bank-type deposits are taxed by everyone. Consequently, they should be in the stability component of the least-taxed investors.

We mentioned that put options can be used to secure some measure of portfolio stability on optionable common stocks. If the put itself is sold at a capital gain, that gain will be taxable as long-term or short-term, depending upon how long it was owned. If the put is exercised, the sale of the underlying stock may generate a long-term or short-term capital gain.

TAX CONSIDERATIONS OF THE INCOME COMPONENT

The purpose of the income component is to produce current income, and, as we've already lamented, current income is taxed as such. For the highest-taxed investors, income from municipal securities, municipal bond funds, and municipal bond trusts often provides the highest aftertax returns. Again, investors who desire the greatest safety with some tax relief will select USGs.

Up to $200 in dividend income for married investors filing jointly may be excluded from federal taxation (but not state and local taxation), so there's some small tax advantage to minimal dividends from common stocks, preferred stocks, and some stock mutual funds. Otherwise, dividend income is as fully taxable just like interest income and earned income.

We observed that writing put and call options generates current income, which is fully taxed.

TAX CONSIDERATIONS OF THE GROWTH COMPONENT

Given that the intention of the growth component is to generate long-term capital accumulations, one hopes that long-term capital gains tax treatment will make the growth component the least-taxed element of the portfolio. Each investor must calculate capital gains from directly held securities after he or she sells them. For indirect investments, mutual funds and other intermediaries will provide year-end statements indicating the reporting status of gains. Any appreciated investment held for the appropriate period—six months and one day under current law—qualifies for reduced taxation under long-term capital gains treatment. Bear in mind, however, that the definition of "long-term" for capital gains has been altered many times, and under some tax reform proposals, favored treatment of long-term gains may be eliminated entirely. Therefore, we may see the day when all long-term gains are taxed as current income without favorable taxation. That will have a dramatic effect upon the tax consequences of the growth element, perhaps even eliminating it as a portfolio consideration.

Capital gains on government and corporate bonds issued before enactment of the 1984 Deficit Reduction Act are still taxable as long-term or short-term. For bonds issued after enactment of that legislation, a portion of the capital gain from bonds may be taxable as current interest income regardless of the ownership period. Capital gains from municipals are taxed as long-term or short-term and are not treated as federally untaxed interest.

Fortunately, capital losses from growth investments are deductible from federally taxable income. Short-term losses offset taxable income on a dollar-for-dollar basis. Losses from long-term holdings offset ordinary income on a two-for-one basis, meaning it takes $6,000 in long-term losses to offset $3,000 in ordinary income. Short-term and long-term losses in excess of the $3,000 offset can be carried forward into future years.

Therefore, the tax-conscious capital growth investor will attempt to match short-term losses with long-term gains. This is advantageous whether the investment is a stock, bond, mutual fund, option, or other vehicle.

TAX CONSIDERATIONS OF THE AGGRESSIVE GAINS COMPONENT

Some types of aggressive gains investments produce both short-term and long-term gains, although they are typically thought of as generating only the former. In general, though, aggressive appreciation and aggressive income investments produce short-term returns that are fully taxable. In managing the aggressive gains component, life cycle investors should be particularly interested in maximum returns regardless of tax consequences, for, after all, the purpose of aggressive gains is maximization of returns. If an aggressive gains component isn't producing aggressive gains, tax consequences are truly secondary.

Investors don't enter into aggressive gains investments because of those investments' tax advantages. However, when they produce short-term capital losses, they can be useful in offsetting other income. When investors pursue aggressive gains with borrowed money, interest paid on borrowings is deductible from federally taxable income. However, rules governing deductibility change frequently, and in some cases interest on borrowed investment capital may be deducted only up to the amount of gains from the investment.

TAX CONSEQUENCES OF THE LUMP SUM COMPONENT

We've discussed lump sum investments for their particular advantages in IRAs and UGMAs, for which tax is deferred in the former case and usually avoided in the latter. We've noted several times that the investments most favored for this portfolio component, zero-coupon bonds and CDs, generate current tax liability even though interest isn't actually received until maturity. Paying tax on income they don't receive dissuades most investors from holding zeros in any vehicle other than IRAs and UGMAs, but it shouldn't do so in every instance.

For starters, some parents might take a lesson from their children. If parents place zeros in a UGMA for their child because the child is in a negligible tax bracket, they might also consider the advantages of one spouse buying zeros and the two of them filing separate tax returns. If one partner earns most of the family's current income, the other partner could own the zeros, declaring phantom interest income on his or her separately filed federal 1040 each year. By so doing, much of the tax disadvantage might be escaped.

In addition, life cycle investors need to be exceedingly cold-eyed about what really happens with interest and dividend payments from current income investments. The unfortunate truth is that interest and dividend payments are too often spent rather than reinvested. Capital that should have been reinvested essentially disappears, even though current tax liability on dividends and interest doesn't, and investors wind up with nothing more than what they initially invested. If investors purchase zeros, they pay tax on unreceived interest, but that interest is still present when the zero matures. If investors aren't disciplined enough to reinvest interest and dividends, they might be better off buying zeros, which have the "disadvantage" of producing no current interest. They'll pay current taxes, but they'll not attenuate their capital.

Finally, another option for the lump sum component is zero-coupon municipal bonds. Munie zeros work exactly like conventional zeros, except that the difference between purchase price and maturity value is federally untaxed interest. Consequently, life cycle investors receive lump sum accumulations exempt from federal (but not state and local) taxation. Municipal zeros are an excellent companion to IRAs, EIPs, and annuities.

ADDITIONAL TAX CONSIDERATIONS FOR LIFE CYCLE INVESTORS

Although we've looked at the tax considerations of the five portfolio components, there are a number of other tax angles we should mention, even at the risk of repetition. Some of those have to do with taxes and investments, and others are more general tax considerations. We'll look at them in no particular order, as each is about equally important and nearly all life cycle investors can benefit by considering them.

It may be insulting to be repetitive, but there are so many life cycle investors who are trying to set aside investments for children in their own names rather than the names of the children that we simply have to repeat a tenet we established in the early chapters. If you're putting money aside for a child's later life, do so through a Uniform Gifts to Minors Account.

How many times has a friend told you, "I'm holding this stock for Johnny"? Well, your friend isn't doing Johnny any favors because when that stock is cashed in on the child's behalf, the tax collector will take capital gains based upon the parent's income. Johnny will receive a lot less because someone is paying more taxes than necessary. There are so many parents, and so few of them have opened UGMAs, and that simply doesn't make any sense.

IRAs, Keoghs, and 401(k) plans raise related issues. These investments reduce taxable income, thereby reducing tax liability. We noted in our earlier example that investors in relatively average tax brackets can save more than $500 per year in taxes by opening an IRA. That $500+ can be used to fund a UGMA or to produce other investment returns. It pays in more than one way to open an IRA, sloganistic though it sounds to say so.

In setting aside funds in illiquid investments like IRAs and most EIPs, however, remember that accumulations from these investments are taxed as current income when withdrawn upon retirement. Therefore, investors will want to remember the advantages of long-term capital gains taxation when allocating funds to IRAs, and especially to EIPs. If investors can generate long-term gains from the growth elements of their portfolios, they might be better off contributing less to an employee investment program, which produces fully taxed income eventually.

If investors are locked into a long-term CD that isn't paying market-level returns, they might be better off in two ways to cash the CD prematurely and pay the interest penalty involved. First, redeeming the CD will permit them to reinvest at market-level rates. Second, the interest penalty from redeeming a CD prematurely is deductible on federal income tax returns.

A similar advantage might accrue in retrieving IRA contributions and earnings prematurely. A number of investment advisors have compared the tax penalties on premature IRA withdrawals against the tax-deferred returns from IRAs and determined ranges within which investors may withdraw contributions prematurely to advantage. Some life cycle investors may discover it pays to cash in their IRA and reinvest elsewhere.

However, there are some special problems in redeeming IRAs prematurely. First, that's a violation of investment discipline. IRAs serve the specific purpose of accumulating funds for retirement, and deciding to do something else with any specially earmarked funds, particularly IRAs, is a breech of discipline. Second, if many investors make a habit of redeeming IRAs prematurely, Congress may move to prevent abuses of the tax law, just as it did with the laws governing annuities. Redeeming IRAs prematurely may offer some short-term advantages, but in the long run it's not wise financially or politically.

Many European and Caribbean nations have established themselves as tax havens with laws that govern financial secrecy more stringently than in our own country. With high levels of international interest rates and the ebullient stock market, many Americans have opened bank accounts and brokerage accounts in foreign countries that do not report gains to American tax authorities. When April 15 has rolled around, some of these Americans have conveniently forgotten to report such gains, and they seem to have gotten away with untaxed income. There's nothing illegal about American citizens transacting investments through foreign fiduciaries, but it is illegal for Americans not to report returns taxable by this country.

Many Americans seeking legitimate ways to reduce taxation are inundated late in each tax year with mailings from partnerships and financial institutions that offer investments providing offsets against current income. Although these may be legitimate and profitable ventures, investors simply aren't wise to go fishing late in the year for tax shelter investments and partnerships. Decisions made hastily late in the year are often repented at leisure for a long time, particularly if the IRA questions a full year of deductions for an investment made in December. Tax-advantaged investments must be made carefully and after a full review of their tax status, to say nothing about a careful analysis of their potential strictly as investments. Too many investors have rushed into these arrangements and discovered too late that they should have studied them at greater length.

There are many tax consequences of investing and many techniques that can legitimately be used to reduce them. As life cycle investors enter high tax brackets and achieve successful gains from their portfolios, they'll need to become more savvy about handling the tax considerations of financial success. Some tax-saving techniques are very simple, such as taking gains in January rather than December and moving them into another tax year. Others require more sophistication. All require planning and what Julian Block, IRS-agent-turned-author, calls "taxwise living."

There are many excellent and readable texts to inform life cycle investors how to reduce tax liability. The Internal Revenue Service publishes many guides that are free for the asking, although in close questions IRS publications and interpretations aren't definitive in tax court. The J.K. Lasser Tax Institute prints useful yearly publications that are available in most bookstores, and many investment books cover tax considerations even though constant revision to the tax laws may date their counsel. One of the most useful tax references for most investors is *Julian Block's Guide to Year-Round Tax Savings* published yearly by Dow Jones-Irwin.

Ultimately, however, life cycle investors will have to rely upon competent legal and accounting advice from trained professionals. There simply is no substitute for authoritative counsel. When income from job and portfolio becomes sufficient, life cycle investors should consult a reputable authority to determine the best way to give less to the IRS.

CHAPTER 20

Managing Investment Advisors

There are thousands of potential financial advisors out there—bankers, stockbrokers, insurance agents, bond salesmen, certified financial planners, precious gem dealers, metals merchants, commodities specialists, mutual fund advisories, newsletter authors, and others in scores of other categories. Life cycle investors will find very few who are outright dishonest (probably fewer than in most professions). They will find that nearly all will be wrong one time or another, and that a sizable number are adept at investments appropriate for one stage of life but not another. They will find many who press a view of the world upon prospective clients, and few who are able to tailor recommendations to the evolving needs of an investor's life.

There are several reasons why life cycle investors will find it so difficult to establish lasting relationships with financial advisors.

First, as financial markets become more accessible, the need to be versed in many types of investments spreads many advisors beyond their interests and abilities.

Second, as markets become more accessible they also become more specialized. If advisors happen to be specialized in a type of investment appropriate for a particular stage of an investor's life, then advisor and client can benefit. Once an investor evolves beyond that stage, the relationship may become dated.

Third, many investment advisors—and stockbrokers particularly are caught in this dilemma—are under enormous pressure to move the securities inventories of their sponsoring companies. If those securities coincide with an investor's specific needs at a given stage of life, then this sales pressure is of little consequence. Otherwise, investors find themselves repeatedly petitioned to acquire inappropriate investments.

Fourth, most investment advisors direct their attention to today's markets rather than to the evolving needs of an investor. They are market-directed, concerned with where current profits are to be made, and not necessarily concerned with where an investor's money should be with respect to his or her position in life. One might be inclined to ask what's wrong with a market orientation. After all, to some extent investors must take what the market gives them. Why not, therefore, go with the market?

Let's hope that anyone who's read this far into *Life Cycle Investing* is prepared with the answer. The problem with a market-directed orientation is that markets may be producing returns in investments that are inappropriate for investors at varying stages of life. In one particular market cycle, perhaps Treasury notes offer the best current possibilities; in another, gold may be producing the greatest gains; in a third, growth stocks; in a fourth, the short side of commodities. Regardless of how profitable each of those investments may be for a particular market cycle, they simply aren't all appropriate for all investors.

Recall the retiree of our preface, the one who made a killing in silver futures. We applauded his good fortune, but not necessarily his good judgment. In many respects, life cycle investors can assess a potential financial advisor by the answer to one question. If you ask, "Where should my money be invested now?" and the answer is to name a particular investment, then you're dealing with a market-directed advisor. The correct answer—"correct" as we use the term—to the question "Where should my money be invested?" is "Where it needs to be invested."

Where money needs to be depends upon the factors we've been discussing—the elements of the portfolio, the importance of those elements at different times of life, the ability of certain types of investments to meet those needs, and our own singular life situation. Where money needs to be is not a decision that should be dictated solely by a current market. This is a difficult lesson for investors to learn, but it's the core lesson in life cycle investing. We want financial markets to reward us constantly, just as we want life to reward us constantly, but the plain fact is that life doesn't reward us all the time, and neither do financial markets.

Each of us can look back on a period when everything seemed perfect, when we seemed invincible and the world seemed to be our oyster, pearl awaiting the taking. Financial markets can give us that feeling, too. What could be more rewarding than compounded profits in growth stocks or high interest rates at the precise moment when it's appropriate for us to be invested in such instruments? But the ideal time of life, whatever it may be for each of us, passes, and so does the coincidence of the ideal market and our own investment needs. It takes great maturity and discipline for investors to admit "This isn't my kind of market" and to leave the big gains to investors for whom it is the right kind of market. Yet such maturity and discipline are the essence of life cycle investing.

If life cycle investors are fortunate enough to meet an advisor with intelligence, experience, market judgment, and sensitivity to their needs, then they may well have found a man or woman for all seasons, someone to stick with throughout a lengthy financial monogamy. What's more likely, however, is that throughout an investment career, life cycle investors will encounter several advisors whose expertise in selected areas is highly useful but whose services don't meet the many needs of a comprehensive and changing portfolio. In this more frequent case, investors find themselves riding herd on a stable of advisors, and it becomes their responsibility to apportion portfolios among the specialties and limitations of many advisors.

Therefore, the first criterion of successful management of advisors is to recognize which one deals in the types of investments appropriate to a particular stage of life. In that sense, managing advisors is quite similar to managing investments appropriate to progressing stages of the life cycle.

ADVISORS AND THE STABILITY COMPONENT

Generally speaking, the "advisor" for this portfolio component will be a banker, a mutual fund representative, or a broker, and the advisor's only real role will be to inform you of the interest rate currently offered on money funds, certificates, or T-bills. This limited role is fine, for rates on such instruments are commonly similar, and one really doesn't need an advisor in order to meet the needs of the stability component.

ADVISORS AND THE INCOME COMPONENT

The best advisors for the income element of the portfolio are a pocket calculator and the yield quotations from *The Wall Street Journal*. However, it would pay life cycle investors to be associated with a major brokerage or institution specializing in new issues of bonds, for those can be purchased without commissions that reduce yields. If investors are in tax brackets sufficient to make municipal securities appealing, it would pay to be associated with a house specializing in municipal bonds, for munies have special considerations regarding maturities, call features, safety, liquidity, and insurance backing that you'll want to discuss in detail.

For lesser-taxed investors fulfilling income needs through a bond portfolio, governments are generally preferable to corporates unless the disparity in yields is several percentage points and sacrifice in quality is minimal. Picking appropriate government bonds and notes is largely a matter of selecting maturity dates that avoid extreme capital fluctuation and selecting yields and payment schedules that provide maximum, regular receipts. Picking suitable corporate issues requires a bit more research into debt coverage, seniority, and agency rating, but such research is within the abilities of a moderately informed investor willing to put in some time investigating.

Life cycle investors generally will not need an advisor to help in developing the income component through bonds, although it never hurts to have someone who will occasionally advise about forthcoming new issues or who can inform you quickly about possible changes in an issue's creditworthiness.

Investors pursuing current income through equity investments, however, will have greater need of an advisor. Given that dividends are declared and not obliged, investors will want to investigate dividend coverage carefully before investing in income stocks, and advisors can be of great help doing so. Attractive income stocks often appear in new offerings sponsored by major brokerage firms, and a well-situated broker can make them available.

ADVISORS AND THE GROWTH COMPONENT

Unless investors are astute at spotting emerging growth stocks, financial advisors are critically important in managing the growth component of the portfolio. A good growth stock advisor will be attuned to markets and will inform you quickly of emerging opportunities, including all the costs and risks necessary in making an investment. Unfortunately, growth advisors can be judged only by performance, and that means they're judged after the fact according to how well their recommendations work out. There are, however, a few ways in which you can appraise a potential advisor before doing business.

Inquire about the performance of a potential advisor's past recommendations. This is something like asking a potential employee for references—you know you're not going to hear anything unfavorable, but you might receive some clue as to past successes.

Another trick is to follow the course of an advisor's recommendations without actually investing. Follow the price movements of the recommended investment in *The Wall Street Journal* or elsewhere. This may cost you profits you could have been earning, but it will also give you an indication of your advisor's savvy, and if the recommendation seems to be making money, you'll have more confidence in future advice.

After you've chosen an advisor and started trading, you'll continue evaluating the advice you're receiving by the profits you're making. However, there are a couple of other measures you can employ.

First, keep track of how long your advisor will let a position turn against you before he or she recommends you dump an investment and put money elsewhere. A conscientious advisor will monitor your downside risks and establish a level beyond which to suggest that you should get out. This is particularly important in managing growth stocks, and it's a point on which many advisors are deficient.

Second, and in company with the first point, keep track of how often your advisor urges you to alter the composition of your portfolio. The growth investor shouldn't be moving money around every few months, but frequent trades mean more commissions and, therefore, more returns to your advisor, who frequently is paid by commission. An important point to remember, though, is that 181 days is now the tax definition of "long-term." Therefore, an advisor could be urging you to change investments twice a year and still be devoted to long-term growth—at least as the taxman defines the term.

Third, monitor how faithfully your advisor adheres to your investment goals. If he or she calls you frequently with recommendations that don't meet objectives the two of you discussed, you're being treated as just another customer, not as an individual investor.

Fourth, and the converse of point three, remember how often your advisor apprises you of new investment opportunities that *do* meet your stated objectives. Contact when opportunities arise means that your advisor has you in mind.

Fifth, be sure to note how efficiently the mechanics of your account are serviced, especially if you elect not to take receipt of securities certificates. Investment mechanics are becoming highly important as the volume of securities trading swells and brokerage "back rooms" are pressed to process everything accurately. Your advisor will provide regular account statements, but it's your responsibility to approve their accuracy. This means that you must monitor the progress of your investments, keeping track of dividend and interest dates, purchases and sales, and other particulars to make sure that all is recorded accurately in your account.

Life cycle investors pursuing long-term growth through mutual funds will have no access to portfolio managers, so their dealings will largely be confined to occasional conversations with funds' telephone representatives and to daily reading of fund quotations in the financial pages. Unavailability of advisors is a great drawback to pursuing growth through mutual funds, although the drawback is minimal when the fund is making money. When the fund isn't making money, your only recourse is to fire your advisor by redeeming the mutual fund shares.

Investors seeking long-term growth through discounted bonds generally will not rely heavily upon advisors, for all the information needed to make decisions is available by applying the yield to maturity formula to the information quoted in the financial pages. It's of little use to have bond advisors for capital growth, as their principal use is in advising about new issues. Some portion of the capital gains from bonds issued after enactment of the 1984 Deficit Reduction Act will be taxed as current interest, meaning that growth-oriented bond investors will be attracted to outstanding issues still eligible for long-term capital gains treatment. Information about them is accessible through conventional sources.

ADVISORS AND THE AGGRESSIVE GAINS COMPONENT

For most life cycle investors, the aggressive gains advisor will be a commodity pool partner, the manager of an aggressive growth fund, or the functioning trader of a similar intermediary, as many investors prefer to pursue aggressive gains indirectly. In effect, these investors have entrusted management of this portfolio component to others, and presumably those others solicit advice from their own sources.

However, many investors also invest directly for aggressive gains, particularly in certain types of stocks, special situations, and commodities. Advisors in this type of investing tend to be highly specialized, concentrating on selected stock groups and isolated commodities. As a practical matter, relying upon aggressive gains advisors for direct investment is much the same as investing indirectly, for unless investors are highly tutored themselves, they usually invest by following their advisor's recommendations. That's not much different from just turning aggressive growth capital over to a pool or mutual fund in the first place.

It's difficult to evaluate aggressive growth advisors. There is, of course, the gauge of profits by which to assess their performance, but even profits and losses don't tell the whole story about an aggressive growth advisor. These investments are highly volatile, and their volatility often is occasioned by circumstances that defy anticipation. Last minute personality clashes kill a merger. A central bank intervenes to support its currency. A banana republic calls off its revolution. All of those circumstances can influence aggressive growth investments, and an advisor couldn't really have been expected to have anticipated them, whether they were money-making developments or not. Losses might not indicate deficiency of an advisor's judgment, nor might gains indicate wisdom.

Obviously, though, the purpose of aggressive investment is to produce aggressive returns, and if you're not receiving them you'll be inclined to look for a new advisor. However, there are other guidelines to be generally observed in managing aggressive growth advisors, whether as an indirect or direct investor.

First, be wary of portfolio turnover. The aggressive growth portfolio will usually be traded more frequently than other types of investments, yet most advisors have a tendency to trade too often in an aggressive account. This is particularly true of commodities accounts. What constitutes too many trades is always a judgment call, but bear in mind that aggressive gains are by nature difficult to repeat consistently. One or two home runs is sufficient for the aggressive growth component, and you don't want your advisor swinging at every pitch.

Second, beware the advisor who attempts to pyramid your account by converting aggressive gains into multiple rather than fractional holdings. Say, for example, that your advisor doubles your money with an investment and then reinvests your gains in additional ownership of the investment. This is inverse pyramiding—essentially constructing a pyramid by starting with the point and building the base into the sky. Picture a triangle standing on one angle instead of a base. The whole thing is a very shaky structure, and sudden portfolio reverses will bring the whole investment down around your ears. A more reasonable strategy is to build the pyramid the right way, taking a fraction of aggressive gains for reinvestment and keeping the rest aside, just as a stable pyramid is erected by making successive layers smaller than the underlying layers. This way a few losses won't destroy the whole aggressive portfolio.

The same is true of advisors using leverage. Great gains can be made using margin and borrowed capital, but doing so adds a dimension of risk that may overshadow potential rewards. Only professional investors or very talented amateurs use leverage profitably and correctly.

Third, by all means find a new advisor when your present one recommends doubling up to recoup losses. If you've just taken a big loss with an investment, accept the loss. We've discussed some of the profitable features of averaging down, but that technique is best used for long-term holdings. Don't use averaging down as an excuse to throw more money into an investment that is inherently volatile.

So far we've talked only about aggressive growth investments, largely because selecting aggressive income investments doesn't require the sustained attention of an advisor. Fortunately, the market quotations will identify aggressive income investments, for they're clearly identified by their higher yields for dividends and interest. However, most major full-service brokerage firms will have a junk bond specialist in affiliation somewhere nearby, and it may be worthwhile to call upon his or her services. Investing in lower-rated income securities is something of a financial specialty, and a good advisor can warn of pitfalls or opportunities that are not apparent.

ADVISORS AND THE LUMP SUM COMPONENT

By and large, life cycle investors will be interested in the services of an advisor who has access to new issues of corporate zeros or to stripped governments reconstituted as zeros, for these newly issued bonds can be purchased without commissions. In addition, investors purchasing zero-coupon municipal obligations will be in strong need of a dealer or advisor who handles these issues, for they are much in demand and consequently snapped up before entering secondary markets, and are frequently held to maturity by initial purchasers. They are also governed by call features, questions about security, or insurance backing that a professional can address.

Otherwise, the features of publicly traded zeros are straightforward enough to be handled without extensive discussion with advisors.

MANAGING MAIL ORDER ADVISORS

For the investor who doesn't require sustained personal contact with an advisor, there are many investment advisory services that correspond with clients through the mails and also, on occasion, offer a hot-line service to apprise clients of sudden moves in monitored investments. These advisories run the range of investment alternatives. Some deal in precious metals, others in corporate stocks, still others in market timing, the movement of money from one investment to another.

Often these mail advisories provide specific recommendations on the purchase and sale of selected investments, such as gold and silver or penny stocks. Most will offer an opinion about the investment climate in general along with their recommendations. Cost ranges from a few dollars per year to $1,000 or more, with the well-known Value Line Investment Survey, which provides exhaustive analysis of corporate stocks, ranking toward the top in both prestige and cost. Fortunately, Value Line is available at many libraries and most business colleges.

Another advisory service of similar distinction and lesser cost is offered by Standard & Poor's Corporation, which we've mentioned in several other contexts. S&P, as it's known in the trade, is a far-reaching investment organization that rates bonds and preferred stocks, runs several indexes of stock market performance, and also provides evaluations of stocks for professional and personal investors.

The S&P 500 Stock Market Encyclopedia and *The S&P Outlook* are two particularly useful publications for life cycle investors. The former is, as its name implies, an extended reference work detailing the financial particulars and market past of 500 stocks that comprise the S&P 500 Index. It sells for $29.95. The latter is a continuing update on market activity and a forecast that, "offers informed recommendations on how you can preserve or enhance the value of your personal portfolio."

Periodically, Standard & Poor's offers introductory subscriptions to its services. By subscribing to the *Outlook* for three months at the trial subscription price of $29.95, you also receive the *Encyclopedia* and a list of currently recommended stocks. You can try out both publications by sending $29.95 to

The Outlook
Standard & Poor's Corporation
Box 992
New York, NY 10275

One advisory service of particular merit to mutual fund investors is the Prime Investment Alert. Prime advises investors on moving holdings among mutual fund families by using switch privileges. It also offers the Prime Tax Alert service, which, by its self-advertisement, "will provide timely tax advice and creative ways to save on taxes." The cost for both services is $100 per year for monthly mailings, occasional special reports, and a telephone hot line, but Prime offers a first-year subscriber rate of $60. The address is

Prime Investment Alert
P.O. Box 10300
Portland, ME 04104
Phone: (207) 772–1679

Finally, the American Association of Individual Investors, a nonprofit educational corporation, publishes a monthly magazine discussing investments, provides investment seminars at modest cost to members, and generally caters to the situation of the small, individual investor. A one-year membership is $44, and a lifetime membership is $350. For further information contact

American Association of Individual Investors
612 North Michigan Avenue
Chicago, IL 60611
Phone: (312) 280–0170

Many investors have found mail order advisors as competent and profitable as personal financial advisors, although they won't be there to complain to if anything goes wrong. Perhaps the most important thing to guard against with mail order advisors is succumbing to those who have a fixed view of the world that governs all of their advice. Regrettably, some of the most prominent and best-selling of today's newsletter writers fall into the category of proselytizers. If you happen to share their world view and like seeing it reinforced every few weeks, that's one thing, but that doesn't mean you're paying for investment advice.

PART IV

The Portfolios of Life Cycle Investing

In the preceding three sections we looked at the concept of life cycle investing and the stages of an investor's life, the investments available and how each can be appropriate at different times of an investor's life, and the management tools life cycle investors can employ in constructing and rearranging their portfolios. Now it's time to pull the preceding information together and see how the portfolios of life cycle investing actually look, their composition and proportions, the blending of their elements, their changes.

There's no perfect set of investments, but there are some norms to examine against which we can make comparisons. Therefore, it's best to regard these sample portfolios as indications rather than prescriptions. No life is the exact parallel of another, but we come to understand our personal singularity by realizing how we differ from the average person. By the same token, each of our portfolios will differ from those of other people in similar circumstances, and by understanding investment norms we are in a better position to evaluate how our investments ought to depart from norms to serve our particular position.

CHAPTER 21

The Minor's Portfolio—
Birth to Age 21

The portfolio of childhood is generally dominated by two elements: growth investments and lump sum accumulations. Parents and UGMA custodians will try to develop those elements within the constraints of the parents' ability to set aside money for their children and within the time allotted for investments to grow. Obviously, the UGMA produces greatest growth when parents open the account when the child is born and contribute to it regularly. The UGMA is least effective when parents suddenly realize that their children will be going to college in a year or two and attempt to generate within a short period the level of returns they should have been striving toward over many years. If parents don't follow the former course, let's at least hope they avoid the latter.

The most straightforward strategy for the minor's portfolio is the accumulation of zero-coupon securities that mature when the minor reaches majority. This strategy offers simplicity and the advantage that early contributions to the UGMA will compound to the greatest sums, for a zero bond maturing in 20 years and purchased today will be cheaper than that same bond purchased 10 or 15 years from today.

In addition, zeros cater to the tax advantages of UGMAs, for they produce income that otherwise would be fully taxed each year even though not received yearly. By holding zeros in the minor's account, a great deal of taxable interest will accumulate untaxed because of the child's minimal or non-existant tax liabilities.

Accordingly, it's not uncommon for 100 percent of the UGMA to be comprised of zero-coupon bonds and certificates of deposit. In many cases, though, conventional corporate or government bonds are included in the UGMA for three reasons. First, like zeros, they offer the advantage of known accumulations within a specified period. Second, conventional bonds produce semi-annual income that can be reinvested in other growth vehicles, such as stocks, mutual funds, or aggressive income securities. Third, long-term bonds often sell at discounts, providing capital gains as well as reinvestable receipts.

Bonds, zero-coupon or conventional, are favored for UGMAs because this special type of account and the special circumstances of young investors short-circuit many drawbacks to fixed-income investments. We've already noted that bonds produce fully taxable income that usually escapes taxation in the UGMA for many years. The child will depend upon parents for all of his or her conventional needs, so there's no worry about interest payments being insufficient for expenses. Because all of the interest will be reinvested and none of it spent for many years, the effects of inflation on a fixed stream of income are minimal. So long as UGMA custodians stay with higher-rated issues, there's little risk of default. Therefore, the UGMA could be populated entirely by bonds and serve its intentions quite well.

If the UGMA eventually produces enough income to incur tax liability, it's possible to convert the bond portfolio to municipal bonds. In general, though, the tax liability of minors isn't sufficient to switch to municipals, for conventional investments will likely produce greater post-tax returns.

Growth stocks and growth stock funds often occupy substantial percentages of the UGMA. Many custodians feel that growth stocks are the best way to produce the long-term gains for which UGMAs are intended. They trade off the predictability of bonds for the potential of greater growth from stocks. If the account is managed by a knowledgable custodian, this trade-off can be profitable.

Parents seeking long-term growth can use dollar-cost averaging by making regular purchases of shares or deposits to a growth-oriented mutual fund established as a UGMA. If parents have decided they should contribute, say, $1,000 yearly to the UGMA, they can capture the advantages of dollar-cost averaging through quarterly deposits of $250. By doing so they diversify the stock holdings of the UGMA and make use of temporarily depressed markets to acquire a greater number of shares for future growth.

Whether invested in stocks or other instruments, mutual funds are a good choice for many parents wishing to set aside sums for children. They achieve all the advantages of the UGMA without requiring large sums. Switch privileges among funds of the same family allow the movement of money among different types of investments, even different types of growth investments. One strategy that parents can follow is to invest half of their UGMA contributions in growth stock funds and half in a lump sum component, achieving known returns while attempting to achieve some level of capital appreciation.

It is somewhat less common, though not unacceptable, for the UGMA to consist of aggressive income investments such as lower-rated bonds. The higher yields on these instruments can provide greater percentage returns when compounded over many years, especially given the lesser tax bite of the minor's account. Direct purchases of high-yielding investments or indirect investment in aggressive income mutual funds can accommodate this purpose, although it's generally preferable to select bonds rather than stocks because interest is more assured than dividends and because the bond will mature to par, whereas no capital gain is inherently promised by aggressive income stocks. In general, 25 percent of the portfolio set aside into aggressive income instruments is a suitable percentage for the UGMA.

It is somewhat less advisable to pursue aggressive capital

growth through a UGMA. The volatility associated with aggressive capital gains investments defeats the purpose of the UGMA, which is, after all, long-term capital growth. An aggressive stock component, perhaps 10 percent of the portfolio, may occasionally be suited for the UGMA if other elements of the portfolio are performing acceptably, but it's best to avoid commodity pools and other aggressive growth investments, for their risk of loss is much higher than is acceptable for the UGMA.

The suitability of precious metals for the minor's portfolio is often debated. It is possible to purchase gold or silver bullion coins for minors, presumably identifying the child as owner in a will or other document, putting the coins in a safe deposit box and hoping that they will produce long-term capital growth. Doing so, however, means the child will likely incur capital gains liability when selling the coins, and that defeats some of the tax advantages of UGMAs. Shares of metals mining companies or metals mutual funds owned in a UGMA are an alternative, but this form of gold and silver ownership is no more advantageous than other types of long-term stock ownership.

CHAPTER 22

The Portfolio of Young Adulthood—Ages 22 to 30

During these years, young investors make their entry into their professional careers and establish financial habits and expectations. It's important that their portfolios begin with the same base of solidity that will support their professional development, and that means attending to the basics of the savings component first.

It's wise for investors of this age group to hold at least 10 percent of their net income in money market funds or other constant-dollar investments before attempting to expand their portfolios into the growth investments appropriate for this time of life. As investors approach the elder extreme of this age group, they would be wise to increase the savings percentage to 20 or 25 percent by including near-term bonds or short-term bond funds in the savings component. The liquidity of these investments makes them preferable over CDs in the savings component for this age group.

If these young investors are contemplating a large lump sum expenditure such as a down payment on a house, the savings component might constitute the entirety of their portfolios for most of this stage of life. In most situations, though, younger people are ready to pursue capital growth once they've amassed 10 to 25 percent of net income in the capital stability component.

Throughout their 20s, it's not uncommon for investors to have 80 to 90 percent of their portfolio in growth investments—directly held stocks, growth mutual funds, and perhaps discount bonds. Of that 80 to 90 percent, up to 5 percent may be located in an employer's EIP.

As we've noted, there are many sources of long-term growth. Most investors select stocks and stock funds for this portfolio element, and investors in their 20s can make ample use of dollar-cost averaging for many years. However, today's younger investors are becoming more acquainted with discounted bonds, and the growth component of their portfolios includes an increased percentage of these instruments to capture built-in capital gains. Even though some of the capital gains may be taxable as interest, that's generally of lesser concern to younger investors, who generally haven't reached maximum tax brackets.

Weighting the growth component with bonds may not be as lucrative as increasing stock holdings, but these investors reason that a constant 11 to 12 percent yield equals the historical return for a broad portfolio of common stocks, provides predictable returns for a known period, and assures some capital appreciation. If younger investors lack interest in growth stock funds or ability to pick growth stocks as a direct investor, discounted bonds can be a logical preference for capital growth. Unless investors happen to be in high tax brackets, they'll generally not buy municipal securities or derivative municipal investments.

Whether these life cycle investors should depend upon employee investment plans for capital growth is an open question. Demographics argue that younger employees change jobs more frequently, with the result that they may fail to achieve the full advantages of vesting. Those whose personal situation parallels the norm may prefer to contribute minimal amounts to the EIP and rely upon other elements of the portfolio for capital growth. On the other hand, if younger investors feel they'll remain with a single employer long enough to become vested, they may prefer to place a higher percentage of their portfolio in an EIP so as to take advantage of company matching and tax deferral. They must remember, however, that they'll lose the advantage of long-term capital gains taxation when withdrawing their money, whether upon retirement or an earlier occasion.

As investors approach 30, they may have accumulated sufficient growth investments or sufficient capital to place a portion of the portfolio in aggressive growth elements. Some advisors believe that 25 percent of the portfolio is an appropriate percentage for younger investors to hold in aggressive vehicles, considering that they have many years in which to regain losses. Those heeding such counsel would have 10 to 25 percent of their portfolio in the constant-dollar element, 25 percent or so in aggressive growth, and the remainder in long-term growth.

However, it may be difficult to obtain diversification in aggressive growth investments, for some aggressive gains vehicles, such as commodity pools, require $5,000 minimums. For younger investors, locating $5,000 to put in one place is difficult enough, to say nothing of the problem of diversifying among investments requiring $5,000 minimums.

Other advisors point out that concentration is the key to achieving success in the aggressive growth portfolio—put the eggs in one basket and watch the basket unblinkingly. Therefore, they counsel younger investors to set aside as much as they wish to risk, using comfort rather than percentages to determine the amount of their aggressive growth investment, and to be more concerned with picking profitable investments than with diversifying to diminish a single loss. Many aggressive growth investments, such as gunslinging mutual funds, require only $500 to $1,000 minimums. Penny stocks and penny funds are available for very modest capital, and they can provide spectacular returns. Publicly listed stock options also provide aggressive gains for minimal capital, as do options funds.

Of course, the problem with aggressive gains investments is that sometimes they occur in markets you can afford and sometimes they don't. Younger investors must guard against skewing their total portfolio in order to enter into aggressive markets. Investors of this age group would also be well-advised to avoid aggressive gains techniques like leverage, which can compound capital losses with burdensome debt.

In addition, it's particularly important that younger investors establish a stop-loss level beyond which they won't wait for an aggressive investment to recover. Younger investors may be able to afford greater losses than other age groups, but that's no reason to persist with undisciplined patience. If you have a deep loss, take it and reinvest elsewhere. Remember: Investors in their 20s and 30s can accrue excellent returns over time at even modest rates of accumulation. If an aggressive investment hasn't performed at least as well as a savings account, you're taking too much risk for too little gain.

Investing for aggressive income is another course open to these younger investors by picking lower-rated bonds and reinvesting the interest rigorously or by setting aside a portion of capital for an aggressive income mutual fund. Option income funds are also an excellent adjunct to the aggressive income element, as they provide returns from a portfolio of professionally managed stocks as well as premium income from the sale of options. If investors can achieve a 12 or 13 percent return from aggressive income investments, they will likely be as well off as if they'd invested in a broader selection of equities.

If these life cycle investors are attracted to aggressive income as a counterpart to aggressive capital gains, then they might have a quarter of the portfolio in savings, a quarter in aggressive income, perhaps 10 percent in aggressive gains vehicles, and the remainder in long-term growth investments.

Conventional wisdom argues that investors younger than age 30 may receive greater post-tax returns by investing for growth rather than setting aside $2,000 yearly for an IRA. Such reasoning also argues that investors in this age group don't usually benefit optimally from the tax offsets that IRAs provide. Further, contributions to an EIP, especially if it's a 401(k) plan may take the place of an IRA.

However, it's also true that investors aren't required to

place the entire $2,000 in an IRA, and they can receive remarkable returns by retirement if they do begin IRA contributions at the earliest time. Consequently, the decision to open an IRA when you're younger than age 30 is a judgment call to be determined by available income, the nature of employment, the eligibility to participate in an EIP, and the investor's overall goals. Once the IRA is opened, however, where to invest is the next question.

For reasons that we've covered earlier, it's generally not wise to invest aggressively with IRA moneys. The volatility of aggressive gains investments negates the purpose of the IRA, which is long-term growth, and capital losses in an IRA account aren't deductible. Many younger investors select growth-oriented mutual funds for IRA deposits, reasoning that they're convenient, require small capital, and offer the mobility of switch privileges. More financially sophisticated younger investors hold IRA deposits in self-directed accounts with a brokerage, selecting the securities appropriate to their investment intentions. For the most part, though, zero-coupon bonds are favored IRA investments for this age group—in fact, for most age groups—because they're inexpensive, secure, and highly predictable.

The mistake that younger investors should avoid is placing IRA deposits in a CD. The chief problem with CDs is maturity. Let's say that in year one you put $2,000 into a two-year CD. In years two and three you do the same. This means that every two years you have a CD maturing, and unless you're willing to pay interest penalties for premature withdrawals, you never get your $6,000 into one place where it can be invested as a consolidated capital mass. Of course, a little juggling of maturities can avoid this problem, but it's easier and probably as lucrative simply to open an IRA money fund with a broker or mutual fund and let the deposits grow until you're able to invest the larger amount.

Whatever the percentages and whatever the exact vehicles comprising them, the portfolio of young adulthood is generally a long-term capital growth portfolio. There is room for aggressive growth and income in the portfolios of these life cycle investors, and there must be room for the

savings component. These years are the time when investors acquaint themselves with financial markets and the
variety of investments available. With a bit of discipline
and self-understanding as well, they can make the most of
them.

CHAPTER 23

The Estate Building Portfolio—Ages 30 to 45

The estate building portfolio extends the portfolio of young adulthood, enlarged and modified as an expanding career, income, and family permit. During these years the financial demands of a family usually restrict the capital available for investment just as professional progression enlarges it. Therefore, the estate building years are a trade-off of capital and necessity.

Life cycle investors in this age group will generally wish to continue the capital growth element as the dominant component of their holdings, although as a practical matter, home, real estate, possessions, and perhaps insurance will comprise the greatest portion of wealth between ages 30 and 45. Among paper investments, however, the growth element of the portfolio will approach 50 percent of total holdings. Whether capital growth is achieved through stocks, discounted bonds, or mutual funds will depend upon market climate to some extent as well as upon the investor's temperament and strategy.

We noted that the capital growth component of the young adulthood portfolio might comprise 80 to 90 percent of total investments, and if the estate building portfolio is largely an extension of that, it may seem curious that the growth component is reduced to 50 percent during these years. These percentages aren't absolutes, of course, but there are some reasons why long-term growth investments account for a reduced overall percentage of the total portfolio for estate builders.

One reason is that taxes become a consideration as investors approach higher-earning years, with the consequence that current income investments, particularly municipal bonds, may comprise a larger percentage of the portfolio than in earlier years. During estate building years, municipals and municipal bond funds may comprise 25 to 35 percent of the portfolio, with growth investments and savings constituting the remainder. If taxes are a consideration, many of these life cycle investors will also be holding their savings component in constant-dollar tax-exempt money market funds.

Zero-coupon municipal bonds are especially conducive to the goals of the estate building portfolio, as they are inexpensive, offer a range of maturities, and compound federally untaxed. As long as investors attend to diversification, insist upon MBIA-type insurance against default, and select higher-rated issues, zero-coupon bonds may rightfully occupy a percentage equal to the capital growth element of the portfolio. Their returns may not be as great as a well-chosen portfolio of stocks or stock funds, but zero munies are likely to rival the aftertax returns of equities and offer greater predictability.

The aggressive gains component can still command a place in the portfolio during the estate building years. Some life cycle investors reason that current demands upon income may reduce available investment capital; consequently, they try to produce the greatest gains with what capital is available for investment. This is generally an acceptable line of reasoning, as these life cycle investors still have two or three decades of employment ahead of them in which to regain any losses. However, the aggressive gains component is somewhat at odds with the nature of estate building, which implies long-term growth, so during this period life cycle investors often restrict aggressive gains investments to 15 percent or so of the total portfolio, whereas 25 percent or more might have been appropriate for the portfolio of young adulthood.

Again, these investors should establish a stop-loss level beyond which they'll accept no further losses. Given that estate building investors are 10 years or more older than investors of young adulthood, they should accept smaller losses, other things being equal. This means their stop-loss level should be a bit higher than that of younger investors.

As a generality, the aggressive income component is less suited for these life cycle investors. Fully taxable interest and dividends, even if providing above-market returns, aren't as rewarding after taxes as capital growth or aggressive capital gains for these investors. Consequently, the aggressive income element is often a very minimal part of the portfolio at this time.

Mutual funds can be rewarding vehicles for estate building investors, as their low minimums for subsequent deposit accommodate what may be reduced capital available for investment during these family years. Option funds, whether aggressive income or growth funds, are excellent choices for investment capital during these years, for the same reasons outlined in the previous chapter.

These life cycle investors may choose to supplement their common stock portfolios with an income options strategy, often writing call options on eligible stocks to secure premium income in addition to dividends and capital growth. Premium income is an addition to the total portfolio, and the decision to write calls, which provide fully taxable returns, will be based upon tax and growth, considerations, for writers of calls risk the possibility of a growing stock being summoned away from them.

A defensive options strategy—buying puts to assure stability against stock price declines—is generally less necessary during estate building years, as these life cycle investors can afford to wait out capital fluctuations. Nonetheless, if the stock portfolio is sizable, buying puts may be selectively warranted.

As investors reach the outer ages of the estate building years, they will wish to give greater consideration to annuities for tax-deferred growth. At age 45, retirement is a not-too-distant consideration, and annuities become more attractive than in previous periods. The decision to select a single premium or variable premium annuity depends upon available capital and the investor's willingness to set aside a given sum in an inaccessible investment. Given the penalties involved in redeeming an annuity before age 59, it's probably best that an annuity comprise no more than 5 percent of the total portfolio. These life cycle investors should also remember that municipal bonds and munie zeros are an excellent alternative to annuities, for they offer not only liquidity but also federally untaxed returns, not merely tax-deferred returns.

Between ages 30 and 45, investors are well-advised to participate more fully in EIPs. With the drain on current income that generally accompanies these years, company matching offers these life cycle investors the opportunity for more immediate, if somewhat inaccessible, returns. If the matching is dollar-for-dollar, employees will want to consider their EIP before undertaking the rest of their growth portfolio.

The percentage of the total portfolio that the EIP constitutes will generally be larger during these years in any event, for the combination of tax-deferred capital growth and company matching will increase its size relative to other investments. The EIP may constitute 8 to 10 percent of total holdings, depending upon how long the employee has been contributing and upon the success of the EIP's investments.

These life cycle investors will also give greater attention to IRAs, for tax offsets and deferred accumulations are more rewarding as investors enter higher brackets. Whether the IRA will emphasize capital growth through stocks or compounding of interest via bonds is a decision of individual strategy. Both can be rewarding choices, but the important point is that these investors do need to set aside capital, the full $2,000 allowed if possible, for retirement-anticipation growth.

It is especially important that estate building investors cultivate relationships with financial advisors. Depending upon the investor's income and investment success, it may be wise to separate joint accounts into individual accounts for husband and wife. A capable advisor can guide these decisions. Also, if there are children in the family, estate building investors will want to consider the UGMA as an adjunct to their own portfolio.

With increasing frequency, however, Americans are marrying later and deferring parenthood as both spouses pursue careers. The dual-income household without children offers life cycle investors extraordinary versatility with their investments. They will have more money to invest and a greater tolerance for losses, meaning that aggressive gains investments are more attractive, but they will also have greater tax liability, with all the investment considerations that implies. Consequently, the portfolio for life cycle investors in this enviable situation may be bifurcated between aggressive gains and tax-sensitive investments. The two-career couple may also be more heavily invested in EIPs, for they generally can afford to have more income tied up in illiquid vehicles to take full advantage of company matching, and tax considerations reward full investment in IRAs.

In summary, the estate building portfolio is largely a capital growth portfolio, but one constrained by the demands of current life. Some aggressive gains vehicles are appropriate, but moderation is the key. Tax-advantaged investments become more attractive during these years, and they'll occupy a greater part of the total portfolio than previously. Long-term, tax-deferred vehicles like annuities, EIPs, and IRAs are also a greater consideration when investors are 30 to 45 years old. In general, these life cycle investors can and should strive for compound growth, and with wisdom and foresight they can achieve it.

CHAPTER 24

The Mature Portfolio—
Ages 45 to 55

Long-term capital growth continues as the presiding element of the portfolio as investors enter the 45 to 55 age group. During these years, at least half of the total portfolio is generally held in growth investments, and the remainder is divided among tax-deferred vehicles like EIPs and annuities, tax-advantaged investments such as municipal bonds and partnerships, constant-dollar savings, and some aggressive growth investments. In addition, the IRA becomes an imperative during these years, and these life cycle investors must make every effort to set aside the maximum permitted.

The mature portfolio accommodates several realities of this time of life. First, investors are likely to be supporting teenaged or college-aged children, who are excising large chunks from their parents' current income. Second, these investors are generally in top tax brackets. Third, their earnings often provide some margin for aggressive speculation. Fourth, their retirement is a more pressing reality, and so is the need to prepare financially for it.

As a consequence, the savings component of the mature portfolio should seek the highest-yielding post-tax vehicles consistent with minimal capital fluctuation and easy liquidity. Near-term municipal bonds are good choices for the savings component of the mature portfolio, although commissions may reduce overall yields to no more than those available from tax-exempt money market funds. A second worthy choice for the savings component is a short-term municipal bond fund with an average portfolio maturity shorter than five years. Abbreviated maturities of such funds minimize capital fluctuations, and the funds otherwise offer the standard advantages of indirect investment, although fees and loads may reduce yields. One particular investment that these life cycle investors should consider for the savings component is the target fund, which we've discussed earlier.

Unless investors are pursuing an income-reinvestment strategy, by which they opt for higher yields as an alternative to capital gains, the income component of the portfolio is minimal during these years. Current income is generally adequate for current needs during these midcareer years, even if it doesn't always seem to be.

Capital growth will be the main concern of investors age 45 to 55. They still have 10 to 20 years of working life ahead of them, and that's sufficient for ample compounding of capital gains. We've discussed long-term gains and the investments appropriate to this portfolio element throughout *Life Cycle Investing*. Those vehicles—stocks, discount bonds, mutual funds—remain appropriate for the mature portfolio, and our earlier examinations will suffice here with little reason to repeat them. By this stage of life, investors can afford to diversify their growth investments into many vehicles, and they should do so, as long as diversification is no greater than they can monitor.

As was true of the estate building portfolio, zero-coupon municipal bonds can be an important addition to the mature portfolio. The tax-free accrued interest rendered by zeros makes them quite attractive to these life cycle investors, and they are an excellent adjunct to long-term capital growth investments. As retirement approaches for investors at the elder perimeter of this age group, the lump sum component of the portfolio gains importance as investors begin to measure the time remaining before retirement. The mature portfolio might contain 25 to 35 percent of its totals in zeros.

The tax status of long-term capital gains and tax-free interest are important to these investors, and so are tax write-offs. For this reason, tax-advantaged oil and gas or real estate partnerships are more suited for these life cycle investors than at previous times. You'll recall from our chapter on these investments that many partnerships offer capital growth, current income, and tax-reducing depreciation. Consequently, many life cycle investors hold around 10 percent of their total portfolio in these vehicles.

Ten percent is also an appropriate figure for the aggressive capital gains element. Pursuit of some aggressive gains is appropriate for these life cycle investors, although tax considerations may in the long term make them better off if they opt for EIPs, IRAs, and annuities. By age 45, investors should be participating earnestly in their employee investment plans to take advantage of tax-deferral and company matching. The same is true of IRAs, and investors must by all means contribute to an IRA by the time they're 55. The decision to purchase an annuity as an addition to the mature portfolio should be weighed carefully. On one hand, the advantages of tax-free compounding can accrue attractive gains over 10 to 20 years. On the other hand, EIPs, especially if they're 401(k) plans, and zero-coupon municipal bonds rival the advantages of an annuity.

There is one unsavory consideration that should influence portfolio planning for live cycle investors after age 50, particularly if they are employed in senior corporate positions. After age 50, senior corporate employees tend to be relatively highly paid in relation to other employees. Not only are their salaries generally higher, but their companies also are contributing greater relative sums to their EIPs, to bonuses, and to other forms of cash, noncash, and deferred compensation. In addition, employees after age 50 present their employers with an impending pension liability. Their years of experience and contribution to the corporation may not outweigh their current and future cost to the organization.

In short, older life cycle investors often need to defend themselves against employers who find them expendable, and they'll need to do so during the years when it's most difficult for them to secure new positions. It's not a pleasant fact, but it is a fact: older employees often find themselves out in the cold, legal protections notwithstanding. Unless these life cycle investors are prepared to enter business for themselves, they may have to rely upon their investments to see them through difficult periods of unemployment.

As a practical matter, this means that liquidity—the ability to convert investments to cash—becomes very important to the mature portfolio because older investors may need that cash to pay bills or to set themselves up in business. Investors need not overemphasize the savings component of the portfolio in order to assure this defensive liquidity, for most growth investments offer liquidity, although selling securities in depressed markets may generate capital losses. It does mean, however, that these investors must be wary of illiquid investments like long-term CDs.

In addition, defensive strategies and investments can help guard against capital losses. We've discussed the uses of puts on portfolios of directly held stocks, and investors should consider their importance in minimizing downside risk. Similarly, bonds with put features and interest rate futures contracts can be useful in case interest rate increases devour the market value of fixed-income investments. Another wise course is to shorten maturities on directly held bonds, thereby minimizing risk of capital fluctuations.

In conclusion, the mature portfolio is still generally a capital growth portfolio, although investors between ages 45 and 55 will look favorably upon tax-advantaged investments as a means of pursuing capital growth. Some aggressive gains investing remains appropriate during these years, and it's likely that a portion of the portfolio should be in tax-advantaged partnerships. The savings component of the portfolio is usually large enough that investors should seek investments offering greater interest consistent with minimal capital fluctuations. The approach of retirement makes lump sum investments and retirement-anticipation investments a greater consideration during these years, and these life cycle investors must remember the importance of liquidity and defensive investment vehicles and strategies.

CHAPTER 25

The Senior Portfolio— Ages 55 to 65

Other things being equal, these are the years when investors apportion their portfolios away from risk and undertake preservation of capital as their main investment concern. In addition, these are generally an investor's highest income years, making taxes an investment consideration. The lump sum component grows in importance as investors contemplate the end of their working careers and recognize the need to accumulate predictable amounts that can be converted to current income investments. The approach of retirement becomes a paramount concern, and along with it comes the increased importance of complete participation in EIPs and IRAs.

During these years, capital growth investments still constitute a plurality of the total portfolio, usually 35 to 40 percent. However, maximum capital gains usually take a back seat to a more moderate equity-income strategy in which dividend reinvestment coupled with less-aggressive capital gains is preferred for the capital growth component. Equity investors realign their portfolios with more conservative stocks and stock funds, and often they use call options to secure additional income along with put options to defend against capital fluctuations. Bond investors typically shorten maturities and direct fixed-income investments into obligations of blue-chip issuers.

Federally untaxed interest makes municipal bonds and bond funds particularly attractive to investors in higher tax brackets. Again, municipal investors seek shorter maturities and maximum safety, usually selecting only issues backed by MBIA-type insurance. Investors in municipal bond funds redirect their portfolios into short-term and intermediate-term funds featuring reduced capital fluctuations. Zero-coupon municipals serve the lump sum component, which typically will equal the capital growth component as a percentage of the total portfolio.

The senior portfolio often contains as much as one third of its total value in current income investments. Reinvesting dividends and interest for growth may be preferable to a capital gains strategy during these years. With 10 years or so remaining before retirement, investors often prefer to convert a portion of their capital growth investments into current income investments so as to assure a steady stream of interest and dividends for reinvestment. If taxes are a large consideration, municipal obligations can be used for this income reinvestment strategy.

Apart from an income reinvestment strategy, these life cycle investors may need current income investments for current expenses. It may be that these investors are undertaking support of an elderly parent just as they are passing the last of their children through college, a common condition at this time of life. Accordingly, the current income element of the portfolio may be a greater percentage of total investments than otherwise would be the case.

Tax-advantaged partnerships may occupy 10 to 20 percent of the portfolio, capturing the inducements of tax write-offs and capital growth. Again, the more conservative partnerships—those investing in operating properties or producing wells—are favored over the more aggressive partnerships.

With conservatism as a guide, the senior portfolio contains a minimal percentage of investments in the aggressive gains component. If investors happen to be especially secure in their employment and generally well-off, perhaps they can retain 5 to 10 percent of their portfolios in speculative vehicles. Otherwise, the volatility associated with aggressive gains is at odds with the conservative needs of the senior portfolio.

Full investment in EIPs is most assuredly warranted for the senior portfolio. After age 55, most employees can direct their contributions into guaranteed insurance contracts providing a contractual rate of return. Most employees of this age would be wise to concentrate their EIP into these arrangements, although the decision to do so will depend upon the performance of the other offerings in the EIP. If the investor's company stock is still performing adequately and is not subject to exceptional volatility, these life cycle investors will keep a fair amount of their contributions in the stock portion of the EIP. A half-and-half split between a guaranteed return and company stock is probably the best course, assuming the company stock is otherwise suited for the needs of a more conservative portfolio. Otherwise, investors may prefer to have 75 percent of their EIP in a guaranteed return investment and 25 percent in company stock.

These life cycle investors may wish to give greater consideration to annuities as a companion to tax-deferred retirement-anticipation investments, weighing their advantages with those of zero-coupon municipals, EIPs, and IRAs in producing growth for an impending retirement.

An IRA is an absolute necessity of the senior portfolio, and these life cycle investors must do everything possible to make maximum IRA contributions, even if they must borrow to do so. Where applicable, investors should open Keogh Plans for self-employment income. It may be possible for investors to pay their spouses for work performed in conjunction with self-employment to assure that they can set aside $2,000 in a spouse's IRA. Investors of this age should contribute the maximum to an IRA even if their company EIP is a 401(k) plan. The tax write-offs and tax-deferred growth of returns make both the EIP and the IRA important.

It becomes particularly important that these life cycle

investors consult competent tax, legal, and estate counsel. Arranging investments to accommodate the best possible returns is important, and so is structuring family holdings to assure they aren't eaten away by estate taxes. These professionals can be well worth the cost of their services.

In sum, the senior portfolio is a conservative portfolio, emphasizing capital gains that minimize downside risk and income investments that offer maximum security. An income reinvestment strategy is often well-advised as a means of securing growth, swelling the percentage of income investments in the portfolio. The approach of retirement is the dominant consideration of the senior portfolio, and life cycle investors must concentrate on investments most inclined toward retirement-anticipation. Taxes, too, are usually an important consideration for these investors. Accordingly, municipal bonds and bond funds should be given greater consideration, as should tax-advantaged partnerships that are consistent with conservative intentions. The lump sum component also attains greater importance in the total portfolio as investors contemplate the known horizon of their working years and seek to arrange their portfolios to secure predictable accumulations within their remaining decade or so of full-time employment.

CHAPTER 26

The Retirement Portfolio—Age 65 and Beyond

As we've observed before, the chief purpose of the retirement portfolio is to supplement pension and social security payments with regular and predictable income. Capital stability is highly important in the retirement portfolio, and some measure of capital growth is appropriate, given today's longer life spans. In general, the aggressive income element is of reduced consequence, for retired investors are interested in quality of receipts. Only in cases where investors are financially very comfortable will aggressive capital gains enter the portfolio. The lump sum component is nonexistent as we've been dealing with it, as the retirement years are one of the periods for which investors have been accumulating lump sum investments. As we'll see, though, lump sum investments can be used as part of the capital growth strategy. These considerations aside, the retirement portfolio is essentially an income portfolio, and it will be heavily weighted—up to 80 percent or more—toward the income component.

For those fortunate retirees who find that income from other sources plus that from accumulated investments still places them in high tax brackets, municipal bonds and bond funds are favored choices for regular current income. These life cycle investors will work with brokers or municipal securities specialists to select high-grade obligations with short maturities and high coupon payments. Investors in municipal bond funds will presumably select funds with high safety ratings and shorter maturities and will elect to receive distributions in monthly checks rather than having proceeds reinvested in additional shares.

These same choices will work with corporate bonds or bond funds, although investors in government bonds are better off investing directly rather than pursuing regular income through government bond funds. As we mentioned in an earlier chapter: distributions from bond funds are fully taxable dividends, whereas interest from direct payments is untaxable by state and local governments; also, loads charged by bond funds will likely exceed commissions for purchase of directly held governments; further, capital fluctuations are indefinite with funds but limited by maturities on direct issues.

Direct purchase of government bonds is a favored strategy for retired investors, as it's possible to arrange maturities to assure both capital stability and current receipts. With government bonds maturing almost every month into the next century, it's easy to arrange near-term maturities that feature minimal capital fluctuation, and with semi-annual payment schedules, selecting six issues will provide monthly income without complicated arrangements.

By comparison, most corporate bonds pay interest on a June–December or January–July schedule, making it more difficult to arrange frequent income with corporates. Of course, most bond funds, corporate, municipal, and government, pay monthly distributions. The price for this convenience, however, is indefinite capital fluctuation.

Some common or preferred stocks and high-dividend stock mutual funds might also be appropriate for the retirement portfolio, not only for their income but also for the possibility of capital gains. Stocks generally pay dividends quarterly, usually on a March–June–September–December schedule, although differing fiscal years may alter dividend payment dates for different corporations. The general similarity of payment dates, however, tends to lump dividend income from stocks during selected times of the year. Consequently, few investors rely exclusively on dividend stocks for current income because they need receipts more frequently than quarterly.

If the income component of the retirement portfolio is 80 percent of the total, it's wise to restrict the stock holdings of the income component to 20 percent—and bear in mind that we're still talking about the *income* component, not the *growth* component. The reasons for this percentage preference are several.

First, bonds offer a fixed maturity, whereas stocks are regarded as perpetuities. The former may offer reduced opportunity for capital gains, but so long as maturities are limited, their capital fluctuation will be minimal. Stocks offer no such assurance.

Second, income from bonds is an obligation, but dividends are not. When one invests for certainty of income, bonds offer it with greater assurance than stocks. However, common stock dividends can be raised; interest payments, excluding those from variable-rate issues, can not.

Third, interest from directly held municipal and government bonds offers tax advantages. Dividend income is fully taxable, except for the modest dividend exclusion and the rare instances of dividends that legally constitute a return of capital. Interest from corporate bonds is fully taxable, which is an important point to remember.

In general, the decision to weight the income component with bonds depends upon the differential in yields between identified fixed-income investments and equities. For the most part, bonds will outyield stocks by several percentage points. When exceptions occur, it may be because of the more speculative nature of the stock, in which case caution should guide the conservative retirement portfolio.

In combination with an options strategy, however, stocks can be lucrative additions to the income component. Writing call options on eligible equities can increase income substantially and can remove some of the sting from price declines. Premiums from the writing of calls can add 10 percent or more to the dividend yield of stocks, and if the calls are written out of the money, chances of having the equities called away are reduced. In evaluating the use of options to generate income, retired life cycle investors should consider option-income mutual funds. These are slightly more speculative vehicles and will need to be monitored carefully, but they can be of use for the income component.

Certificates of deposit, T-bills, and money market funds can also be wise investments for current income. All are constant-dollar investments providing market-level returns, and all may be purchased without commissions, fees, or loads. Investors can arrange to receive interest from CDs by check rather than have it reinvested, although most institutions will pay direct interest only quarterly. For the largest denomination CDs, however, some institutions will make monthly interest payments. Income from T-bills will vary with prevailing rates at the time of renewal, and monthly checks from money market funds will rise and fall with the performance of the instruments in their portfolios. Neither pays a contractual amount, as do CDs, but both are more liquid than CDs.

Retirees can become quite innovative in planning their current income from many types of investments. They can combine semi-annual bond payments with monthly interest checks from certificates of deposit and quarterly dividend payments from income stocks, for example. Retirees who really get a charge from clipping coupons can be even more intricate: they can mate government bonds, which pay interest at midmonth, with corporate bonds, which usually pay interest at the end of the month, and with municipal bonds, which usually pay interest at the beginning of the month.

As other sources of income, participation in real estate or oil and gas partnerships can be as lucrative as stocks and bonds. Of course, retired life cycle investors will be interested in the more conservative partnerships, those dealing in existing, high-quality real estate with steady rental income or in oil and gas partnerships confined to producing wells. As a rule of thumb, 5 to 10 percent of the retirement portfolio is sufficient investment in these vehicles. If the retired investor is still in need of some tax shelter, he or she should consult a reputable dealer or advisor to assess the uses of partnerships offering tax advantages over current income.

All the investments we've noted as appropriate for capital growth remain appropriate for the retirement portfolio. The emphasis will be on more conservative capital growth, probably from blue-chip stocks and stock funds if the investor selects equities as the growth vehicle. Investors who've been managing their money for many years and have developed some market sophistication may wish to pursue capital growth through special situation stocks and stock funds, both of which can provide capital growth. Life cycle investors who have learned to profit from the cyclicality of markets can by all means continue to do so with equity investments.

For fixed-income investors, discount bonds from quality issuers can also provide capital growth, some of which might be taxed as current income, when issues purchased below par mature. Bond funds can provide capital gains for investors who follow interest rate fluctuations astutely, just as they can provide indefinite capital losses for those who don't.

Zero-coupon municipal bonds can be used to secure capital growth with tax advantages for investors who have satisfied their income needs with the current income component. For retired investors, this twist on the lump sum component of the portfolio is appropriate, provided that maturities are kept short and attention to liquidity is maintained. The built-in increment in value of zeros makes them predictable sources of capital growth, even though the growth comes from interest rather than capital gains. If retired life cycle investors find that they have a little unneeded income, purchasing zero-coupon municipals can be a wise use of the extra cash. Unless tax considerations are minimal, investors will buy municipal zeros, for corporate and government-backed zeros will generate current tax liability despite failure to pay current interest, whereas municipal zeros won't.

In some cases, retired investors may find that they

needn't invest for capital growth. If income from social security, pensions or EIPs, and a portfolio is sufficient for current needs and permits some room to accommodate unexpected expenses, an income reinvestment strategy may prove more lucrative than a growth investment strategy. Reinvesting temporarily unneeded cash in a money market fund or in zero-coupon issues will provide predictable returns without the capital fluctuations often associated with growth investments. Retired investors might achieve greater returns from growth investments, but if income is sufficient for requirements, it could be that higher levels of growth merely gild the lily.

There's little question that retired investors need to build capital rather than merely living off a fixed mass of investments. Capital growth is necessary if for no other reason than at some date retirees may need greater current income, which in turn means they will need capital growth in order to convert more capital into current income investments. However, in arranging the growth component investors shouldn't forget the advantages of compounded interest from an income reinvestment strategy.

For life cycle investors recently retired, the first pressing problem is how to go about arranging a portfolio to suit current and expected needs. Typically, investors find their capital spread out among the EIP, an IRA, a retirement plan or two, and their other investments—here a CD, there a money fund, a few stocks scattered about. Such dispersion may prevent the newly retired from gathering their capital together in a coherent whole for strategic reinvestment. There are several guides to follow in drawing a retirement portfolio together.

Obviously, the first step is to assess current income requirements and balance them against retirement benefits payable in an income stream. Social security, pensions, and corporate retirement plans typically pay recipients in monthly checks rather than in a lump sum distribution. Income from rental property, part-time employment, and miscellaneous sources is also payable in a continuing stream. This income, which generally is highly predictable, can be earmarked against fixed expenses, which also can be calculated with high certainty during retirement.

Next, the recent retiree needs to calculate the total value of other investments. For example, most employee invest- ment plans pay retirees a lump sum distribution upon re- tirement. The company will provide a statement of accumu- lated value in the EIP and will make the payment shortly after retirement. Investors need to calculate the total value of IRAs, Keoghs, and other investments, like annuities, that have accrued to a known amount. Added to this will be the current value of other investments. Knowing these amounts, investors can calculate the current income they could receive if all their holdings were converted to income securities.

Say, for example, that the value of these holdings is $100,000. If converted to a portfolio of government bonds yielding an average of 10 percent, $100,000 will yield $10,000 yearly throughout the term of the bonds. Add the $10,000 to the income stream from pensions, social security, and other sources, and investors know the base level of cur- rent income they'll have to live on.

Once recent retirees know the receipts they can receive by converting everything into income investments, they can better judge how to apportion their portfolio. Perhaps there will be no need to convert some holdings into income in- vestments. These life cycle investors can plan for growth investments, or perhaps sell some holdings for a world cruise as a retirement caprice. It may be that a substantial part of the portfolio can be left where it is, continuing to grow. Otherwise, adjustments need to be made.

In particular, newly retired investors will have to decide how they wish to receive returns from their EIP. As we noted, the EIP is usually paid in a lump sum distribution. In many cases, companies will arrange to have the EIP con- verted to an annuity—by law, a joint and survivor annuity that pays regular income for the life of the retiree and spouse unless the spouse agrees in writing to a lifetime an- nuity for the retiree only. The annuity may not be the best course, for if the EIP is reinvested in an IRA rollover account, returns may be greater than those provided by the annuity.

As always, competent tax and investment counsel is warranted in making such decisions. Tax counsel is especially needed for the newly retired, because sudden lump sum payments may push them temporarily into higher tax brackets that devour their retirement nest egg. Competent advisors can tell you whether you'd be better off accepting lump sum payments, if you're eligible for income averaging or special 10-year averaging, or whether you should redirect lump sum payments elsewhere.

Converting holdings in an IRA or Keogh Plan presents similar dilemmas. The investments held in these tax-deferred accounts might well be growth, rather than income investments. Given that investors must begin receiving distributions by age 70 years and 6 months, at least under current law, investments within the IRA will need to be sold or rearranged.

One strategy for rearranging the investments within the self-directed IRA is to buy T-bills or money fund shares as stocks are sold or as bonds mature. For IRAs with other intermediaries, mutual fund shares can be switched to money funds within the same fund family, and maturing CDs at depository institutions can be redirected into short-term deposits or transferred to another custodian. Converting these investments to near-cash holdings permits their subsequent reapportionment with greater ease. T-bills and money funds are "close to cash" because of their liquidity and broad markets.

Another decision that retired life cycle investors need to make is when to begin receiving social security payments. As a general rule, investors should begin receiving social security as soon as possible, for current payments, even at reduced levels, can be reinvested to advantage. Even if entitlements are greater at age 65, investors will have deferred three years of investable or consumable income by electing later payments. The larger payments at a later age may not be sufficient to offset deferred income that could have started years earlier.

However, with social security in its present straits and

with each new Congress seeking "solutions" to the problems of social security, future retirees may not be able to elect early receipts. You'll have to see what the law is when you retire.

Deciding how to accept payment from an annuity is a similar problem. We discussed payment options in our chapter on annuities, where we noted that investors trade income for time and vice versa: the shorter the guaranteed period of payment, the higher the payments; the longer the contractual payment period, the smaller will be each payment. The decision to accept one of the payment schedules we examined in the annuity chapter will depend upon tax considerations, the performance of other investments, current needs for income balanced against current income available, and the investor's desire to assure income for survivors.

All in all, the retirement portfolio brings us full-circle from the portfolio of young adulthood. Where current income was inconsequential, it now becomes paramount. Retired life cycle investors should be in the position of enjoying the rewards of a lifetime of investment and work—letting their money work for them rather than the other way around. If the retired portfolio is predominately an income portfolio, it's income that is earned by having deferred consumption. Continuing capital growth is of some consequence, but after age 65, investors generally need maximum current, regular income with predictability and stability of capital. Fortunately, there are many investments to provide what they need and to reward a lifetime of labor.

Conclusion

We finally come to the end of *Life Cycle Investing,* but let's hope we've just started life cycle investing as a financial strategy for a lifetime. Regardless of our age or income or present portfolio, each of us can do more to make our investments productive for now and for the future.

Although we've examined many investment alternatives, our emphasis has been on the investor, not the investment. We have addressed the investor's needs first and the investments meeting those needs second. In this way, life cycle investing is an investor-directed approach rather than an investment-directed approach.

As we've seen, one way to examine our investment needs is to look at our place in life, examining how our investments can complement earnings and how our portfolios will need to change as we enter new stages of life. By understanding where we are and where we're going, we can better understand what our portfolio can and will need to do. Our investments become part of the context of our lives, and the context of our lives helps us to arrange our investments accurately and appropriately.

As we've also seen, dozens of investments can hold an

appropriate place in meeting the strategies suited for an evolving life, whether that strategy calls for aggressive or conservative courses. We can achieve the balance, proportion, and measure we seek in a portfolio, and we can be comfortable recognizing that different times of life will call for a portfolio that emphasizes one of the five portfolio elements over another. The end result of such awareness is that we can live our lives fully, and that, after all, is what investment is all about.

INDEX

A

Aggressive gains component, 13–14,
  212–23
  mathematics of, 254
  tax considerations of, 263–64
Aggressive growth, 13, 41–43
  defined, 13–14
  investments providing, 13–14, 77–78,
    119, 124
Aggressive income, 13
  defined, 13–14
  investments providing, 77, 220–22
Allen, Everett T., Jr., 151
American Association of Individual
    Investors, 280
Annuities, 142–49
Averaging down, 242–43
Averaging up, 243–44

B

Berlin, Howard M., 80
Beta coefficient, 203
Block, Julian, 268
Boeckh, Anthony J., 231
Bonds, 25, 75–80, 194–95
  and estate building portfolio, 83
  and mature portfolio, 83–84
  and minor's portfolio, 80–81
  and retirement portfolio, 25, 85–87
  and senior portfolio, 84–85
  and young adult's portfolio, 81–83
  convertibles, 77

C

Capital growth, 12–13
  defined, 12
  investments providing, 12–13, 86,
    102, 211
Certificates of deposit, 30–32, 191, 193,
  266
Clasing, Henry K., Jr., 66
Collins Commodities, 125
Commodity pools, 121–26
  and estate building portfolio, 127
  and mature portfolio, 128
  and minor's portfolio, 126
  and retirement portfolio, 129
  and senior portfolio, 128–29
  and young adult's portfolio, 126–27
Coughlan, Richard T., 231
Countercyclical industries, 200
Cyclical industries, 200

D

Depository institutions, 29–32
  and estate building portfolio, 33–34

Depository institutions—*Cont.*
  and mature portfolio, 34
  and minor's portfolio, 32–33
  and retirement portfolio, 35
  and senior portfolio, 34–35
  and young adult's portfolio, 33
Dividend exclusion, 39
Dollar-cost averaging, 236–42
Dow, Charles H., 206
Dow Theory, 207–9
Droms, William G., 90

E

Elements of a portfolio, 9–15
Employee investment plans, 150–60
Estate building portfolio, 293–97

F

Fabozzi, Frank J., 66, 80
Fischer, Donald E., 202
Friedman, Milton, 2
Futures, 121–23
  financial, 78

G

Gordon, Gail, 78
Gordon, Robert J., 3
Gould, Bruce G., 126
Graham, Benjamin, 202
Growth component of the portfolio,
  12–13
  managing growth component,
    198–212
  mathematics of, 250–54
  tax considerations of, 262–63
Growth industries, 199–200

H–I

Hale, Norman B., 90
Income component, 11–12
  managing income component, 192–98
  mathematics of, 248–50
  tax considerations of, 262
Income investments, 11–12
  defined, 11–12
  investments providing, 12, 76, 93,
    104, 117, 119
Individual Retirement Accounts, 21, 22,
  109, 161–75, 177–78
Inflation, 229–35
Inflation hedges, 231
Investment advisors, 269–72

319

J–K

Jarrow, Robert, 66
Jordan, Ronald J., 202
Keogh Plan Accounts; *see* Individual Retirement Accounts
Keynes, John Maynard, 2

L

Lasser, J. K., Tax Institute, 268
Life Cycle Hypothesis of Income, Consumption, and Saving, 2–4
Life cycle investing, 4–5
Limited partnerships, 114–20; *see also* Commodity pools
Loosigian, Allan M., 78
Lump sum investments, 14–15, 23
  defined, 14–15
  investments providing, 15, 79
  managing lump sum component, 223–28
  mathematics of, 256–58
  tax considerations of, 264–65

M

Margin, 43–44
Mature portfolio, 298–302
Minor's portfolio, 283–86
Modigliani, Franco, 2
Money market funds, 106–9
  and estate building portfolio, 110
  and mature portfolio, 111
  and minor's portfolio, 109
  and retirement portfolio, 112–13
  and senior portfolio, 111–12
  and young adult's portfolio, 110
Municipal securities trust, 91
Mutual funds, 89–95, 195–97
  and estate building portfolio, 97–98
  and mature portfolio, 98–99
  and minor's portfolio, 95
  and retirement portfolio, 102–4
  and senior portfolio, 100–102
  specialty funds, 91
  switch privileges, 93
  and young adult's portfolio, 96

N–O

Nix, Susan, 45
Nix, William, 45
Noddings, Thomas C., 77
O'Brien, R. J., & Associates, Inc., 125
Options, 52–66
  call option, 53, 56–57, 72–73
  combinations, 55

Options—*Cont.*
  and estate building portfolio, 68–69
  and mature portfolio, 69–71
  and minor's portfolio, 66–67
  put option, 53, 57, 73
  and retirement portfolio, 72–73
  rules for price movements, 60
  and senior portfolio, 71–72
  trading symbols of, 53–54
  and young adult's portfolio, 67–68

P

Platnick, Kenneth B., 78
Pollack, Irving M., 80
Precious metals, 131–37
  and estate building portfolio, 138
  and mature portfolio, 138–39
  and minor's portfolio, 137
  and retirement portfolio, 140
  and senior portfolio, 139–40
  and young adult's portfolio, 137–38
Price-earnings ratio, 202

R

Rebell, Arthur L., 78
Retirement-anticipation investments, 152, 176–85; *see also* Annuities; Employee investment plans; *and* Individual Retirement Accounts
Retirement portfolio, 307–15
Rosenbloom, Jerry S., 151
Rudd, Andrew, 66
Rugg, Donald D., 90

S

Self-tithe, 190
Senior portfolio, 303–6
Short sales, 43
Stability of principal, 9–11, 24–25
  defined, 9–10
  investments providing, 25, 107
  tax considerations of, 261
Stability component of the portfolio, 9–11, 75–76
  managing the stability component, 189–92
  mathematics of, 245–48
Stages of an investor's life, 16–26
  childhood, 16–19
  estate building, 21–22

Stages of an investor's life—*Cont.*
  portfolio maturity, 22–23
  retirement, 24–25
  senior portfolio, 23–24
  young adulthood, 19–20
Stock index futures, 45, 50
Stocks, 37–46
  aggressive growth and income, 41–43
  and estate building portfolio, 48
  growth stocks, 39–41
  income stocks, 37–39
  and mature portfolio, 48–49
  and minor's portfolio, 46–47
  preferred, 45–46
  and retirement portfolio, 50
  and senior portfolio, 49–50
  and young adult's portfolio, 47

T–U

Target funds, 101
Taxes, 17, 21, 40, 83, 117–19, 259–60, 265–68
Technical analysis, 204–5
Trusts, 94–95
Uniform Gifts to Minors Account, 18–19, 283–86
USA Metals, 134

Y–Z

Young adult's portfolio, 287–92
Zarb, Frank G., 66
Zero-coupon bonds, 15, 79, 82, 180, 223–28, 284
Zero-coupon CDs, 15, 31, 223, 284